**Praise for**

***Paris Histories and Mysteries***

"I've lived in Paris for more than twenty years, yet John Frederick has found a way to tantalize me from page one with his series of tales about my adopted city. If you like Daniel Boorstin's *The Discoverers* or Bill Bryson's work, you will appreciate Frederick's raconteur style, which meanders about the city that has exerted its extraordinary influence on the world throughout the ages.

"In the manner of a true Parisian flâneur, revealing hidden details and surprising connections to life in today's modern world, *Paris Histories and Mysteries* is more than a simple litany of dates and events. This book is about context, placing the reader directly 'at the scene of the crime' (literally!) in all its most delicious and gruesome details.

"So, grab a croissant and a café au lait, and be ready to explore the heights, the depths, and the heart of Europe's cultural capital—Paris!"

— Keri Chryst, Jazz Ambassador and
Founder of Arts Embassy International (Paris)

"In *Paris Histories and Mysteries*, John Frederick fills his stories of Paris thoroughly with historical and cultural facts, which gives me a new outlook on some of the Parisian landmarks I pass by every day. He also narrates in vivid detail how these old stories still echo today through the rest of the world. It's a very entertaining and educational journey that makes me see the city I live in in a whole new light."

— Maylin Pultar, Singer/Songwriter and Film Maker (Paris)

"John Frederick squires us around his beloved city of Paris in the great tradition of the American flâneur, ready to be amused, educated, or surprised by unexpected adventures on any street corner. If you are traveling to Paris, he will help you to see things from fresh angles, and lift the hem of histories and mysteries large and small. If you are going to travel in the mind from your easy chair, he'll arouse your inner senses with sights and smells and amuse-bouches. This book is a delightful stroll through the Paris of the heart."

— Robert Moss, Bestselling Author of
*The Secret History of Dreaming*

"The romantic City of Lights, renowned for its great history, art, and literature, has a darker side too. Paris—home to some strange and unsettling mysteries from medieval times to World War II—has changed the world and affected our lives in amazing ways. In this powerful book, John Frederick has documented some of the most fascinating, spooky, thrilling, and fun tales Paris has to offer."

— Susan Friedman, CSP, International Bestselling Author of
*Riches in Niches: How to Make It BIG in a small Market*
(New York)

"John Frederick presents a panorama of Paris' most enchanting mysteries, from the Phantom of the Opera to Nicolas Flamel, providing historical background and taking readers on a time-traveling tour from Roman times to the modern day. Every page of *Paris Histories and Mysteries* intrigued me. I feel like I truly know Paris now in ways that will greatly enrich my next visit. *C'est magnifique!*"

— Tyler R. Tichelaar, PhD and award-winning author of
*Melusine's Gift* and *The Gothic Wanderer* (Michigan)

October 2023

To Barb —
With love for
you and for Paris

# Paris Histories and Mysteries

## How the City of Lights Changed the World

Love
John

John A. Frederick

***Paris Histories and Mysteries: How the City of Lights Changed the World***



Published by: John A. Frederick



Published by:

Aviva Publishing

Lake Placid, NY 12946

518-523-1320

www.avivapubs.com

Address all inquiries to:

John A. Frederick

911 Central Avenue, Box 205

Albany, NY 12206

parishistorymystery@yahoo.com

www.johnafrederick.com

ISBN: 978-1-63618-241-4

Library of Congress Control Number: 2022917098

Editors: Tyler Tichelaar and Larry Alexander, Superior Book Productions

Book Layout: Larry Alexander, Superior Book Productions

Author Photo Credit: John A. Frederick

Every attempt has been made to properly source all quotes.

Printed in the United States of America

*To my greatest romantic loves*
*Patty, Willie, Bill, Mark, and Paris, France*

**Acknowledgments**

My gratitude to Robert Moss, who encouraged me to dream and write (and dream some more), and to my editors, Tyler Tichelaar and Larry Alexander.

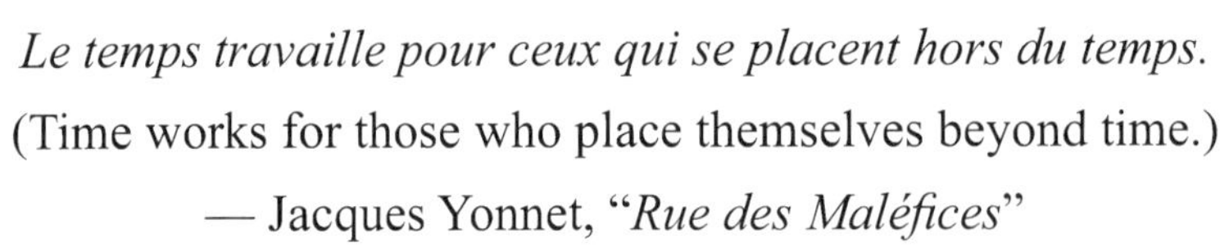

*Le temps travaille pour ceux qui se placent hors du temps.*
(Time works for those who place themselves beyond time.)
— Jacques Yonnet, "*Rue des Maléfices*"

*Quand j'ai la terre et mer avironnée*
*Et visité en chacune partie*
*Jérusalem, Egypte et Galilée,*
*Alexandrie, Damas et la Syrie,*
*Babylone, le Caire et Tartarie,*
*Et tous les ports qui y sont,*
*Les épices et sucres qui s'y font,*
*Les fins draps d'or et soies du pays*
*Valent trop mieux ce que les Français ont :*
*Rien ne se peut comparer à Paris.*
*C'est la cité sur toutes couronnée,*
*Fontaine et puits de science et de clergie*

When I have circled earth and sea
been to all places, every one:
Egypt, Jerusalem and Galilee,
Damascus, Alexandria, and Babylon,
Cairo, Syria and Tartary,
and all their ports,
seen the spices and sweets they make,
their fine gold cloth and silks
are dearer than what they have in France:
Paris is quite beyond compare.
She is the city crowned above all others,
Fountain and well of wisdom and of learning.
— Eustache Deschamps (c. 1346-1406)

Contents

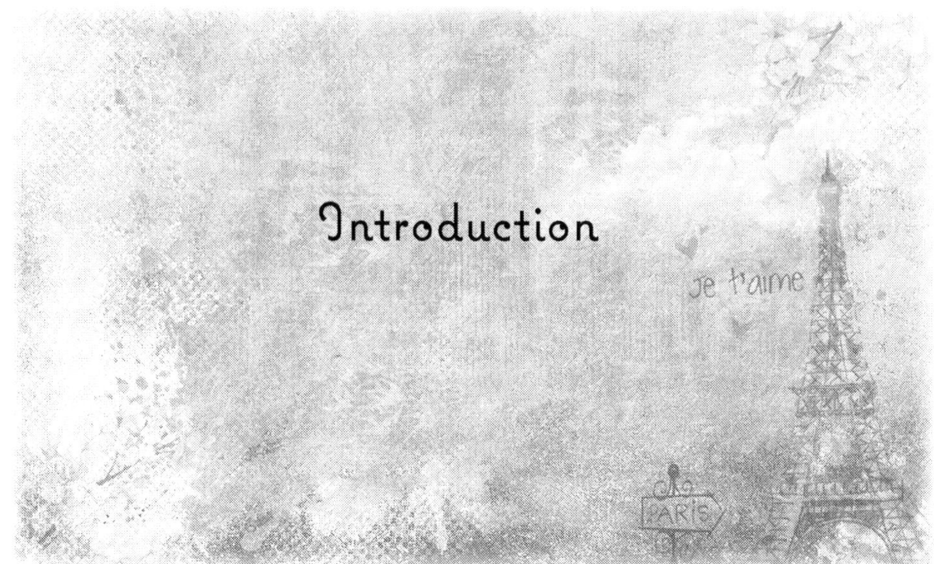


# Introduction

Does the world need another Paris book? Plenty of books already chart Paris' sweeping journey through time, exploring the life of this king or that queen, a particular neighborhood or street, a period of history or a singular event. This book is not meant to be a scholarly work. It is reasonably well-researched by an amateur historian, but it does not pretend to be anything like a doctoral thesis.

There are also plenty of travel books. You can buy city-wide guides, walking tour guides, Ten-Must-See-Sites-in-Paris guides, guides to restaurants, and guides to the seamier side of Paris. This book is a reasonably helpful guide to the places and events discussed. It is written for the traveler to Paris, but perhaps more so for the person who, alas, will never visit Paris....

Frankly, everyone—*everyone*—has been to Paris. Paris lies deep in our subconscious. It is so much a part of the world's understanding of itself, Paris colors the minds and imaginations of everyone on the planet, so much so that even a person who has never *heard* of Paris (nearly impossible) has in effect *been* to Paris.

Paris as an idea is so fixed in the human psyche that when someone visits Paris for the first time, the city meets their expectations: Those who believe Paris is dangerous will find a scary city. Those who believe Parisians rude will find rudeness all around. Those who believe in a city of romance will find romance everywhere.

But even the greatest of expectations fade as the mystique and beauty of Paris takes hold, with its subtle, powerful energy; with its skies that seem closer and bluer than elsewhere, clouds sailing by like great ships along the Seine; with its cobbles that will twist your ankle and its crazy *velo* and *moto* riders who somehow manage to stay alive commuting in the crazy Paris traffic.

People come to Paris to dream, to create, to be inspired, to find love. Yes, all cities have their own energy, rhythm, and style and all have contributed their share to the world. But the energy of New York or London, Tokyo or Toronto, Rio or Cairo do not compare to the energy of Paris.

If there is a crossroads of the world, since at least the fifteenth century, it is Paris.

In his beautiful book, *Time Was Soft There: A Paris Sojourn at Shakespeare & Co.*, Jeremy Mercer writes:

> Just like nobody ever dreams of being a payroll clerk at a software company when they are a child, nobody ever dreams of living in my city. In a place like Paris, the air is so thick with dreams they clog the streets and take all the good tables at the cafés. Poets and writers, models and designers, painters and sculptors, actors and directors, lovers and escapists, they flock to the City of Lights. That night at Polly's, the table spilled over with the rapture of pilgrims who have found

> their temple. That night, among new friends and safe at Shakespeare and Company, I felt it too. Hope is a most beautiful drug.

So the world needs this book, *Paris Histories and Mysteries*, for *another* reason, beyond the interesting tales from Paris history, beyond the Travelers' Tips:

Because these Paris events have reverberated across time and have affected the whole world. Whether you know it or not, these events have affected you. Your life is different, you are different because of these twelve tales, events that happened in Paris.

Let me tell you how….

*John A. Frederick*

Paris, France

# Chapter 1
# The Unknown Girl of the Seine

## (*L'Inconnue de la Seine*)
## (Nineteenth and Twentieth Centuries)

*"He feels himself buried in those two infinities, the ocean and the sky, at one and the same time: the one is a tomb; the other is a shroud."*
— Victor Hugo, *Les Misérables*

*"There are too many ways to drown even if you don't want to drown."*
— Charles Bukowski

THE BANKS, BRIDGES, and *quais* of the Seine are many things to many people: A spot for fishing. A place to dream away an afternoon. An out-of-the-way respite from the busy city. A romantic lover's setting—perhaps the most romantic setting in all of Paris.

Or....

A dank and seamy place for a quick and meaningless encounter. A solitary place where one can contemplate the existential questions of life, love, art, meaning, sex, loneliness, and death. A jumping off place, where the chains of the world can be loosed, and a soul can swim free....

The waters of the Seine run slow, deep, and dark through Paris, in turns colored moss green, mud brown, or slate gray, in movement indolent, turbulent, or like smoky glass barely rippled. The name "Seine" comes from the Celtic goddess of the river, "Sequana," patron of the Sequanae tribe who lived near the headwaters of the Seine near Dijon. But a seine is also a net to catch fish, and perhaps not coincidently, *le sein* is the French word for a "bosom," a synonym for the breast or the heart. The history of the Seine is in many ways the history of the people of Paris and the heart—the bosom of all of France. These are forever intertwined, linked by forces both temporal and spiritual.

And speaking of fishing nets, the Seine has a history of bodies found floating in its watery arms or washed up on its banks. While there are, of course, accidental drownings—a drunk who perhaps trips on a nightly stumble home—the bodies are too often victims of violence. The murdered corpse of some unlucky tourist, sucker gambler, or one of those unfortunates caught up in the brutal barbarity of the many massacres, revolutions, or political uprisings that have occurred throughout the centuries may bob to the surface. Many such have ended up in the river.

For example, in August 1572, during the infamous St. Bartholomew's Day massacre, Protestant men, women, and children were murdered in a two-day orgy of violence, their bodies flung into the Seine by the hundreds.

And this kind of horror is not a thing of centuries past. In October 1961, during the French war in Algeria, thousands of Algerians marched to protest against a targeted curfew. Contemporary accounts tell of police attacking the demonstration and rounding up hundreds of protesters. Decades later, the French government acknowledged the events of October 5, 1961, when a number of Algerians (estimates range from forty to more than 300) were beaten, tortured, and murdered, their bodies thrown into the Seine from the Pont St. Michel. The Paris police chief, Maurice Papon, who commanded the forces that day, would later be tried and found guilty, not for the police violence against the Algerian protestors, but for his role in deporting Parisian Jews to the Nazi death camps.

And finally, perhaps saddest of all are those lonely souls who have committed suicide by throwing themselves into the Seine. The Seine seems to be an obvious place to look to escape from life, a reasonable place to commit an unreasonable act. A leap off of a Paris bridge has a romantic appeal, while also being a venture from which there fairly certainly can be no turning back. The lazy waters of the Seine gladly takes these deaths too, with barely a ripple.

*La Traversée de Paris*, as the Seine's indolent waters that wind their way through Paris are called, has received many of these poor souls over the centuries. Such deaths were so commonplace and unexceptional that at one time the local authorities strung a net across the river at St. Cloud to catch any undiscovered corpses floating downstream on their way to the sea.

Recounting his travels from America to France in 1831, Alvan Stewart, New York lawyer and ardent abolitionist, wrote in his diary of a day he spent with American author James Fenimore Cooper who was living in France at the time. On a carriage journey to Versailles, he wrote:

> Near St. Cloud we again crossed the Seine by a bridge which is five miles below Paris, and at this bridge is a curious weir to catch the dead bodies of those who commit suicide in Paris by jumping from its numerous bridges, into the Seine, or those who are murdered and

> are thrown into the River, or those who may have been accidentally drowned, and it is supposed that this weir catches two or three a day through the year. One of the bridges, which I passed the oftenest last week, called Pont Royal, four persons threw themselves from it during the week, all of which except a young woman were drowned. Mr. Cooper saw two of them jump in, and the woman was one whom the humanity of the spectators saved.

More recently, in 2019 Paris news reports discussed one week when four bodies were pulled from the Seine, including a young woman who, sadly, succumbed to the freezing waters shortly after being rescued.

So it was not too remarkable when sometime in the late 1880s (nobody knows exactly when) a young woman was pulled lifeless from the river near the Quai du Louvre. She was young, perhaps no more than sixteen or so. And she was beautiful, as anyone who saw her would attest. She was so beautiful, in fact, that someone—an enthralled morgue attendant perhaps—made a death mask of her, something not done regularly with anonymous corpses.

She was likely a suicide. No evidence of violence, marks, bruising, or wounds were found on her body. She had died very recently. No evidence of decay or decomposition was noted. Had the river held her for even a day or two, deterioration and hungry fish would have left their mark. Later, controversy over the exact manner of the girl's death would erupt.

This *ecadavre feminin inconnu* ("unknown female cadaver" as she was first logged into the morgue's records) may not have drowned after all. But drowning, water, and femininity are powerful images in the imaginations of a population hungry for intrigue, mystery, and a good diversion to talk about on the streets and at parties. And so she soon became known as *l'inconnue de la Seine* (the Unknown Girl who had drowned in the Seine).

In those days, as now, when an unknown person is found dead, they go to the morgue. In this case, the Paris morgue. Originally, *morgue* comes from the Old French verb *morguer*, "to look solemnly" or "to stare." *La Morgue* was the informal name given to a small basement room in the large Parisian fortress known as *la Grande Châtelet.* Once a notorious prison, all that remains of it today is its name on the largest mètro station, Châtelet.

The *Dictionnaire de l'Académie* of 1718 describes, *la Morgue:*

> [A] place at the entrance of a prison, where those who are being imprisoned are kept for a while, so that the jailers can take a good look at them, to recognize them. "We held him for a long time in the morgue."
>
> (*Endroit à l'entrée d'une prison, où l'on tient quelque temps ceux que l'on escrouë, afin que les Guichetiers puissent les regarder fixement, pour les reconnoistre ensuite. On l'a tenu long-temps à la morgue.*)

Eventually, this informal viewing room was moved out of Châtelet and into a building expressly built for this purpose by order of Napoleon's Prefect of the Seine. In 1804, the new morgue opened for business on the Île de la Cité, on the Quai de Marché near the Pont St. Michel. Situated in a very visible location, it was also close to the river (to more easily transport bodies), to the police station, and to the courts, from which sometimes the accused would be brought to stand before the murder victim, in the hopes that the sight would elicit a remorseful confession.

In 1864, during the reign of Emperor Napoleon III, his Prefect of the Seine, Baron Haussmann demolished the morgue on the island and replaced it with a newer, more modern morgue located behind the cathedral of Notre Dame. It is here you can find on contemporary maps of the day "the rue Morgue" (see Chapter 4, Edgar Allan Poe's Rue Morgue).

So however these unfortunates came to find themselves in the morgue, each unclaimed corpse was laid out on a black marble slab behind a viewing window in hopes family or friends would come looking for their missing loved one. Water from above dripped onto the bodies, a crude method of cooling and preserving the corpses as long as possible. More modern methods of refrigeration were not available and would not be installed until after the 1880s. Families and friends could view the deceased, their clothes hanging on the wall just behind them, and perhaps identify the sad remains.

*Fig. 1 - Interior view of the morgue in 1855 (Paris)*
*(Brown University, public domain)*

This arrangement had another side to it—morbid curiosity. Thrill seekers came by the scores to view the bodies, a cheap, ghoulish form of entertainment that quickly became popular. Contemporary tourist guidebooks highlighted this "must-see attraction" along with other aspects of Paris' mysterious underbelly. One noted, "There is not a single window in Paris that attracts more onlookers than this."

Émile Zola, novelist, playwright, realist, naturalist, and chronicler of ordinary life in nineteenth-century France, created a stark and gruesome picture of this phenomenon in his novel, *Thérèse Raquin* (1867):

> Laurent imposed on himself the task of passing each morning by the Morgue, on the way to his office. He had made up his mind to attend to the business himself. Notwithstanding that his heart rose with repugnance, notwithstanding the shudders that sometimes ran through his frame, for over a week he went and examined the countenance of all the drowned persons extended on the slabs....
>
> Each morning, while Laurent was there, he heard behind him the coming and going of the public who entered and left.
>
> The morgue is a sight within reach of everybody, and one to which passers-by, rich and poor alike, treat themselves. The door stands open, and all are free to enter. There are admirers of the scene who go out of their way so as not to miss one of these performances of death. If the slabs have nothing on them, visitors leave the building disappointed, feeling as if they had been cheated, and murmuring between their teeth; but when they are fairly well occupied, people crowd in

> front of them and treat themselves to cheap emotions; they express horror, they joke, they applaud or whistle, as at the theatre, and withdraw satisfied, declaring the Morgue a success on that particular day.

In a February 1885 edition of the *Harvard Crimson*, an unknown student wrote a sophomore theme entitled, "A Description of the Paris Morgue":

> Brutal, gashed, and swollen faces; wide gaping mouths, which opened for the last time to utter the death-shriek, and are now fixed forever in rigid agony; jagged, discolored teeth, sunken cheeks, knitted brows, dead, sodden eyes, awful contortions, ghastly smiles, hideous leers, faces of men and faces of women, faces of the young and faces of the old, faces which reek with the slime of years of vice and misery and despair; faces which Dante, groping among the damned, might have dragged from hideous, steaming depths of Lethean mud, and flung forth to front the unwilling eye of day; faces mutilated into every shape into which the human countenance can be bruised or flattened or slashed or puffed or putrified—such is the sight which greets the visitor upon his entrance to the Paris Morgue....
>
> An eager throng is surging to and fro in front of a long, low window; men are crowding and elbowing each other; old hags are pointing toward the glass, and croaking to one another; pretty women are gazing with white faces of pity, but with none the less thirsty greediness, upon some fascinating spectacle; little children are being held aloft in strong arms, that they

> too may see the dreadful thing, and they do see, and they toss their tiny, wavering arms aloft and crow right gleefully....
>
> Ah, Paris has her seamy side!

Charles Dickens, too, was fascinated by the macabre spectacle. A journalist with an eye for detail, he wrote:

> Whenever I am in Paris, I am dragged by an invisible force into the Morgue. I never want to go there, but am always pulled there. One Christmas Day, when I would rather have been anywhere else, I was attracted in, to see an old grey man lying all alone on his cold bed, with a tap of water turned on over his grey hair, and running, drip, drip, drip, down his wretched face until it got to the corner of his mouth, where it took a turn, and made him look sly. One New Year's Morning (by the same token, the sun was shining outside, and there was a mountebank balancing a feather on his nose, within a yard of the gate), I was pulled in again to look at a flaxen-haired boy of eighteen, with a heart hanging on his breast—"from his mother," was engraven on it—who had come into the net across the river, with a bullet wound in his fair forehead and his hands cut with a knife, but whence or how was a blank mystery.

And so it was in this manner that our heroine was found, brought to the morgue and displayed. But no one stepped forward to claim the body of the poor *l'inconnue de la Seine*. The story of *l'inconnue* spread throughout the city. People came in droves to see her at the morgue.

All Paris society became enthralled, attracted by talk of her beauty and her mystery. People speculated about her life and death. Who was she? Where did she come from? How did she die? And why had no one come to claim her?

And why was she smiling?

In the days after she was discovered and brought to the morgue, debate about the manner of the young girl's death was particularly lively. The common wisdom, that she had drowned in the river, was certainly the most likely cause of death. Others disagreed. No drowning victim would be smiling, looking so peaceful in their last moments. No body that had spent even a few hours in the river would look quite so well-preserved. The water would quickly begin to transform the body, bloating being the primary effect.

Nonetheless, however she had lived and died were quickly lost in the rising tide of fame that awaited her. Like all unclaimed souls, her body was displayed for a time and then she had to be removed from the morgue to make room for new arrivals. She was buried somewhere, there is no record of where, but likely she was placed in a pauper's graves on the outskirts of Paris. She was gone, but not forgotten, thanks to her death mask, fashioned by the unknown morgue assistant.

With the advent of photography, death masks are a thing of the past. Usually death masks were made only of famous people, or by a family who wanted to preserve the memory of a loved one. Rarely was a death mask made of some poor or unknown person, like our drowned heroine.

Using "Plaster of Paris" (another Paris story), the mask needed to be made soon after death. The face and any facial hair were treated with grease or oil. Then several layers of plaster gauze were applied to create the form and outline the features. After this had set, plaster was built up covering the entire face and allowed to harden. Once removed, the mask was cleaned and sometimes filled with plaster or wax to keep the three-dimensional features intact.

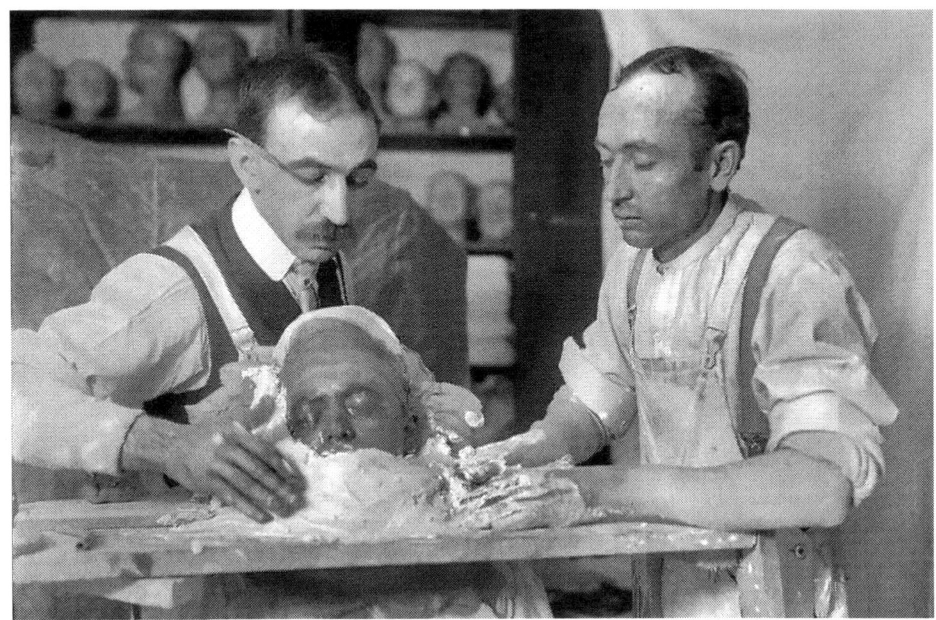

*Fig. 2 - Two men making a death mask (Wikimedia Commons, public domain)*

Someone, perhaps the death-mask maker, made copies of the death mask and they began to be sold around Paris. From these copies even more casts were made. Souvenir shops stocked up on copies of the mask and fascinated Parisians bought them by the scores, decorating their Paris apartments and shops. High society and bohemian circles were equally captivated by this face.

Something about *l'inconnue* spoke from the grave to the human heart and soul. People speculated that, with her mystifying smile and a visage that spoke of a beatific calm, she had died (of all things) "in a moment of extreme happiness."

Her image continued to grow in popularity, and in a very short time, her fame spread across Europe. Painters and sculptors used copies of the mask as a model for their art. Writers in France found much mystery in her image. Albert Camus, the renowned French philosopher, remarked that she was "the drowned Mona Lisa," or "The Mona Lisa of the Seine." Richard le Gallienne, English author and poet, referred to her as "a modern Ophelia."

Soon novelists and poets from all over Europe were writing odes and stories with a copy of the death mask mounted over their desks. Novellas, poems, and short stories attempted to capture the unsolved riddle of the drowned girl of Paris and flesh out the narrative of her life and death.

Vladimir Nabokov's 1934 poem, "L'Inconnue de la Seine," written in Russian, is a meditation on our mysterious heroine:

Hastening the outcome of this life,
Loving nothing on earth,
I'm still looking at the white mask
From your lifeless face.
In the strings dying to infinity
I hear the voice of your beauty.
In the pale crowds of drowned young people
You are more pale and bewitching than all of them.
At least in the sounds stay with me!
Your fate was stingy with happiness,
So respond with a posthumous mocking smile
From your enchanted gypsum lips.

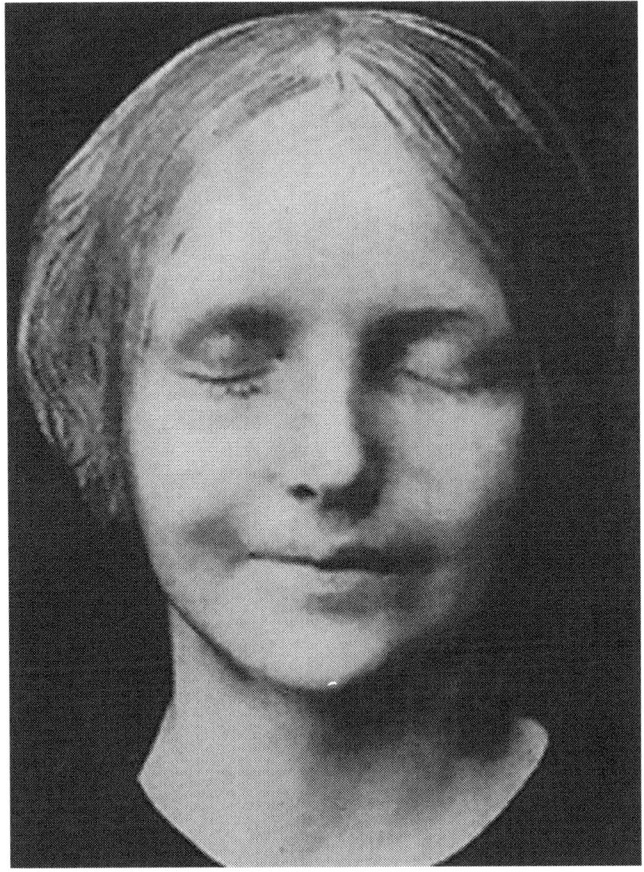

*Fig. 3 - L'Inconnue de la Seine, Death Mask*
*(public domain)*

Others reflected on the effect she was having on art and the current zeitgeist. In his only novel, *The Notebooks of Malte Laurids Brigge*, written in 1910 while he was living in Paris, poet Rainer Maria Rilke wrote:

> The caster I visit every day has two masks hanging next to his door. The face of the young one who drowned, which someone copied in the morgue because it was beautiful, because it was still smiling, because its smile was so deceptive—as though it knew.

And so in death, and in the imagination of thousands of people, the mysterious girl lived on.

But eventually, the story, the allure, the novelty, the importance of *l'Inconnue de la Seine* faded into a distant memory, as all fads eventually do. Her visage eventually disappeared from drawing rooms and parlors, short stories and etchings as new ideas, new fascinations, new mysteries appeared and took her place.

And so this story, as interesting as it is, might have ended here but for another twist of fate in her improbable journey. Around 1957, the unknown girl of the Seine came back to life! Our heroine moved out of Paris, away from the grisly morgue and the drawing rooms of polite society, only to be revived amid the pine forests and the fjords of Norway. Some seventy years after her body was first discovered she miraculously gained new life and new purpose.

Norwegian toymaker Asmund Laerdal worked mostly in wood and metals in his small but efficient factory. He was an energetic man, full of curiosity, and an accomplished inventor. After World War II, he began experimenting, making toys out of a new material—plastic. This new soft plastic was especially suited for manufacturing dolls' faces and bodies. Molded plastic, supple and malleable, made the dolls more life-like and durable, and it was better and cheaper than porcelain or cloth.

Laerdal's most successful creation was the "Annie Doll" which was a huge seller, a tremendous success for his toy company and for Laerdal personally. It was so popular it was named Norway's "Toy of the Year" in 1957. Laerdal was riding high. He had a family and business was good. He was a successful entrepreneur and inventor.

Then, tragedy nearly struck. His son, two-year old Tore, almost drowned. He was saved only by his quick-thinking father, who hauled him out of the water and began applying an early form of artificial respiration, which saved the boy's life. This event proved to be a turning point for Laerdal's life's mission. The shock of his son's near drowning led him to become interested in the current science for reviving people who had stopped breathing, either by drowning or for other reasons.

This led him to contact medical professionals in Scandinavia and in the United States. He attended a Scandinavian medical conference in Norway where a fortuitous meeting took place. The idea for a mannequin was first proposed at the time when Laerdal was speaking with doctors and people from the Red Cross about the newest discoveries in artificial respiration. Something was needed to allow people to practice the latest techniques.

Could Laerdal and his toy company make such a device? With the well-known Annie Doll riding high in popularity, it was logical to approach him with the idea. Not only had he recently experienced the near drowning of his young son, but his company had also recently expanded to making artificial, real-looking body parts with injuries for teaching people to properly dress wounds.

Laerdal seized the opportunity to help. He flew to the United States to meet the leading doctor in the field of artificial respiration. Their conversations gave Laerdal the ideas he needed to begin work.

Much thought went into the design. The mannequin's chest had to inflate and deflate. Its "pulmonary system" had to resemble the workings of an actual human body. Its neck had to swivel side to side. It needed to be portable. Everyone agreed the doll had to be a woman. Men would be highly reluctant to put their lips on a male mannequin.

Early versions were good, but not yet to the high mechanical, esthetic, and medical standards Laerdal demanded. For one thing, the face was not human enough. It did not resemble a real, unconscious person.

Two years later, after several prototypes, Laerdal revealed his gift to the world: Resusci Annie, the first doll used to teach people how to apply artificial respiration. But although the doll worked perfectly mimicking an unconscious person, the look on the face was not right. It was too flat, not realistic enough to satisfy Laerdal. The problem continued to frustrate him.

One day, shortly after revealing the mannequin to the scientific and medical community, Laerdal was visiting his wife's parents. The face of a young woman hung on their parlor wall. It was a copy of the death mask of *l'inconnue de la Seine*. The idea struck him like a lightning bolt. Here was Annie. Here was the face of the drowned girl who would save the lives of millions.

Laerdal borrowed the decoration from his in-laws and took it back to the factory. Soon, Resusci Annie had a new look. She is, even today a face kissed by millions upon millions of people all over the world: the unknown girl who drowned in the Seine!

**Travelers' Tips**

Ⓜ **Métro Station Pont Neuf, Line 7 (Quai du Louvre)**

Ⓜ **Métro Station Châtelet, Lines 1, 4, 7, 11 or 14**

Ⓜ **Métro Cité, Line 4 (Quai de l'Archevéché) — Memorial to the Martyrs of the Deportation**

Most of the sites discussed in this chapter are long gone. Both morgues have been demolished, and of course, casual visits to the present-day Paris morgue are discouraged. Nor is anything left of the old Châtelet fortress turned prison, except the name on the largest Métro station in Europe.

Walking along the Île de la Cité and behind Nôtre Dame, you will see the lovely gardens and the place where the rue Morgue and *the* morgue that Dickens visited once stood. In that place today stands something that is worth visiting. On the spot of the old morgue you will find the Mémorial des Martyrs de la Déportation (Memorial to the Martyrs of the Deportation).

This site is a solemn memorial to the 200,000 souls deported from France by the Vichy government to the Nazi death camps during World War II. It was inaugurated by Charles de Gaulle in 1962. The French survivor's group, *Reseau de souvenir*, described the memorial as a crypt, "hollowed out of the sacred isle, the cradle of our nation, which incarnates the soul of France—a place where its spirit dwells."

The memorial, shaped to recall the prow of a ship, can be accessed by two staircases leading to a rotunda and two chapels that each hold some earth and the bones of victims of the camps, and the tomb of an unknown deportee killed at the camp in Neustadt. Inside the enclosed and darkly lit space, giving a feeling of claustrophobia, are glass crystals that shine with light, one for each of the 200,000 deportees who died in the concentration camps. A single bright light shines at the end of the tunnel.

### *Quais (Banks) of the Seine*

*L'Inconnue de la Seine* was found in the waters of the river off the Quai du Louvre. While, hopefully, you will not encounter any floating corpses, lovely or otherwise, a leisurely stroll along the Paris quais is a marvelous way to spend a few hours. Parisians love the river—in the summer it is turned into *Paris Plage* or "Paris Beach." The city goes all out, trucking in tons of sand, setting out beach chairs, beach volleyball courts, concession stands, and more for a seaside experience in the heart of the city.

For that true Parisian experience, pack a picnic lunch like the Parisians do: wine, cheese, bread, charcuterie, olives, crudités, and whatever else pleases your palate, and head to the banks of the Seine for a summer picnic!

*Fig. 4-5 - Memorial to the martyrs of the deportation (photo by the author)*

*Fig. 6 - Welcome to Paris Plages*
*(photo by the author)*

## How Paris Shaped Our World

A drowning in the Seine was not unusual, nor was a murder nor an unclaimed body. But somehow fate had a memorable story to write about the unknown girl of the Seine, *l'inconnue de la Seine.*

The mystery of her death and the nature of her beauty led her to an afterlife of fame—first as an intriguing mystery to the people of Paris, then as an image, a death mask. Then she became a muse and inspiration for artists, poets, and writers. With that aura, she became a presence, a decorative fixture in homes, galleries, and salons across Europe and the United States.

Then the story took another twist. From a near drowning in the family of a man with an innovative mind, resources, imagination, and willingness to take on the challenge to create a model to help people learn artificial respiration, our heroine went on to be the face that helped save millions of lives. This lifesaving "doll" came from a chance meeting of minds at a medical conference and a flash of inspiration at seeing our heroine on the wall of his in-laws' home.

All these forces came together to elevate one poor, anonymous, dead young woman to the kind of fame and fate few will ever experience, nor could anyone have planned. She lived in death in a way she certainly never did in life, nor could she have dreamed of her fame and fortune in the decades since she died.

The truth is, indeed, stranger than fiction.

Today, Laerdal Medical is an international corporation. Its mission is simple: *Helping save lives.*

Its vision statement is also simple and powerful: *No one should die or be disabled unnecessarily during birth or from sudden illness, trauma, or medical errors.*

Laerdal Global Health (LGH) is a not-for-profit company dedicated to helping save the lives of mothers and newborns in low-income countries. The Laerdal Foundation supports research into best practices and practical implementations in acute medicine, supporting 1,800 international research projects with millions of dollars in funding.

And the "Unknown Girl of the Seine" is still influencing artists today. In 1986, Michael Jackson wrote and recorded his album Bad. He also happened to be taking a CPR course at the time. In these classes, students practice CPR on an Annie doll. They are taught that the first thing you do is ask, "Annie, are you okay?" before starting CPR.

In the song, “Smooth Criminal,” Jackson repeats the CPR-inspired phrase, “Annie, are you okay?” over and over and over, incorporating this basic CPR technique into the song. He also mentions mouth-to-mouth resuscitation in the song lyrics.

If you have ever taken a CPR class, you have kissed *l’inconnue de la Seine.* She has touched your mind, heart, and soul. Perhaps she has saved your life or the life of someone you love. We all owe her an impossible debt of gratitude. We owe it to her memory to honor all those who come among us and pass on unnoticed.

Merci! to the Unknown Girl of the Seine!

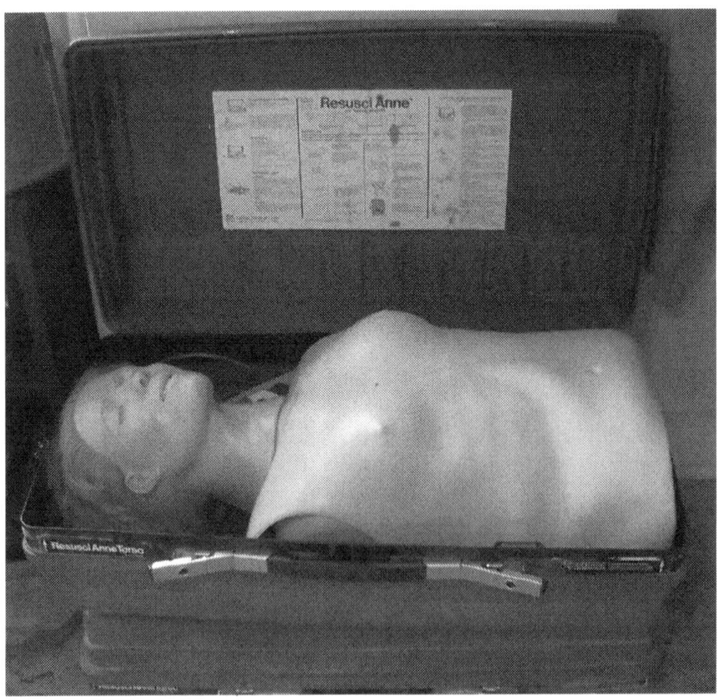


*Fig. 7 - Resusci-Anne by Laerdal Medical (Creative Commons)*

## Chapter 2

# The Most Popular Attraction in Paris

(Sixteenth and Seventeenth Centuries)

*"I only understood the Parisians when I finally crossed the Pont Neuf."*

— Benjamin Franklin,
US Ambassador to France, 1775-1785
P. L. Jacobs, Curiosités de l'Histoire du Vieux Paris (1858)

IN THE MODERN era, the most popular attraction in Paris is the Eiffel Tower, one of the most visited monuments in the most visited city in the world. Seven million visitors a year is something worth discussing…but another time.

Today we travel back to July 1606, when the most popular attraction in Paris was le Pont Neuf (the new bridge) which recently opened to traffic crossing the Seine at the top of the island, the Île de la Cité. The Pont Neuf was, and still is, the heart of Paris. It was the Eiffel Tower of its time, visited by throngs of people day and night. It changed the course of history because it changed Paris, and because it changed Paris, the Pont Neuf changed the world.

Never mind that the "*New* Bridge" is four centuries old and is now the *oldest* bridge in Paris. When it opened, le Pont Neuf was a marvel of engineering and design the likes of which had not been seen in the Western world since Rome 1,500 years earlier. Indeed, when King Henri IV inaugurated the bridge in 1607, it had already begun to remake Paris in significant ways, ways mostly hidden from the casual observer today. Two of these significant innovations will come into focus—*if* you know what to look for.

**Travelers' Tips**

 **Métro Station Pont Neuf, Line 7**

Coming out of the Métro, you are on the Right Bank where you will immediately see the river Seine and the Pont Neuf. On the bridge, you first cross the longer of the two spans before the short section that spans the Île de la Cité, and then another span to the Left Bank.

Visitors and tourists likely cross the bridge with barely a thought. Yet they are standing on top of an engineering marvel that was innovative for its time. Let's travel back to an age when the Pont Neuf really was the *new bridge* and see the innovations it brought.

The first innovation can't be seen *because it is a feature that is not there!* The second innovation you *will* see immediately—and completely overlook—because it is something so common today as to be unremarkable.

Bridges are essential to a city or region's life and commerce, their vitality, and health. But bridges cost money to build and maintain and monarchs were more interested in spending tax money on luxuries, wars, fortresses, and palaces. They were reluctant to build bridges. Hence, if they *had* to build a bridge, they would build the cheapest bridge possible—small, narrow, functional, and barely stable. Whenever possible, they built it using other people's money. For example, because floods had already destroyed the Petit Pont thirteen times over the centuries, when floods destroyed it yet again in 1393, the king funded its replacement by taxing the Jews of Paris.

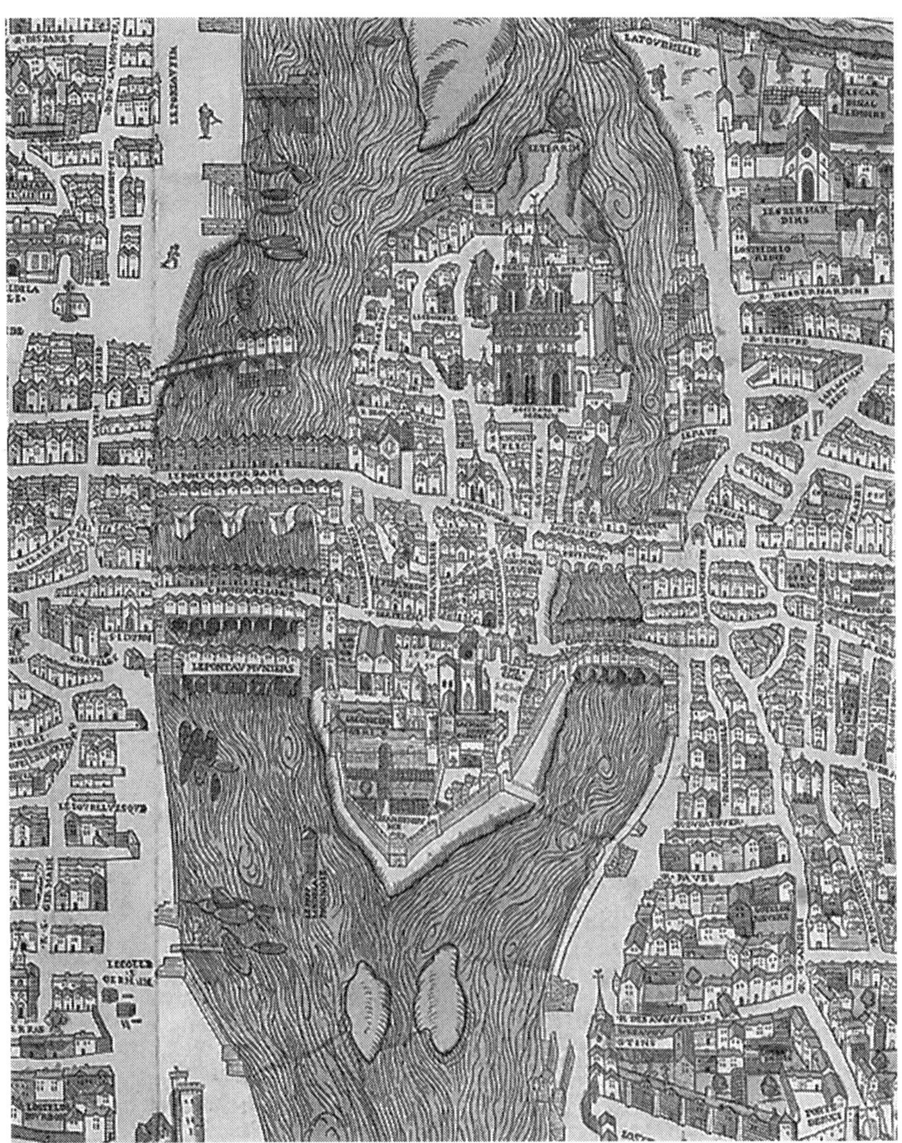

*Fig. 8* - The Center of Paris 1550 *by Olivier Truschet and Germain Hoyau (public domain)*

Up through the sixteenth century until the time of the Pont Neuf, there were only five bridges in all of Paris, three on the Right Bank (the Pont au Change, the Pont aux Meuniers, and the Pont Notre Dame), and two on the Left Bank (the Petit Pont and the Pont St. Michel). What was worse for the people of Paris, none crossed the Seine directly from right bank to left, so to get from one side of Paris to the other, one needed to walk a long and circuitous route.

Then, in the early 1500s, King François I began to reshape Paris from a medieval city to a modern Renaissance capital. He started transforming the Louvre from a medieval fortress into a Renaissance palace. It was François who sent explorers like Jacques Cartier and Giovanni da Verrazano to explore the Americas. He built Paris' new city hall (Hôtel de Ville), and he ordered that every library in France receive a copy of every book published in France.

And it was François I who summoned the Italian painter and inventor, Leonardo DaVinci to Paris. DaVinci, who brought with him a little painting which the French call *la Joconde* but most of the world calls the *Mona Lisa*. François liked the painting so much that he had it hung in his palace at Fontainebleau—in his privy (his toilet)! Today, of course she resides in the Louvre, a much more auspicious place.

François' successors continued the process of making France a modern country, and making Paris the preeminent city in Europe. Of course, a world-class city needed a world-class bridge befitting its status and its burgeoning needs. After all, a modern city couldn't have narrow, rickety, wooden bridges subjected to frequent destruction by spring floods, winter ice floes, and fires all year round.

In May 1578, Henri III accompanied by his mother, Queen Catherine de Medici, and his wife, Louise of Lorraine, laid the first stone of the new bridge. Work progressed for a time, but it halted in 1588 due to the violence of France's bloody and intractable Wars of Religion—the roiling political conflict between Catholics and Protestants—that eventually resulted in the horror known as the Saint Bartholomew' Day Massacre.

The assassination of Henri III in 1589 brought Henri of Navarre to the throne. Crowned King Henri IV, he was France's first Protestant king. Although he converted to Catholicism, that did not lessen the religious conflict. In fact, it exacerbated it. Henri was so embroiled in the strife consuming France that construction of the bridge didn't resume until 1598, when he issued new orders for its completion. Henri, a talented and thoughtful visionary, drew up new plans for the Pont Neuf. His design modifications made the Pont Neuf less elaborate, but they incorporated several new and radical ideas.

Up until then, European bridges were lined with houses and shops along both sides. Taxes and rents from the buildings financed the bridges' construction and maintenance. The upside (for the monarchs) was that the money didn't have to come out of the royal coffers.

Bridges with houses and shops of course had to be sturdy enough to hold their own weight, but as a result, they could not hold heavy traffic. The narrow roadway could accommodate riders on horseback, small carts, and wagons, but not larger, heavier vehicles. By the end of the sixteenth century this was a growing problem because a new kind of transportation was emerging: the personal carriage. These new vehicles were a rare sight on the streets of Paris in the 1500s—so rare the king had just one. But by the close of the century, their numbers were growing with the emergence of the middle class — the bourgeois, merchants, artisans, etc. and more and more carriages began to fill the streets of Paris.

*Fig. 9* - The Pont Neuf, the Samaritaine and the Pointe de la Cité,
*Nicolas-Jean-Baptiste Raguenet (1715-1793);*
*painting at the Carnavalet Museum, Paris (public domain)*

*Fig. 10 - Nicolas-Jean-Baptiste Raguenet,* The joust of the sailors, between the Notre-Dame bridge and the Pont-au-Change, *1756*

Henri knew his growing city needed a bridge that could support larger vehicles *and* more traffic overall, so the old bridge designs were scrapped. The revolutionary innovation on the Pont Neuf you *can't* see becomes obvious once pointed out:

There are no houses and no shops on the bridge.

The bridge is clear and unobstructed on both sides. With no houses and shops to tax, Henri financed his new bridge by levying an import duty on every cask of wine that entered the city. The joke on the streets of Paris was that the rich and the drunk paid for the Pont Neuf.

A bridge without houses was a new sight, and it caused an immediate reaction among the public. To understand why this was such a shock and a delight, you must imagine yourself in medieval Paris, which at the time was a dense maze of streets. Most streets were close and narrow, with both sides hemmed in by tall houses that bulged in the middle, as was the style of medieval construction.

*Fig. 11 - 1577 Artist's Rendering of Henri III Design for the Pont Neuf (Musée Carnavalet, public domain)*

Most Parisians lived in these confining *quartiers* (neighborhoods) cramped streets twisting right or left. Most Parisians rarely left the safety of their small neighborhood, living their whole life having never seeing an expansive vista—unless they had come from the country. And they surely had never seen a manmade panorama such as what awaited them when they first came to the Pont Neuf.

The sight was stunning—a wide, almost limitless vista. This stunning view of the city quickly attracted throngs of people. Look! You could see the Seine. You could see the Louvre Palace. You could see the Concierge with its three towers and clock. People flocked onto the bridge in droves, idling about, looking at the Seine, the sky, and the cityscape. They discovered Paris was beautiful.

Writing in 1670, French travel writer and physician François Bernier exclaimed in his book, *Travels in the Mogul Empire*, "Yes, my friend, when you are on the Pont Neuf at Paris, you may boldly aver, on my authority, that your eyes behold the grandest of all artificial scenes in the world.... What will this view be, what will be its beauty when the Louvre is completed!"

This new vision of the city arguably had an expansive effect on people's consciousness. Those standing on the "New Bridge" saw an unobstructed panorama stretching as far as the eye could see. Perhaps for the first time in their lives, they saw their physical environment—and their lives—from a larger perspective. The sight must have broadened people's horizons, giving the Parisians a new outlook, new vitality and energy. The reactions and events that followed were a direct result of the architecture of the Pont Neuf.

And it is clear that this dramatic effect was something Henri IV undoubtedly had in mind. What evidence is there to assert this bold claim?

Put yourself back in 1607, and then step onto the bridge. Look to your right and to your left. What do you notice built into the stone barriers on either side?

There are alcoves in the stone railings, balconies like theater boxes, expressly designed for people to step out of the flow of traffic and pause to look, with seats carved out of the stone allowing people to sit and relax. This design clearly creates a dramatic engagement for the viewer between city, river, sky, and Paris herself.

Just as dramatic, perhaps more so, is the vast open area in the center of the bridge that holds the statue of Henri IV on horseback. It is the perfect gathering place for people to meet and mingle with their fellow Parisians. From the start, this area became a stage where one could find, day or night, all manner of diversion. Jugglers, acrobats, actors, orators, poets, news criers, and comedians entertained, delighted, and provoked the crowds into the wee hours of the morning.

Long before the first theaters opened in Paris (the Comédie-Française would not be established until 1680), the "stage" of the Pont Neuf, under the statue of Henri IV, was the place people went to hear news, gossip, and watch entertainers. Comedians were a crowd favorite, poking fun at everything and everyone, including the royals themselves, much to the delight of the populace and the dismay of the nobility.

It is clear Henri IV anticipated his people's reaction to the views of Paris. Removing the last vestiges of the medieval fortress on the Right Bank, he wanted people to see the magnificence of his new *Grande Galerie of the Louvre*, being built at the time. Running over a quarter mile along the Seine, the *Grande Galerie* was at the time the longest building in the world.

Yet all of this magnificence would have been for nothing if people could not appreciate it, if they were forced to cross the Pont Neuf in the crush of traffic. Nobody could linger and look if they were too concerned with their own safety. To prevent this, Henri added something else: the innovation that you *do* see and is still there today, right under your feet....

Sidewalks.

Henri added sidewalks, a feature not seen since Roman times and never before in a European city. These modern marvels (that you probably don't think twice about) right under your feet, in 1607 they were new—and revolutionary.

*Fig. 12-13 - Theater Box on the Pont Neuf, Barrier (photos by the author)*

As you observe the roadway and traffic, continue to imagine yourself 400 years ago. In those days, everyone would walk in the narrow, muddy streets, where people, wagons, herds of pigs being driven to market were all vying for space trying to navigate through the crowds.

Here comes a gang of youths, roughhousing and stealing caps. There goes an elegant gentleman and a lady trying to keep her skirts clean. A walk anywhere was a struggle with horses, livestock, children, carts—all in the muddy roadway trying to get through the streets of Paris. The image of Sir Walter Raleigh putting his cloak down to let Queen Elizabeth traverse a mud puddle comes to mind.

The phenomenon of sidewalks was so new that the French didn't even have a word for them or for those who walked *on* the sidewalks. Official documents refer to the people as *gens de pied* (people on foot). Later, a new word would be coined, *piéton* (pedestrian). And, eventually, *trottoir* would be settled on as the preferred name for these new walkways.

In his 1639 guidebook, *France, dressé pour l'instruction & la commodité tant des François que des estrangers (France, prepared for the instruction and convenience of both the French and foreigners*), Claude de Varennes describes the bridge and the pedestrians this way:

> The deck floor is divided into three: in the middle pass the carriage and the horses; the two sides are two aisles that rise two feet more than the middle, and only pass people [on] feet.
>
> (*Le sol du pont est parti en trois: au milieu passent les carosse et les chevaux; les deux côtez sont deux allées*

> *qui s'elevent de deux pieds plus que le milieu, et n'y passent que les gens de pieds*.)

De Varennes knew his readers would be unfamiliar with this new structure, so he felt his guidebook should highlight the fact that "sidewalks" were only for pedestrians.

The Pont Neuf's original design had the sidewalks elevated two feet higher than the roadway, so people could walk safely and confidently, free from the dangers of trundling carts and herds of cows. They could relax, at ease to stroll, talk, and enjoy themselves and the view.

Later, the French would invent a word for someone strolling along, relaxed with no destination or goal in mind: *un flâneur*. The word has no real English equivalent. (See Chapter 3: Smoke and Mirrors.) Both a noun and a verb, it describes an *insouciance*, free of any care or concern, open to whatever one comes across in their stroll, ready to be educated, entertained, amused, or thrilled by an unexpected adventure. A flâneur has hours, days, a lifetime to enjoy life without thought or agenda. Being *un flâneur* takes practice, mindfulness, and skill—and it would not be possible without sidewalks.

The combination of the sidewalks and the open-air scene resulted in another modern phenomenon, one we still suffer from today: traffic jams. Rather than alleviate traffic congestion with a larger, more expansive roadway and bridge, the Pont Neuf increased traffic considerably. It is a counterintuitive fact even in today's modern urban planning that the more room you make for traffic, the more traffic you will get.

So almost immediately, the bridge was crowded with throngs of people, horses, carts, and carriages. Even though the Pont Neuf was much wider than any bridge built before, it quickly became a snarled mess as word spread and people came to see for themselves what Good King Henri had given them. On the sidewalks and on the roadway, a great cacophony of noise, and a tremendous surge of humanity converged on the New Bridge.

*Fig. 14* - The Louvre from the Pont-Neuf*, around 1666-75, painting by Hendrick Mommers (Museum: Department of Paintings of the Louvre) (Courtesy Wikimedia, public domain)*

Some came just to cross over, as a part of their daily travels. But some came just because it was there, to look, to gawk, to buy or sell, to see and be seen. Besides its functional use, the bridge became *the place* to meet, talk, gossip, hear news, buy merchandise, and be entertained. Soon after it opened, posters were everywhere, telling people the latest news and events. Peddlers and vendors began hawking their wares.

Pamphleteers and booksellers set up makeshift stalls. These met with immediate protests from the established bookshops on the Left Bank. The itinerant booksellers drew customers away from the bookstores, which paid taxes while these transients did not. The bookstores were also more easily subject to inspection and censorship by government officials and the church. The second-hand booksellers were accused of offering seditious materials against the king, and perhaps even worse, forbidden writings by a new, radical religious sect—Protestants!

Chased off, arrested, their provocative publications confiscated, the booksellers quickly regrouped along the approaches leading to the bridge. A settlement in 1649 prohibited selling books on the Pont Neuf. But by a century later, accommodations would be made for these itinerant booksellers. The green boxes you see along the Seine on either side, les bouquinistes, are their direct descendants. Today, the green boxes of les bouquinistes line the walls along both sides of the riverbanks (quais). It is said that the Seine is the only river in the world that runs between two bookshelves.

The lack of houses and the addition of sidewalks on the Pont Neuf forever changed Paris, and the world you live in today. The origins of these changes is something scholars and academics continue to debate and discover more about. Hopefully, this book—part history, part guidebook to Paris—sheds some light and makes what you are seeing (and *not* seeing) a little more interesting and meaningful.

## How Paris Shaped Our World

Nothing like the bridge and its popularity had ever happened before; the Eiffel Tower of its day, Pont Neuf attracted visitors from far and wide. The bridge is credited with many things, and some contend it was integral in the development of three phenomena that have affected the world we live in today: French fashion, burgeoning commerce, and ideas of egalitarianism.

### *Paris Fashion*

As the hub of social activity, entertainment, news, and gossip, people planned their day around a trip to the Pont Neuf. All classes, especially the nobles and the rapidly growing middle class (bourgeoisie), realized they would see other important people, and more importantly, *be seen* by them. Hence, the need to look one's best. Quickly, it became *de rigeur* to be dressed to impress the people one might meet while strolling the Pont.

Over the next one hundred years, the Paris fashion industry came to completely dominate Europe. Changes in shopping habits, marketing, innovations in manufacturing, and the romantic and compelling idea that *la mode* was Paris, and that Paris was *la mode* were among the many contributing factors that made Paris the fashion and style capital of the world.

Some contend the origins of this phenomenon can be traced back to the new "see and be seen" atmosphere of the Pont Neuf. People of means had to have new outfits made so they could be observed in their finest dresses and cloaks by all of Paris. Historical documents and guidebooks, which talk extensively about the Pont Neuf, make special note of the styles that appeared among the crowds. They also warn travelers of the notorious and dangerous gangs of thieves who would steal ladies' handkerchiefs and scarves and especially the large men's cloaks (manteaux), garments which could cost a small fortune.

French dominance of the fashion world, which has created the mystique of Paris as much as anything, is well known and continues to the present day. French fashion brands, Chanel, Louis Vuitton, Dior, and Lacroix, began in Paris and are headquartered here. Along the Champs-Élysées, Avenue Montaigne, and the Rue du Faubourg

Saint-Honoré the luxurious houses of upscale fashion, jewelry, and beauty, many of which were founded in the seventeenth century still reside.

Many forces came together to make *la mode* what it is today. The start of the French fashion industry was supported by new methods of transmitting news and information. Under Louis XIV, the monarchy itself was responsible for the creation of a new concept: the fashion press. By the mid-1670s the fledgling fashion industry was benefiting from the king's fashion press marketing new designs to the public. The concept of a "fashion season" and the periodic change in styles, all contributed to the "need" to buy and wear exclusive French fashion.

The concepts of fashion are so ingrained in our consciousness today that, like sidewalks, they are barely noticed. And like sidewalks, the origins of the entire multi-billion-dollar worldwide fashion industry can likely be traced back to the Pont Neuf.

### *Commerce and Trade*

Almost at the exact moment the Pont Neuf opened, it became a magnet drawing all walks of life to stroll its wide sidewalks and view the broad expanse of the Paris skyline. Vendors, merchants, food stalls, orators, hucksters, booksellers, peddlers hawking everything from souvenirs to medicines along with pickpockets and thieves saw an opportunity and set up shop. Commerce became a meaningful and pervasive presence in day-to-day life along the Pont Neuf.

One of the most prolific groups of thieves were the clothes-thieves, often organized gangs or merely kids stealing on a lark or a dare. For those wealthy people with fancier garb, to go near the Pont Neuf meant risking the loss of an expensive cloak or a silk handkerchief, scarf, or other item of clothing. Other crimes flourished as well, especially pickpockets, prostitutes, quack "doctors" selling miracle cures, and hustlers with all kinds of cons, like the shell game one can still find today in the touristy parts of Paris.

But obviously, most commercial activities were not criminal. Besides the legitimate vendors, and the aforementioned booksellers, jugglers, acrobats, actors, puppeteers, clowns, mimes, artists, and entertainers of all sorts came to the Pont Neuf to make their living and use its perpetual stage to entertain and amuse the passersby.

Many merchants found the crowds on the Pont Neuf to be a source of customers eager to buy. Sellers of luxury items made a good living on and around the bridge. A prime example is the Quay de Orfèvres named for the gold merchants who set up along this stretch of the river, beating gold into fine jewelry.

The forerunners of the modern newspaper also started here, with those who sold periodic newssheets and pamphlets. As a social gathering place, people came to hear the latest reports, news, and gossip and learn what was going on in Paris and the world outside. *Heard it on the Pont Neuf* became common slang for "I already knew that."

Not long after the opening of the bridge, new ways of marketing and selling merchandise appeared in other parts of Paris. Shops became more than just places to store goods, which were then carted to a customer's home. Display windows enticed people to come in and look at what was on offer. Shopping arcades, predecessors to today's shopping malls, soon followed. Shopping became a social activity and a form of entertainment in and of itself. The importance of the Pont Neuf to today's modern commerce is unmistakable and yet little understood by most who just see a bridge.

### *Political and Philosophical Ideas of Egalitarianism*

In the years before the Pont Neuf officially opened, all of Paris waited in high anticipation. *Everyone* was attracted to the bridge, and throngs came to see it soon after it opened.

All of Paris gathered there; every strata of society gathering at the same time.

They came and stayed...and returned day after day. Poor, lifelong city dwellers who had rarely been out of their neighborhood, country peasants newly arrived, bored homemakers, itinerant peddlers, knife-grinders, acrobats, criminals, children, all had to go see and be a part of this marvelous thing.

The newly minted *bourgeoisie*, who were quickly growing wealthy and climbing the social ladder, were equally drawn to the bridge. Even the nobility, some disdainfully, some happily, threw themselves into this sea of people, as eager as anyone to be a part of the Pont Neuf experience.

Different classes of people suddenly coming together generated all sorts of reactions. Peasants, who had never laid eyes on a duchess, found themselves standing nearby one. At first, this might inspire awe, but over time, perhaps they saw that this duchess was not so different from them, nor from anyone else.

It might be a little harder to imagine noblemen and women having the same reaction. Would they look at a filthy street beggar and feel a kinship? Maybe not. Yet never before had the various classes of Parisian society mixed and mingled daily in a sustained fashion such as they began to do on the Pont Neuf. Over time, it clearly would have dawned on some that being a noble was a matter of luck and birth, not some God-given right.

Add to that the availability of the latest news, read from the broadside sheets mysteriously appearing in the middle of the night—the "seditious" pamphlets and books that were available, the comedians speaking truth and confronting power and society's incongruities with their barbed humor, plus a growing sense that the world was larger than one's small *quartier* (neighborhood)—it should not be surprising that new philosophies, new energy, new ideas, and new possibilities emerged.

Could the seventeenth-century Pont Neuf social mix have been one of the contributing factors to the eighteenth-century ideas of Rousseau, Montesquieu, and Voltaire? Rousseau especially speculated on questions of justice, fairness, and egalitarianism in his *Discourse on Inequality*. He saw that human inequality was deeply ingrained in society with its different classes dominating and exploiting each other. Rousseau's reflections led him to develop ideas of equality that eventually influenced Thomas Jefferson, leading Jefferson to write, "all men are created equal."

Perhaps these radical ideas began to awaken in 1607, here on the bridge in late Renaissance Paris where, for the very first time, a public space brought together people from the different social strata, the first glimmerings of Enlightenment ideas of equality and egalitarianism, ideas that eventually played a role in the American and French Revolutions.

In sum, the origins of Paris fashion, the broadening of ideas, Enlightenment concepts, and modern ways of buying and selling goods and services are all deeply rooted in the foundation stones of Henri IV's bridge, which also gave us the now commonplace wide, sturdy bridges sans houses and shops, with paved roadways for traffic only, sidewalks for people on foot, and the understanding that government has a duty to build public works projects that benefit the entire populace.

Make your way onto the bridge, but don't hurry across. Stop and look at the city and river laid out before you in an unbroken vista and imagine that the expanse of water, monuments, palaces, and sky opening to the horizon is a new sight. Imagine you have been hemmed in all your life by the cramped and narrow streets in the small neighborhood from which you have rarely ventured.

Then you come to the Pont Neuf for the first time and see not only a view virtually unknown in 1607, but you are surrounded by all manner of people and news of places you've never heard of.

And what's more, this goes on virtually day and night in all manner of weather. You'll want to come here again. And again. Where before the center of your world had been the baker, the butcher, and the dram shop one street over, now your world has expanded. The Pont Neuf and all its activity and wonder is now part of your world. It has become a center of daily life. It is the center of Paris.

The changes the Pont Neuf wrought in the world cannot be overstated. Another bridge like it would not be seen in Europe for more than 150 years, not until 1750 when Westminster Bridge in London opened. Made of stone so it was fire- and flood-proof, with sidewalks and a paved roadway, the Pont Neuf's design introduced or reintroduced many things, reimagining and remaking Paris herself. With broad and safe sidewalks, a new term had to be invented: *piétons* (or pedestrians), a word hitherto unnecessary because people did not stroll through cities for enjoyment and stimulation.

The economic and creative influence of the commerce generated and practiced on and around the bridge, with sellers of all manner of goods plying their wares on the Pont Neuf's broad stage, created new ideas, energy, methods, and commercial enterprises that still affect us today. We have the word *souvenir* (in French literally "a memory" or "to remember") because of the trinkets and novelties sold to tourists visiting the Pont Neuf.

The Eiffel Tower is today the most visited monument in the most visited city in the world, but in the seventeenth century the most visited site was the marvelous, unique, and unforgettable heart and soul of Paris, which was, is, and always will be the Pont Neuf.

# Chapter 3
# Smoke and Mirrors

je t'aime

## (Eighteenth and Nineteenth Centuries)

PARIS

*"All political power is primarily an illusion....*
*Mirrors and blue smoke, beautiful blue smoke rolling*
*over the surface of highly polished mirrors, first*
*a thin veil of blue smoke, then a thick cloud that*
*suddenly dissolves into wisps of blue smoke, the*
*mirrors catching it all, bouncing it back and forth."*
— Jimmy Breslin, *How the Good Guys Finally Won:*
*Notes from an Impeachment Summer (1975)*

THE HALL WAS pitch black. The only sound was the rustling of women's dresses, which lent a nervous energy to the atmosphere around the people in attendance already on edge standing there in the dark. Imperceptibly, a pale green light slowly crept in, but from whence did it come? Its source was unclear. It grew, and then stole across the room as if possessing a will of its own. Then, just as suddenly as it had appeared, it vanished, leaving everyone in darkness once more.

A moment passed. The temperature in the room dropped noticeably, as if the winter weather outside had also made an entrance. Abruptly, the light reappeared, now behind them. It was accompanied by a low and wavering sound, like someone singing a dirge, but underwater. This startled everyone and made them look for the exits, invisible in the gloom. The green light began to coalesce, forming a human shape. It moved in and out of focus before resolving into the figure of an elderly man. He was dressed in last century's garb; his hair was stringy and thin, his mouth gaunt and wrinkled, his eyes sunken and hollow.

Several women gasped, one screamed, and a few of the men grabbed their walking sticks to use as cudgels should the apparition move toward them. But the ghost just floated there, slowly moving his head, surveying the crowd. His hands and arms reached out as if to implore the people to do something to help him. As he did this, he let out an awful moan that grew louder and louder as his weightless form rose up. It drifted toward the high ceiling—and right through it!

The green ghost-light was gone once more, plunging the room back into blackness. Pandemonium erupted as men and women rushed as one to find the exit leading out of the salon, falling over each other, heedless and panicked.

In the very back of the room, one man did not move. He chuckled to himself and fingered the coins in his pockets. An overflow crowd had paid well to be admitted to his new show, Robertson's *Phantasmagoric Spectacle*, at the Pavillon de l'Echiquier in Paris. To Robertson's delight, the night went off better than he could have ever imagined.

It was January 23, 1798. Étienne-Gaspard Roberts, Belgian scientist and artist, had returned to Paris. He had already made a name for himself in Europe as an early explorer of lighter-than-air flight in hot-air balloons.

He had studied the sciences, physics, optics, and mathematics. He was a remarkable artist—and he had had an almost obsessive interest in the macabre, in spirits and ghosts and the supernatural since he was a very young boy.

Roberts, using the stage name "Robertson," thrilled all of Europe and especially France during the French Revolution, and in the decades after. His combined talents and interests lent him the skills he needed to pull off some of the most amazing spectacles ever seen.

Charles Dickens commented after seeing one of Robertson's shows:

> He was a charmer who charmed wisely—who was a born conjurer, inasmuch as he was gifted with a predominant taste for experiments in natural science—and he was a useful enough man in an age of superstition to get up fashionable entertainments at which spectres were to appear and horrify the public, without trading on the public ignorance by any false pretense.... [His] is the story of an honourable and well-educated showman....

Robertson's fame would fade, but to this day, practitioners of magic, illusion, spectacle, and visual legerdemain revere his work as groundbreaking, and his show-business lineage continues on in literature, theater, film, and in many other forms of entertainment.

In Robertson's memoirs, *Mémoires, Recreatifs, Scientifiques et Anecdotiques*, published in two volumes in 1831 and 1833, he gives a comprehensive account of his life in these diverse and often revolutionary fields. He also recounts in sometimes gory detail his childhood fascination with the occult, his desire to master the abilities and secrets some people were believed to possess—of conjuring, weaving spells, and the dark arts of magic.

MÉMOIRES

RÉCRÉATIFS

SCIENTIFIQUES ET ANECDOTIQUES

DU PHYSICIEN-AÉRONAUTE

E. G. ROBERTSON,

Connu par ses expériences de Fantasmagorie, et par ses Ascensions Aérostatiques dans les principales villes de l'Europe; ex-Professeur de Physique au Collége central du ci-devant département de l'Ourthe, Membre de la Société Galvanique de Paris, de la Société des Arts et des Sciences de Hambourg, et de la Société d'Émulation de Liége.

ORNÉS DE PLANCHES ET FIGURES.

TOME PREMIER.

A PARIS,

CHEZ L'AUTEUR, BOULEVARD MONTMARTRE, Nº 12;
ET A LA LIBRAIRIE DE WURTZ, RUE DE BOURBON, Nº 17.

1831.

*Fig. 15-16* - Mémoires : récréatifs, scientifiques et anecdotiques *Robertson, E. G. (Etienne Gaspard), 1763-1831. Harry Houdini Collection (Library of Congress Rare Book and Special Collections Division)*

de bonnes raisons pour cela. Mais comme l'écrivain qui lui a reproché cette crédulité n'a point cité les passages où se trouve cette confession, et que je ne l'ai point vérifié, je ne prends pas la chose au sérieux. Qu'est-ce qui n'a pas cru au diable et aux loup-garous dans ses premières années! Je l'avoue franchement, j'ai cru au diable, aux évocations, aux enchantemens, aux pactes infernaux, et même au balai des sorcières; j'ai cru qu'une vieille femme, ma voisine, était, comme chacun l'assurait, en commerce réglé avec Lucifer. J'enviais son pouvoir et ses relations; je me suis enfermé dans une chambre pour couper la tête d'un coq, et forcer le chef des démons à se montrer devant moi; je l'ai attendu pendant sept à huit heures, je l'ai molesté, injurié, conspué de ce qu'il n'osait point paraître : « Si tu existes, m'écriais-je en frappant sur ma table, sors d'où tu es, et laisse voir tes cornes, sinon je te renie, je déclare que tu n'as jamais été. » Ce n'était point la peur, comme on le voit, qui me faisait croire à sa puissance, mais le désir de la partager pour opérer aussi des effets magiques. Les livres de magie me tournaient la tête. La *Magia naturalis* de Porta, et les *Récréations* de Midorge me donnaient surtout des insomnies. Je pris enfin un

Who didn't believe in the devil and the werewolves in his early years! I honestly admit, I believed in the devil, in the evocations, in the enchantments, in the infernal pacts, and even in the witches' brooms; I thought that an old woman, my neighbor, was, as everyone assured, in regular trafficking with Lucifer. I envied his power and his relationships; I locked myself in a room to cut off the head of a rooster, and force the leader of the demons to appear before me; I waited for seven to eight hours, I molested, insulted, taunted that he dared not appear: "If you exist, crush me." I slapped my table. "Come out of where you are and let's see your horns, otherwise I will deny you, I declare that you have never been...."

*Fig. 17 - Illustration of a performance by Philidor, from a 1791 handbill (courtesy wikimedia, public domain)*

*Fig. 18 - Étienne Gaspard Robertson,* Spectale Fantasmagorie, *frontispiece from his Mémoires (Library of Congress)*

A talented artist since his youth, Robertson knew, he must leave his childhood home, Liège, and head to Paris, the place where all artists must go if they wish to make a name for themselves. Robertson arrived in 1789, on the eve of the French Revolution, a dangerous but exciting time to be in Paris. He survived the Revolution and the Reign of Terror, and was a witness to the horrors of the guillotine, while continuing his many and varied scientific pursuits.

In 1793, Robertson attended a spectacle by a popular performer and promoter, Paul Philidor, who staged "magic lantern" shows. The magic lantern (in Latin, *Lanterna Magica*) was the early forerunner of the modern slide projector. Developed in the 1600s (or perhaps even earlier—there is evidence of Leonardo DaVinci drawing a similar device), it projected images by shining a light source through pictures, paintings, prints, and later, photographs embossed onto glass plates. The light shone through a lens that threw the image onto a wall or screen. Sunlight, candles or lamps were used, but the latter were usually too dim to be effective.

However, in the late 1700s, a new type of lamp was invented that produced a much stronger and brighter glow. In Paris, Thomas Jefferson, then US ambassador to France, wrote to James Madison in 1784 about this invention—a bright-burning lamp that gave "a light equal as is thought to that of six or eight candles." Madison replied asking Jefferson to bring some of these new "Argand lamps" back to America. Jefferson was particularly intrigued because the Swiss inventor, Ami Argand, had accomplished something that Benjamin Franklin had tried but failed to achieve. Jefferson wrote:

> The improvement is produced by forming the wick into a hollow cylinder so that there is a passage for the air through the hollow. The idea had occurred to Dr. Franklin a year or two before: but he tried his experiment with a rush, which not succeeding he did not prosecute it.

Philodor, or Phylidor (who also went by the stage name "Paul de Philipstal") developed his magic lantern shows in Berlin. He toured Europe presenting what he called *Fantasmagorie*, which he billed as "black art" or "natural magic." These types of shows were not new. Records and depictions of "ghosts and spirits" being "conjured" using a light source and optics go back to at least the 1400s and perhaps even earlier. However, with advances in science, the shows were becoming more varied and sophisticated.

After several successful years, Philidor left Paris, taking his show to London in 1802. Soon after, Marie (Madame) Tussaud would also leave for England to set up her waxworks displays. Tussaud had been apprentice to Dr. Philippe Curtius, who had his own "Chamber of

Horrors" first in the Palais Royale in 1776, and later on the Boulevard du Temple. Curtius called his show, *Caverne des Grands Voleurs* (*The Cavern of the Great Thieves*), and he displayed wax figures of notorious French criminals who had been executed. Later, he added French royals, such as Marie Antoinette and Louis XVI, who had been guillotined on the Place de la Revolution (today's Place de la Concorde) during the French Revolution.

Fig. 54.—Phantasmagoria (Robertson).

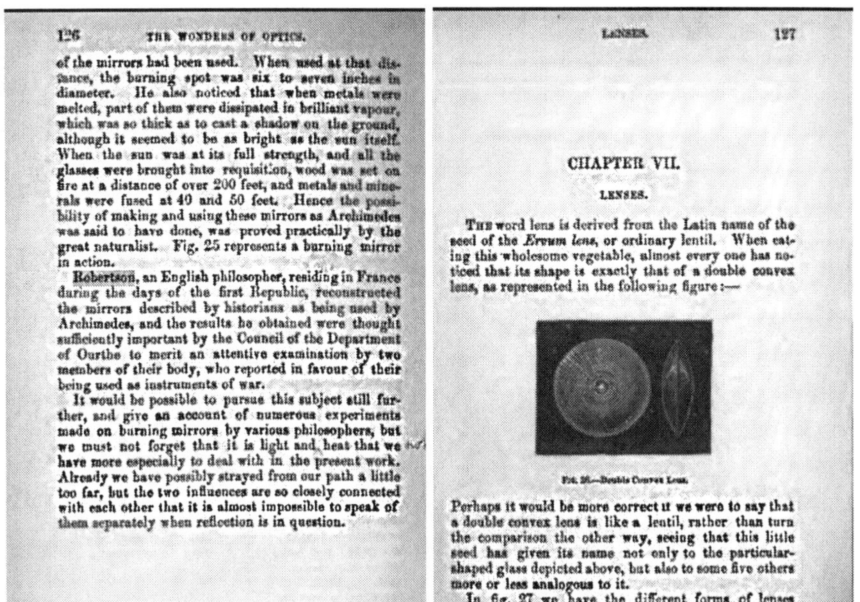

126 THE WONDERS OF OPTICS.

of the mirrors had been used. When used at that distance, the burning spot was six to seven inches in diameter. He also noticed that when metals were melted, part of them were dissipated in brilliant vapour, which was so thick as to cast a shadow on the ground, although it seemed to be as bright as the sun itself. When the sun was at its full strength, and all the glasses were brought into requisition, wood was set on fire at a distance of over 200 feet, and metals and minerals were fused at 40 and 50 feet. Hence the possibility of making and using these mirrors as Archimedes was said to have done, was proved practically by the great naturalist. Fig. 25 represents a burning mirror in action.

Robertson, an English philosopher, residing in France during the days of the first Republic, reconstructed the mirrors described by historians as being used by Archimedes, and the results he obtained were thought sufficiently important by the Council of the Department of Ourthe to merit an attentive examination by two members of their body, who reported in favour of their being used as instruments of war.

It would be possible to pursue this subject still further, and give an account of numerous experiments made on burning mirrors by various philosophers, but we must not forget that it is light and heat that we have more especially to deal with in the present work. Already we have possibly strayed from our path a little too far, but the two influences are so closely connected with each other that it is almost impossible to speak of them separately when reflection is in question.

LENSES. 127

CHAPTER VII.

LENSES.

The word lens is derived from the Latin name of the seed of the *Ervum lens*, or ordinary lentil. When eating this wholesome vegetable, almost every one has noticed that its shape is exactly that of a double convex lens, as represented in the following figure:—

Fig. 26.—Double Convex Lens.

Perhaps it would be more correct if we were to say that a double convex lens is like a lentil, rather than turn the comparison the other way, seeing that this little seed has given its name not only to the particular-shaped glass depicted above, but also to some five others more or less analogous to it.

In fig. 27 we have the different forms of lenses

*Fig. 19-20* - The Wonders of Optics *by Fulgence Marion (not in copyright, from internet archive)*

Tussaud herself had been arrested and was in danger of being guillotined, but friends intervened and secured her released. Her talents were then in high demand, and she was commissioned to make the death masks of many famous victims of the Reign of Terror, including King Louis XVI, Marie Antoinette, Marat, and Robespierre.

In 1802, Revolutionary France had been at war with England. When the two countries made peace that same year, Philidor invited Madame Tussaud to London to exhibit her work alongside his phantasmagoria show, which was then being staged at the Lyceum Theatre. She accepted and made London her home, eventually setting up a permanent exhibit with a separate "Chamber of Horrors," for which she charged an additional fee.

But Robertson saw the *Fantasmagorie* show while Philidor was still in Paris and was enthralled. He immediately grasped how the show was devised and began to think up ways to improve and expand the effects. In addition to being a talented artist, Robertson was grounded in many scientific disciplines including optics, physics, and mathematics.

His studies in optics were useful when mounting his own *Fantasmagorie* shows and proved useful in other areas as well. During the recent war with England, Robertson devised a modern version of a weapon from ancient Greece: the mirrors of Archimedes of Syracuse. Archimedes proposed using large mirrors to focus the rays of the sun on the Roman ships that had besieged Syracuse, harnessing the sun's power to set the ships ablaze. In *Wonders of Optics* (1870), the prolific French author, Nicolas Camille Flammarion, writing under the pseudonym *Fulgence Marion*, noted:

> Robertson, an English [sic] philosopher, residing in France during the days of the first Republic, reconstructed the mirrors described by historians as being used by Archimedes, and the results he obtained were thought sufficiently important by the Council of the Department of Ourthe to merit an attentive examination by two members of their body, who reported in favour of their being used as instruments of war.

Fulgence Marion wrote more than fifty books, including *Wonderful Balloon Ascents; or, The Conquest of the Skies* (1870). He speaks of Robertson's experiments in ballooning, along with the Mongolfier brothers, early French pioneers in flight. Of Robertson, Marion said:

> Robertson is regarded by many as a sort of mountebank; yet such men as Arago have put themselves to the trouble of examining the aerostatic feats of this aeronaut, and of examining the results of his observations.
>
> The first time that Robertson appears in the annals of aerostation is in 1802, on the occasion of the sale of the balloon used at the battle of Fleurus.... But three years previously he had been instructed to make a balloon of an original form, which should ascend in honour of the Turkish ambassador at the garden of Tivoli. The fête was completely successful. Turks, Chinese, Persians, and Bedouins will always be welcome, as on this occasion, at Paris, appearing as they do only at rare intervals, and for a short time.

Robertson's artistic skills, his technical and scientific interests, and his youthful fascination with the occult and the spirit world all combined to fire his imagination after seeing Philidor's show, compelling him to carry out even more grand and harrowing spectacles.

He immediately set about fashioning his own, vastly improved version of the magic lantern which he called a "fantoscope." Marion touts Robertson's innovations, saying, "It is undoubtedly to Robertson that we owe most of the improvements in the phantasmagoria. The success of his performances in Paris during the first Revolution has never been equalled."

Images which Robertson himself drew were projected from the fantoscope onto smoke billowing unseen in the darkness on stage, giving the eerie and quite realistic impression of translucent bodies floating through the air. He developed increasingly elaborate effects, using multiple lanterns. Some were on wheels or tracks, so the images could grow larger, move across the room, or fade in and out of focus. Some were fixed, to project scenes of graveyards or deep caverns. Many of Robertson's effects and techniques prefigured today's Hollywood cinematographers' bag of tricks with panning shots, fade-outs, dolly shots, and images projected from the rear.

"I am only satisfied if my spectators, shivering and shuddering, raise their hands or cover their eyes out of fear of ghosts and devils dashing toward them," Robertson wrote in *Mémoires*.

Robertson had actors and ventriloquists speaking for the images. He could conjure up, seemingly upon request, nearly any famous person his audience desired: Voltaire, Marat, Rousseau, Madame du Barry, although requests for the recently executed king and queen, Louis XVI and Marie Antoinette, were politely refused for fear of inciting reprisals or even arrest, should he be accused of promoting the monarchy in Republican France.

His shows in Paris were so realistic and frightening that many attendees left convinced they had seen actual ghosts. Word spread and soon the authorities shut the performances down, perhaps because of the possibility of the late king reappearing in Revolutionary Paris, perhaps because of the belief that witchcraft and sorcery were involved.

Robertson left Paris and took the show on the road. However, he soon returned, setting up this time at the Couvent de Capucines, a decrepit Gothic convent. Phantasmagoria shows were best staged in these forlorn and abandoned places, their somber ambiance perfect for the show's atmosphere. The cloister was an ideal setting, with the ancient tombs and effigies surrounding the spectators. Long since demolished, the site of the cloisters today can be found on the rue de la Paix (Nos. 2-6) just off the Place Vendôme.

The spectacles were much more than the appearance of simple apparitions. They could take the form of elaborate tableaus with scripts and actors voicing the characters. Robertson described scenes from one of his shows in *Mémoires*:

> A gravedigger, with a lantern, looking for treasure in an abandoned temple; he opens a tomb, there is a skeleton, whose head is still adorned with a jewel; when he tries to remove it, the dead man makes a move and opens his mouth; the gravedigger drops dead of fright. A rat was housed in the skull.

Often scenes from history or well-known works of literature were depicted in ghostly shadows of light and darkness, smoke and mirrors. Robertson describes one such scene:

> The king shows up at Macbeth's house; it is received with demonstrations of respect for a submitted subject. Macbeth's wife, spurred on by ambition, urges him to kill the king: he is indecisive. His wife will find three witches, who appear and promise him the throne: he no longer hesitates, and kills the king. Appearance of the vengeful shadow and punishment of Macbeth.

He performed his eerie and astounding spectacles in Paris for the next four years, before taking the show worldwide, including to the United States. Audiences everywhere were shocked, surprised, bewitched, and above all, frightened by the seemingly real appearance of Robertson's "ghosts and demons," which pleased him greatly.

Ever the entertainer, Robertson's elaborate displays were not limited to the appearances of the spirits and demons, but in his stagecraft in evoking them as well. Marion describes a portion of Robertson's show in *Wonders of Optics*, including the methods Robertson used to bring forth his ghosts:

> Robertson immediately threw upon a brasier containing lighted coals, two glasses of blood, a bottle of vitriol, a few drops of aquafortis, and two numbers of the *Journal des Hommes Libres*, and there instantly appeared in thc midst of the smoke caused by the burning of these substances, a hideous livid phantom armed with a dagger and wearing a red cap of liberty. The man at whose wish the phantom had been evoked seemed to recognise Marat, and rushed forward to embrace the vision, but the ghost made a frightful grimace and disappeared. A young man next asked to see the phantom of a young lady whom he had tenderly loved, and whose portrait he showed to the worker of

all these marvels. Robertson threw on the brasier a few sparrow's feathers, a grain or two of phosphorus, and a dozen butterflies. A beautiful woman, with her bosom uncovered and her hair floating about her, soon appeared, and smiled on the young man with the most tender regard and sorrow. A grave looking individual sitting close by me suddenly exclaimed "Heavens! It's my wife come to life again," and he rushed from the room, apparently fearing that what he saw was not a phantom.

**Travelers' Tips**

Ⓜ **Métro Station Bonne Nouvelle, Line 9 — 46 rue de l'Echiquier (10th arr.)**

Ⓜ **Métro Station l'Opera, Line 8 — 2-6 rue de la Paix (1st arr.)**

Ⓜ **Métro Station Gambetta, Line 3 — Père Lachaise Cemetery (20th arr.)**

Robertson died in 1837, and is buried in Père Lachaise cemetery.

At Métro station Bonne Nouvelle, you are standing on the Boulevard Poissonnière (boulevard of the fishmongers), one of les *Grands Boulevards* of Paris. The Grands Boulevards exemplify classical Paris, perfectly made for strolling, window shopping, and dreaming romantic dreams. They are the setting for many plays, books, and movies—the very image people the world over think of when they think of Paris.

In the summer of 1894, at No. 20, one of the first movies was shown in Paris, on a kinetoscope, an early movie projector. This exhibition inspired the Lumière Brothers to develop their highly successful movie projection system. This bit of movie history lives on at No. 24, at the Max Linder Panorama; an elegant art deco cinema opened in 1912 that is still in business today.

A short walk north off the Boulevard Poissonnière is the site of the Pavilion de l'Echiquier at No. 46. However, there is not much to see today. The Pavilion is long gone, and all that stands there now is a drab apartment building.

Heading to Métro Station Opera and the rue de la Paix, you will find the Boulevard des Capucines, another of Paris' Grands Boulevards. These wide streets were created when the walls surrounding Paris were demolished during the reign of Louis XIV.

While the convent of the Capucines is also long gone, the convent gardens were located on the south side of the Boulevard des Capucines. At No. 2, at the corner of the rue de la Chaussée-d'Antin, was the Hotel de Montmorency, which later became the Théâtre du Vaudeville in 1869, and then the Paramount Opéra movie house in 1927. It has been the Gaumont Opéra since 2007, with its main hall, the former "grand salon" of the old hotel and its rotunda having been kept intact. The Romantic composer and cellist Jacques Offenbach lived at No. 8, moving there in 1876, and dying in 1880, just before his opera, *The Tales of Hoffmann*, premiered.

No. 35 Boulevard des Capucines, was the home and photography studio of Gaspard-Félix Tournachon, who used the pseudonym *Nadar*. Nadar was a photographer, caricaturist, journalist, and novelist; as an amateur balloonist, he is credited as the first person to take aerial photographs.

In April 1874, an upstart group of young artists, including Renoir, Manet, Pissarro, and Monet, mounted an exhibition of their works in Nadar's studio. Eleven years earlier, in 1863 they had been denied admission into the official Paris Salon. They protested and Emperor Napoleon III intervened. He felt the public should see their works and judge for themselves, so he let them have their own salon, which became known as the *Salon des Refusés* (Salon of the Refused).

At the 1874 exhibit, Monet presented his painting, "Impression, Sunrise." Established artists long believed that these works were not real paintings, but were just mere unfinished sketches. They were only *impressions*. Mocking Monet's work, a newspaper critic derided these "Impressionists." Thus, Impressionism as a word and as a movement began with that exhibit here at No. 35.

Since these places no longer exist, to get a feel for Robertson's domain and his effect on the imagination of the people of his time, head out to Père Lachaise and search for his tomb, located to the right of the main entrance, in Division 8. It's hard to miss. It is like the man himself, an unforgettable and spooky sight to behold. Owls carved of stone peer out at you. A tableau depicts the ghastly specters that filled the air and frightened his audiences. One audience member covers her eyes in fright.

The cemetery's atmosphere is peaceful, yet this spot holds some vibrant energy that seems to keep Robertson alive today. Allow your imagination to run away with you—but not too much. It is "Mysterious Paris" after all, and in that cemetery, there may be more than imagination at work, rising up out of the ground to scare you.

And as we know, Robertson loved to give people a good scare.

## How Paris Shaped Our World

Although Robertson's experiments in aerodynamics and other scientific pursuits might seem more important and serious, it is for his ghostly and demonic magic lantern shows—and their influence on the minds and imaginations of people, during his lifetime and after—that he is best known.

The phrase "Smoke and Mirrors" has its origins in the illusions presented by Robertson and others of his time, scientific "magicians"

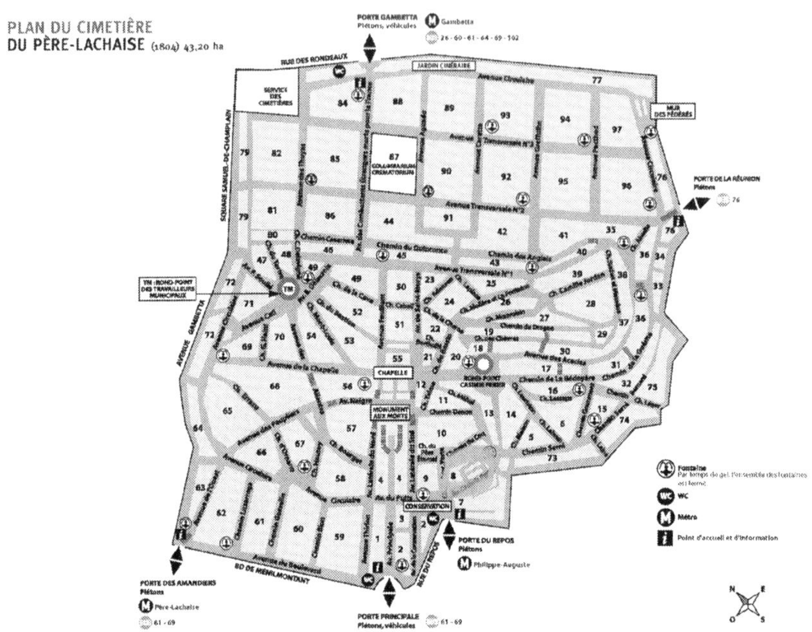


*Fig. 21 - Plan du cimetière du Père-Lachaise à Paris Map of Père Lachaise Cemetery. Robertson's tomb is located in Division 8 (courtesy wikimedia, public domain)*

*Fig. 22-24 - Robertson's Monument in Père Lachaise (photos by the author)*

who used new technology to produce ghostly and supernatural apparitions for audiences throughout Europe in the mid- to late-eighteenth century. Indeed, Robertson would open his shows by emphasizing to his audiences that these apparitions were the product of science and its application using technology. Entertainer that he was, he would soon pull the rug out from under his audience, using mystical incantations and satanic rituals to call forth the dead.

Although Robertson used smoke, mirrors, and other equipment and techniques, the actual words "smoke and mirrors" never appeared together as a phrase until used by New York City journalist and author Jimmy Breslin in his 1975 book, *How the Good Guys Finally Won: Notes from an Impeachment Summer:*

> All political power is primarily an illusion.... Mirrors and blue smoke, beautiful blue smoke rolling over the surface of highly polished mirrors, first a thin veil of blue smoke, then a thick cloud that suddenly dissolves into wisps of blue smoke, the mirrors catching it all, bouncing it back and forth.

The parts of Breslin's phrase had long been in the English lexicon. In *Thesaurus Linguae Romanae & Britannicae* (*Thesaurus of the Roman Tongue and the British* [1578]), English theologian and Bishop of Winchester Thomas Cooper wrote:

> *Verborum & argutiarum fuliginem ob oculos audientium iácere.*
>
> To speake obscurely: to cast a darke smoke or mist before their eyes.

Along with references to "smoke," the word "mirrors" was also often used to describe illusions and effects of misdirection.

> The magician began with one or two sleight-of-hand tricks, presenting each illusion with a topical patter. "Very clever. Very clever," murmured Mr. Barber in his stentorian undertone. "They say those tricks are handed down from generation to generation. I think it's all done with mirrors myself."
>
> — *Mystery Mile by Margery* Louise Allingham (1930)

But it seems nobody had combined the ideas into the common phrase used today, slightly abbreviated from Breslin's original "*blue* smoke and mirrors." Breslin is writing about power, and more importantly, the perception—the illusion—of power. If someone *appears* to have power, then they have power, whether in the halls of Congress or in a local club or organization. Breslin explains:

> If people think you have power, then you have power. If people think you have no power, then you have no power. This is a great truth in politics that I was able to recognize....

As with a magician or illusionist, the image, the perception of something is everything. Since the early Greek philosophers, people have been fascinated with ideas of truth, reality, perception, illusion, and how do we see what we see. Add to that the fascination with and the attraction to the macabre, the eerie, the grotesque, haunted, and the fantastical and you have a compelling situation from which people cannot tear their eyes away.

Images of and fascination with the dead have always been a part of the human psyche. From time immemorial, ghosts, spirits, demons, and devils have fascinated and frightened humankind. In the late eighteenth century, these things were finding new expression in various ways. Robertson's occult performances were just one arena for expression. The debate about religion, mysticism, magic, the occult, the "realness" of reality—what is true, what is provable, what is illusion—all these questions took on new energy in the light of the Age of Reason and the rapid advances in science that were rushing society into the modern era.

The rise of horror as a form of entertainment was a product of the times, and Robertson played a vital part in it. Ghost stories and Gothic novels were becoming quite popular, with writers such as Horace Walpole, William Beckford, and Ann Radcliffe. The events of the mid-to late eighteenth century, in the wake of the Age of Enlightenment, created disillusionment in a world once given "certainty" by religion. Now, science and reason were replacing the old religious superstitions. The French Revolution attempted to use rational thought to govern the affairs of humankind. The results swung wildly from advances like the metric system to the bloody Reign of Terror, which Robertson's audiences had witnessed and survived.

Gothic romance novels, paintings, literature, and other forms of popular entertainment began to feature the macabre. The psyche of the masses sought release in the mysterious and the terrifying. William Blake, mystical and visionary poet, was on this same wavelength in 1790, writing his epic, *The Marriage of Heaven and Hell*. Blake overturns and examines many accepted religious, social, and political norms, looking past the illusions of the world and the old dogmas—smoke and mirrors—to gain a greater and closer look at a truer reality beyond the veil.

Blake, perhaps echoing Plato's *Allegory of the Cave*, writes, "If the doors of perception were cleansed everything would appear to man as it is, Infinite. For man has closed himself up, till he sees all things thro' narrow chinks of his cavern."

*Fig. 25* - Witches' Sabbath, *Francisco Goya (Spanish: El Aquelarre) 1798, currently in the Museo Lázaro Galdiano, Madrid.*

The phrase "the doors of perception" found new life in the title of Aldous Huxley's seminal work, *The Doors of Perception*, written about his experiences with the hallucinogen mescaline. He used the psychedelic drug as a means to remove his persistent spiritual myopia and cleanse his vision. His book, in turn, gave its name to the legendary and mystical rock band, The Doors.

Around the same time as Robertson was performing and Blake was writing, in Spain, Francisco Goya was working on his "Black Paintings," a series of fourteen haunting scenes done on his farmhouse walls later in his life. Executed in secret, and never discussed or mentioned by the painter during his lifetime, Goya's images could easily have shown up in one of Robertson's shows.

*Fig. 26* - Witches' Flight*, 1797 Prado Museum*

The artist obviously intended for the paintings to remain where they were, affixed to the walls. But after Goya's death, the owner of the farmhouse had them removed and placed on canvases. Although seriously damaged by the move, and needing to be restored and repainted, which ruined significant portions of the artist's work, they were brought to France and shown at the Paris *Exposition Universelle* of 1878.

*Fig. 27* - The Sleep of Reason Produces Monsters *(No. 43), from Los Caprichos, engraving by Goya (public domain)*

Goya once said, "Fantasy, abandoned by reason, produces impossible monsters; united with it, she is the mother of the arts and the origin of marvels."

The modern mind, scientific in nature, rational and reasoned, looked with new eyes on the macabre, the ghostly, the blurred lines between fantasy and reality, between imagination and truth, between spiritual and physical realities. In the centuries after the

Enlightenment, not only scientists but writers, poets, painters, philosophers, religious and spiritual thinkers, and even political and social theorists felt the pull of these millennia-old mysteries. And in the decades after the American and French Revolutions and the troubles in Spain, the beginnings of the Industrial Age and the weakening grip of the Catholic Church on the minds and souls of humankind, these forces gained steam and flowed together to inspire new thinking.

In the United States, Edgar Allan Poe was spinning his own web of phantasmagoric tales in the 1830s and '40s. His brand of macabre horror was in keeping with the increased interest in the Gothic, the grisly, and the ghoulish of the era. His influences on the genre of horror, and his creation of a whole new genre of detective fiction (See Chapter 4: Edgar Allan Poe's Rue Morgue), have only grown larger in the ensuing centuries, in literature, in cinema, and in popular culture.

For example, in modern video gaming, Roberta Williams cites Poe's works as the inspiration behind her successful 1995 horror video game, *Phantasmagoria*. And the modern master of horror fiction, Stephen King, stands out atop this mountain of the macabre as a most prolific inheritor of phantasmagoria. Inspired as a youth when he discovered a book of H. P. Lovecraft's short stories, King has gone on to publish an astonishing collection of major horror fiction, both short stories and novels, starting with *Carrie* (1975).

Indeed, throughout Robertson's lifetime and well afterward, from the late eighteenth into and throughout the nineteenth century, people were becoming spellbound by horror, from Mary Shelley's *Frankenstein* (1818) to Bram Stoker's *Dracula* (1897). The Romantic poets—Byron, Shelley, Keats, and others—all dove deep into these subjects. Indeed, the Victorian era stands out for its strong associations to fantastic, gruesome, and terrifying literature: the Brönte sisters, Dickensian plots and motifs, Robert Louis Stevenson's *The Strange Case of Dr. Jekyll and Mr. Hyde* (1886), Oscar Wilde's *The Picture of Dorian Gray* (1891), and on and on.

In France, authors like Charles Nodier and Alexandre Dumas wrote plays about vampires, and Eugène Sue and Paul Féval developed crime literature using Gothic elements. And on and on, up until the early twentieth century when Gaston Leroux's novel, *The Phantom of the Opera* (1910) appeared (See Chapter 10: The Phantom's Lake).

Notably, the French poet Charles Baudelaire, inspired by such influences as Edgar Allan Poe, the occult, and mysticism (and an addiction to opium), wrote his genius, scandalously creative work, *Les Fleurs du Mal* (*The Flowers of Evil*). Starting in 1857, he would continue to revise and change his work throughout his lifetime, often due to censorship.

In "Les sept vieillards" (The Seven Old Men) he begins:

Swarming city, city full of dreams,
Where the specter in broad daylight hangs on the passerby!

*Fourmillante cité, cité pleine de rêves,*

*Où le spectre en plein jour raccroche le passant!*

Some scholars say that the original title for Baudelaire's poem was "*Fantômes parisiens*" (Parisian Ghosts). The poem tells the story of a man who recounts meeting seven old men/ghosts, one after the other on Paris' foggy and lonely streets, after which he flees back home, his reason nearly gone. The reader was left asking: Are these real encounters? Hallucinations? Or is the poem an allegory for the modern encountering the old and failing to make peace with it?

Writing when industrialization had taken firm hold of and was encroaching on every aspect of society, at a time when Baron Haussmann was ripping through old Paris, razing streets, neighborhoods, buildings, churches, erasing centuries of history, Baudelaire used these phantasmagorical images to highlight the clash between the old and new. How destabilizing current events were! As in a Robertson spectacle, one couldn't tell what was reality and what was illusion, what was solid and what was fleeting. But this was not in the controlled environment of a stage show. This was on the street, in the neighborhood.

Baudelaire dedicated the poem to Victor Hugo, author of the novel *Notre-Dame de Paris* (*The Hunchback of Notre Dame*). Written in 1831, Hugo's book is specifically an homage to the then 600-year-old cathedral, at the time in serious disrepair and in danger of being torn down. Hugo wanted all of France to wake up to the beauty of the decaying Gothic architecture. The situation was dire. After all, could anything be more solid than Notre Dame? Yet it appeared ephemeral; the cathedral and all it represented could very well be lost forever. Hugo warns us of the dangers of rapid, thoughtless change as two eras collide, with the new about to obliterate the old.

The modernization of Paris—and rapidly changing modern life in general—brought up feelings of intense alienation and anxiety in many of Baudelaire's generation. No place was safe; the old anchors that stabilized life, reason, consciousness, and identity, were gone or going away fast. Baudelaire saw the city itself as a phantasm. It was an illusion, ephemeral, set like a stage where one could never be sure of anything. Reality was crumbling!

In this context, a new concept appeared, a new person entered the Parisian stage: the *flâneur.* (See Chapter 2: The Most Popular

Attraction in Paris.) A *flâneur* is one who walks the city with no set destination in mind. With no plan, he or she becomes a voyeur strolling in the middle of (yet separate from) the passing scenes, open to whatever wonders and experiences present themselves. This was an entirely novel and French concept, one that has no counterpart in English.

In "The Painter of Modern Life" (1863), Baudelaire paints the *flâneur* as an artist and poet, an observer reacting to the sights, sounds, smells, and life in a modern city:

> The crowd is his element, as the air is that of birds and water of fishes. His passion and his profession are to become one flesh with the crowd. For the perfect flâneur, for the passionate spectator, it is an immense joy to set up house in the heart of the multitude, amid the ebb and flow of movement, in the midst of the fugitive and the infinite. To be away from home and yet to feel oneself everywhere at home...the lover of universal life enters into the crowd as though it were an immense reservoir of electrical energy. Or we might liken him to a mirror as vast as the crowd itself; or to a kaleidoscope gifted with consciousness, responding to each one of its movements and reproducing the multiplicity of life and the flickering grace of all the elements of life.

Walter Benjamin, a German-Jewish philosopher and literary critic, wrote a treatise called "The Arcades Project" (*Das Passagen-Werk*). In it, he takes these concepts of phantasmagoria and *flânerie* even farther, into the realms of philosophy and political discourse. Benjamin writes about Parisian city life in the nineteenth century, especially about the Passages—the covered ways that made *flânerie* possible when inclement weather kept people off the streets and boulevards. Here, the "phantasmagoria" is seen in the shops, the merchandise, and the illusions enthralling passersby with ephemeral objects, obscuring with "smoke and mirrors" a deeper, truer reality—real people, real feelings, real suffering, real joy.

The concepts and ideas generated by phantasmagoria also made their way from Robertson's Gothic grottos into philosophy, politics, and all forms of entertainment: poetry, literature, theater, music, dance, movies, and television. Robertson strongly influenced magician, illusionist, and escape artist Harry Houdini. The Harry Houdini Collection in the Rare Book and Special Collection Division at the Library of Congress holds Houdini's personal copy of Robertson's *Mémoires*.

As a master of illusion, Houdini's act moved from straight magic into escape artistry, a form of illusion and a statement of defiance against the apparent solidity of things: constraints, bonds, government authority, and modern restrictions. His phantasmagoria was the illusion of solid steel, strong rope, closed burlap sacks, locked handcuffs, and "escape-proof" jail cells. He escaped watery graves over and over. No small town or big city lockup could hold him.

He walked through walls, an illusion that caused a sensation when he first performed it in 1914. While Houdini performed his act, a nine-foot-high, ten-foot-wide wall was rolled out and placed so that the audience could see either side. Houdini invited audience members to hammer on the wall, showing it was solid. He then stood on one side of the wall. A screen was placed in front of him and another was put on the other side. Seconds later, both screens were removed. Lo and behold, Houdini was on the other side of the wall.

Press reports the next day said: "The audience sat spellbound for fully two minutes after his feat was accomplished, too dumbfounded to applaud."

Houdini took his professional stage name from the French magician Jean-Eugène Robert-Houdin, probably the most famous magician and illusionist the world has ever known. He perfected many illusions still performed today. Houdin as a child was destined to become a clockmaker, following in the family business. But fate intervened. In the mid-1820s, the young Houdin ordered a two-volume set of books on clockmaking, *Traité de l'horlogerie* (*Treatise on Clockmaking*) by Ferdinand Berthoud. When the package arrived, instead of books on clocks he found a two-volume set on magic: *Scientific Amusements*. Instead of returning the mixed-up order, he began to read them and practice the tricks inside.

Houdin later studied magic through an apprenticeship and by attending magic shows before he arrived in Paris. Once there, he was ready to open his own spectacle in an elegant theater he built in the Palais Royale, the funds coming from a stroke of good fortune. Houdin's knowledge of clocks and complex mechanical devices—called "automata"—led him to begin building these fascinating gizmos. In 1844, he built a small android for the French Industrial Exposition in Paris, for which he was awarded a silver medal. The android was purchased by American circus impresario P. T. Barnum—for the astounding sum of seven thousand francs.

The lineage of phantasmagoria extends from Robertson to Robert-Houdin and Houdini and then beyond to early cinema and the astounding innovations of pioneer filmmaker, Georges Méliès. Houdini, in his book, *The Unmasking of Robert-Houdin* (1906), writes:

From the date of his return to St. Gervais to the time of his death, June 13th, 1871, Robert-Houdin devoted his energies to improving his inventions and writing his books.... He was survived by a wife, a son named Emile, and a step-daughter. Emile Houdin managed his father's theatre until his death in 1883, when the theatre was sold for 35,000 francs. The historic temple of magic still stands under the title of "*Théâtre Robert-Houdin*," under the management of M. Méliès, a maker of motion picture films.

*Fig. 28 - The Joueuse de Tympanon (circa 1772) owned by Marie Antoinette, restored by Robert Houdin (1864) (Image Musée des Arts et Métiers)*

— 472 —

bien exécutés à des prix très-réduits; l'importance de sa production et la bonté de sa fabrication le fait juger digne d'une médaille de bronze.

MENTION HONORABLE.

M. DUCRET, à Épinal (Vosges).

M. Ducret présente à l'examen du jury des mouvements de pendules dans lesquels les tiges et les assiettes des roues sont supprimées par le montage de la roue sur le pignon lui-même; la bonne disposition de toutes les parties de ces mouvements confectionnés par M. Ducret, à l'aide de procédés mécaniques, le rend bien digne d'une mention honorable.

*Outils d'horlogerie et pièces détachées.*

MÉDAILLES D'ARGENT.

M. ROBERT-HOUDIN, à Paris, rue de Vendôme, 9.

M. Robert-Houdin ne s'est pas complu inutilement dans l'exécution de quelques pièces mécaniques difficiles; la branche qu'il exploite avec succès est devenue en ses mains une véritable industrie. Ce ne sont donc pas des chefs-d'œuvre curieux qu'il soumet au jury, ce sont les produits habituels et plusieurs fois répétés de ses ateliers. Le jury se plaît à reconnaître l'intelligence et l'habileté dont M. Robert-Houdin a fait preuve dans l'emploi et le groupement des divers organes

*Fig. 29 - Robert Houdin, Silver Prize (1844)*
*French National Industrial Exposition*

The area around the Théâtre Robert-Houdin was demolished in 1923, but at that time, it was located at 8 Boulevard des Italiens. Robert Houdin sold the theater to aspiring stage magician and film pioneer Georges Méliès. Méliès had begun visiting the Théâtre Robert-Houdin in his youth. He was enthralled by the magician's feats of magic and began practicing magic on his own. Soon he was performing his own shows at the *Cabinet Fantastique* of the Grévin Wax Museum, which still exists today.

Méliès bought the Théâtre Robert-Houdin with proceeds from the sale of his family's business, and he did much to improve the entertainment staged there. In 1895, Méliès saw an early demonstration of cinema put on by the Lumière brothers. Enthralled, he found and purchased a "cinematograph" for his own theater. He began showing short films there, many of them created by Thomas Edison. Méliès eventually turned from showing films to making films. His pioneering work is still regarded as legendary, some of the finest and most inventive movie-making created during the birth of the cinema.

In his lifetime, Méliès directed 500 films between 1896 and 1913. His short films are exercises in special effects similar to the shows produced in his magic theatre. He employed tricks and novel (for the time) cinematic techniques to show viewers impossible events. Things disappeared and reappeared. Objects changed size or morphed into entirely new things. His early special-effects films were a product of trial and error, his own inventiveness, and sometimes even mistakes that produced novel effects. The "stop trick" was a result of his camera jamming during a shot. Other techniques like multiple exposures, time-lapse photography, dissolves, and hand-painted color—all common cinematic techniques today—flowed from Méliès' mind. Méliès has been referred to as a *cinemagician* due to his genius.

Perhaps his most famous film is the 1902 *Le Voyage dans la lune* (*A Trip to the Moon*). Based on Jules Verne's story, *From the Earth to the Moon*, it is considered by many to be the first science fiction film. In it, Méliès used all his tricks, incorporating both live action and animation, making use of miniatures and matte-painting to tell the fantastical story. *A Trip to the Moon* was named one of the 100 greatest films of the twentieth century by *The Village Voice*, and the scene when the rocket carrying the voyagers lands smack in the middle of the Moon's eye is one of the most iconic images in the history of cinema.

*Fig. 30 - Frame from the only surviving hand-colored print of Georges Méliès' 1902 film, Le voyage dans la lune (courtesy Wikimedia, public domain)*

Méliès' genius lives on today in the cinematic techniques he created or perfected and in popular literature. He is an essential character in

Brian Selznick's 2007 novel, *The Invention of Hugo Cabret*, and its 2011 film adaptation, *Hugo*, directed by Martin Scorsese, in which Méliès is played by Ben Kingsley. From *Nosferatu* to *Ghostbusters*, *Friday the 13th*, *Nightmare on Elm Street*, and beyond, movies have picked up the mantle from Robertson and Méliès with special effects that would delight them today.

Modern "phantasmagoria," other than in the cinema, is probably the best known in the effects at Disneyland and other theme parks and attractions. Indeed, thrilling excursions such as the Haunted Mansion, where holographic ghosts fly, moan, laugh, and scare the crowds, or in Disney's live show, *Fantasmic*, which features images projected onto water screens, are directly descended from Robertson's bag of tricks.

Other amusement parks and even museums employ modern technology to create phantasmagoric illusions. Some use live actors and film projection, such as can be seen in the Mystery Lodge at Knott's Berry Farm in Buena Park, California. The Abraham Lincoln Presidential Library and Museum in Springfield, Illinois, has its "Ghosts of the Library" exhibit which uses these techniques. At Universal Studios in Florida, the Hogwarts Express attraction is designed so park-goers who are seen entering "Platform 9¾" seem to disappear into a brick wall, just like in the Harry Potter movies.

Ghost stories and medieval superstitions leapt to life in the phantasmagoria shows of Philidor and Robertson at the start of an era when in various places and seemingly all at once, the macabre and the gruesome infused modern thought, art, entertainment, and politics.

Chances are you have never heard of Etienne-Gaspard Roberts (aka Robertson). I had not until I came upon his crypt in Père Lachaise cemetery. And yet we have all been influenced by him and his work, his innovations and his contributions to our modern sensibilities and our love of horror in all its forms. Robertson's *Fantasmagorie* lives on today in ways we never notice because they are such a part of the fabric of our lives. With simple materials—glass plates, a few strong lamps, smoke, and mirrors—and the power of imaginations, he weaved illusions so solid they leapt right into our consciousness in ways still vibrant and vital today.

The next time you are curled up watching a horror movie, enjoying a good scare, take a moment to think of Robertson and thank him for what he helped bring into the world. And don't be surprised if, in a smokey French accent, you hear a disembodied voice bid you, "*Bienvenue Mesdames et Monsieurs. Welcome, come on in....*"

# Chapter 4
# Edgar Allan Poe's Rue Morgue

(Nineteenth Century)

*"The first time I opened a book he [Poe] had written, I saw with equal measures of horror and fascination, not just the things that I had dreamed of, but actual phrases that I had designed and that he had penned twenty years earlier."*

— Charles Baudelaire, in a letter to Théophile Thoré (1864)

In 1846, a desperate man living a little north of New York City wandered from his lowly cottage off the Kingsbridge Road in the Bronx toward the High Bridge. Although well past midnight with no moon to illuminate the path, he did not hesitate or falter, for he had walked this way innumerable times in the months since he had moved here with his wife and mother-in-law.

He was troubled. His wife was dying of tuberculosis, but he could not get his head around the thought; he would not allow the idea to coalesce clearly in his mind. Instead, he mused along its edges, with hopes and schemes of a miraculous cure or some other fantastical scenario turning over and over in his mind whereby she arose healed and well from her fevered sickbed to walk with him along these very paths, not in the dead of night, nor in the dead of winter, but in the dappled sunlight of a spring morning.

Soon enough, however, the truth would be inescapable. And yet even after she had died, he would be driven out of his bed at all hours to wander in all weather to the cemetery to continue to sit in vigil over his beloved wife and cousin, Virginia.

Poverty was their lot. He had no means by which to purchase any meagre comfort to ease her suffering, much less a cure. They had moved to the bucolic village of Fordham to ensure Virginia's health. Here she could breathe the fresh, wholesome country air, instead of the noxious and foul airs of New York City. This area of Westchester County, north of the old Bronck's Farm, was well-known in those days for its pleasing and tranquil environs, a place to rest and recuperate. That tiny cottage, now situated in the Borough of the Bronx, was Poe's final home. It can still be seen today where it stands along the Grand Concourse near Fordham Road, near Fordham University.

Poe, the penniless American writer of more than seventy poems and sixty short stories, wrote three short stories set in Paris. The first, "The Murders in the Rue Morgue," published in 1841, is credited as the first detective/murder mystery—the story that started the whole genre of modern detective fiction. But did Poe ever live in or even visit Paris? Is there or was there ever a rue Morgue?

> *"We proceeded at once to the Rue Morgue. This is one of those miserable thoroughfares which intervene between the Rue Richelieu and the Rue St. Roch."*
> — "Murders in the Rue Morgue"

These lines have fascinated scholars and Poe enthusiasts, sending them on a search for the street on which the murders allegedly happened. Both the rue Richelieu and rue Saint Roch escaped Baron Haussmann's bulldozers as he modernized Paris. They exist to this day, both begin at the rue de Rivoli. The rue Richelieu borders the Palais Royale. The rue Saint Roch passes by the church for which it is named, running all the way up to the Boulevard des Capucines.

Between these two virtually parallel streets, a number of smaller streets ran in a haphazard manner, as Paris streets often do, zig-zagging in ways that can sometimes boggle the mind; clearly no planning or forethought went into this jumbled maze of a city. Haussmann leveled many of those streets in the *quartier* in the mid-nineteenth century to make room for l'Avenue de l'Opera.

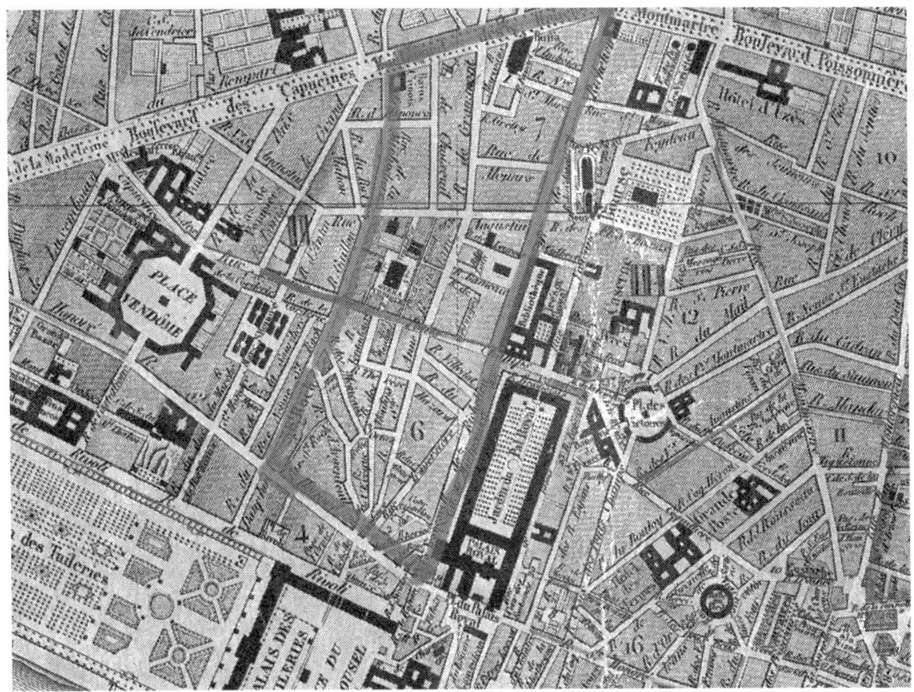


*Fig. 31 - Map of Paris, drawn by X. Girard, published in 1820, reviewed and considerably augmented in 1830 (public domain)*

In the time before the Second Empire and the reign of Napoleon III, the layout of the streets was infinitely worse! Paris was a virtual rabbit-warren of tiny, closed-in streets, lanes, alleys, passages, and cul-de-sacs that had never been accurately mapped until serious attempts were made beginning in the eighteenth century. The Turgot map of Paris (1734-36) gives some indication of what Paris looked like then.

For example, the rue de Rivoli did not exist until Napoleon Bonaparte ordered its construction, running from the Place de la Concorde alongside the Tuileries gardens and the northern length of the Louvre. On the Turgot map, you can see some of the streets and buildings that disappeared to make way for the construction of the rue de Rivoli.

But Bonaparte's efforts to remake Paris pale in comparison to the wholesale re-creation of Paris by his nephew, Louis Napoleon (Napoleon III), who allowed Baron Haussmann, Prefect of the Seine, to launch the wholesale bulldozing of medieval Paris. Starting in 1853, and continuing on until 1870 and the fall of the Empire in the Franco-Prussian War, Napoleon III and Baron Haussmann remade Paris, demolishing small streets and whole neighborhoods to make way for grand, wide boulevards and the uniform streetscape of the "Haussmannian" buildings that are synonymous with the look and feel of Paris today.

The Haussmann building is highly functional and gives Paris the clean style you see and may not even notice. You are looking at urban planning forcibly imposed by an emperor on his subject people. True Haussmann buildings *always* have these elements: on the ground floor, commercial space. On the first floor, an apartment for the shop owners. (Note: In France, the first floor is the floor above street level).

*Fig. 32 - The rue du Jardinet on the Left Bank, demolished by Haussmann to make room for the Boulevard Saint Germain. Photographer unknown, but likely Charles Marville (courtesy Wikimedia, public domain)*

On the second floor is a larger apartment for wealthier tenants, which has a real balcony. The third and fourth floors have similarly large apartments. The fifth-floor apartments has a faux balcony railing, not a true balcony. The sixth (top) floor sports a Mansard roof, underneath which are small servant's quarters.

Haussmann destroyed whole blocks to carve out wide new boulevards, like the *Boulevard St. Michel, rue Turbigo,* and the *Boulevard Malesherbes*. But in Poe's time, the only wide boulevards were natural spaces created by the removal of the medieval walls that had once surrounded and protected the city. These spaces, dubbed *les Grands Boulevards*, include the *Boulevards Beaumarchais*, *Filles-du-Calvaire*, *Temple*, *Saint-Martin*, *Saint-Denis*, *Bonne-Nouvelle*, *Poissonnière*, *Montmartre*, *Italiens*, *Capucines*, and the *Madeleine*.

Haussmann, creating these new boulevards had a secondary objective, what twentieth-century urban planners would call "slum clearance." Haussmann rammed his new boulevards straight through homes, shops, churches, streets...and straight through the lives of thousands of people in a style that New Yorkers in the 1930s and beyond knew all too well. Baron Haussmann's style of urban renewal would later be copied in and around New York City by his American counterpart, Robert Moses.

So the street that gives its name to Poe's detective story, "The Murders in the Rue Morgue," was located in the area around the Avenue de l'Opera. One can envision the maze of streets and alleys that existed before Haussmann's boulevard smashed through the old quartiers, opening up the area to light and air and eliminating most of the medieval buildings and crooked, narrow streets.

An additional reason for this wholesale removal of much of old Paris was the cholera epidemic of 1832. Paris' closed-in streets hemmed in by three- and four-story houses was half the problem. The other was that Paris had no sewer system to speak of. People threw their garbage, human and animal wastes, and other trash into the center of the street where rain eventually washed it away to the Seine River—whence came the city's drinking water! As a result,

Paris streets were a muddy, filthy, and disease-ridden mess people had to slough through daily.

The stench of Paris was well recorded. In *The Great Stink of Paris and the Nineteenth-Century Struggle against Filth and Germs*, David S. Barnes writes, "In the late summer of 1880 in Paris, death was in the air, and it smelled like excrement." It had been so for centuries....

The smells and bad air of the entire city, with a population rapidly growing to more than a million, were increasingly intolerable. The worldwide cholera outbreak spread rapidly in France, eventually killing 20,000 people in Paris and its suburbs. Everyone felt something drastic had to be done. Scientists would not figure out until many decades later that cholera was spread through the water. Before the real cause was discovered, the obvious culprit seemed to be "bad air," or "miasma"—and Paris had that in abundance.

Those studying the problem noted that over half the deaths were concentrated in relatively small areas of the city, those which happened to have the highest population density. Hence, a call arose for better hygiene, for space, air, light, and better systems for sewage and garbage removal. This situation in large measure drove the emperor's urban renewal project.

In the macabre way that people meet a crisis or an epidemic, during this time of cholera, many masked balls were given in which the personification of cholera was an invited—or sometimes uninvited—guest. The poet Heinrich Heine attended one such party in 1832. In his journal he noted:

> ....when all at once the merriest of the harlequins felt that his legs were becoming much too cold, and took

> off his mask, when, to the amazement of all, a violent-blue face became visible.
>
> It was at once seen that there was no jest in this; the laughter died away, and at once several carriages conveyed men and women from the hall to the Hôtel Dieu, the Central Hospital, where they, still arrayed in mask attire, soon died. As in the first shock of terror people believe the cholera was contagious, and as those who were already patients in the hospital raised cruel screams of fear....

He goes on to say that the "dead were said to have been buried so fast that not even their checkered fool's clothes were taken off them; and merrily as they lived, they now lie in their graves."

Another chronicler of the Paris cholera epidemic was Nathaniel Parker Willis (1806–1867, also known as N. P. Willis). Considered one of the best and certainly one of the highest paid magazine writers of his day, Willis was especially known for voluminous texts about his travels around the world.

In 1835, he published his book *Pencillings by the Way*, a compilation of a series of letters he wrote and first printed in *The New York Mirror* in 1832, where he was the foreign editor and correspondent. In one of his many letters from Paris, he wrote:

> I was at a masque ball at the Théatre des Varietés, a night or two since, at the celebration of the Mi-Careme, or half-Lent. There were some two thousand people, I should think, in fancy dresses, most of them grotesque and satirical, and the ball was kept up till seven in the morning, with all the extravagant gaiety, noise, and fun, with which the French people

> manage such matters. There was a cholera-waltz, and a cholera-galopade, and one man, immensely tall, dressed as a personification of the Cholera itself, with skeleton armor, bloodshot eyes, and other horrible appurtenances of a walking pestilence. It was the burden of all the jokes, and all the cries of the hawkers, and all the conversation; and yet, probably, nineteen out of twenty of those present lived in the quarters most ravaged by the disease, and many of them had seen it face to face, and knew perfectly its deadly character!

Willis was one of Poe's professional and personal friends, and Poe certainly knew of this letter. While editor of the *Evening Mirror*, Willis published Poe's poem "The Raven" in the January 29, 1845 issue. Willis said "The Raven" was "Unsurpassed in English poetry for subtle conception, masterly ingenuity of versification, and consistent, sustaining of imaginative lift.... It will stick to the memory of everybody who reads it."

Willis helped Poe financially during his wife Virginia's illness and, after Poe died, Willis vigorously defended Poe's reputation against some vicious slander perpetrated by a Poe rival, Rufus Wilmot Griswold.

The 1832 Paris cholera epidemic inspired Poe's famous short story, "The Mask of the Red Death," written in 1841. Poe would not have needed to visit Paris during the cholera outbreak to get the ideas in the story. Accounts of the disease in Paris, written by Willis and others, were widely read in America, which also experienced illness and death from the pandemic.

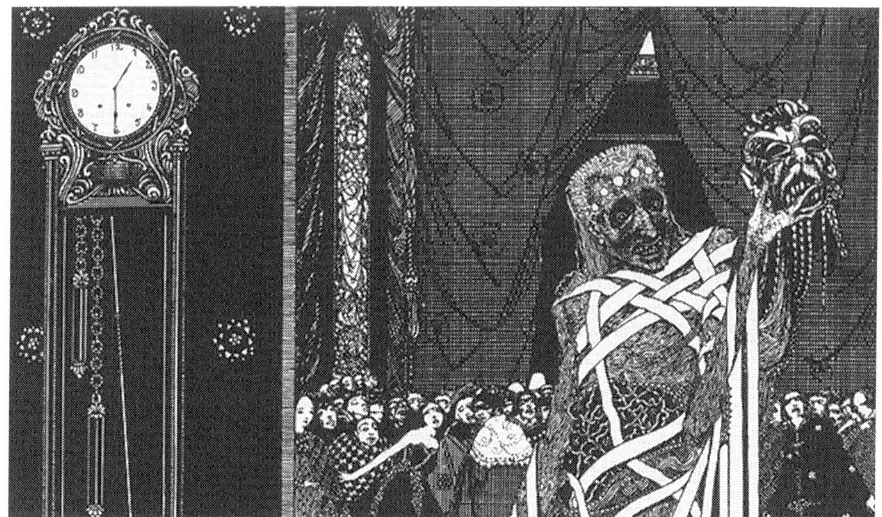

*Fig. 33 - The dagger dropped gleaming upon the sable carpet—From Tales of Mystery and Imagination... Illustrated by Harry Clarke, by Edgar Allan Poe. London: G. G. Harrap & Co., 1919. (British Library item 12703.i.43). Illustrating The Masque of the Red Death.*

But what about "The Murders in the Rue Morgue" and the other two whodunits set in Paris, "The Mystery of Marie Rogêt" and "The Purloined Letter"? How did Poe come by his knowledge of Paris and its streets? Was there a rue Morgue where Poe situates it? And had Poe ever visited Paris?

No evidence exists of a rue Morgue in the area between the rue Richelieu and the rue St. Roche, and no street of that name shows up on any early maps, like the Turgot map or the 1830 map by Girard. In any case, if there *had* been a small street, alley, or *passarelle* in the vicinity, it would have likely been destroyed when Haussmann bulldozed through the quartier in 1864.

However, in the 1874 edition of the *Dictionnaire des Rues de Paris* which corresponds to *le Guide Topographique of C. Chevalier, Chef des bureaux de l'Administration des Pompes Funèbres de Paris*

(*Administrative Bureau of Funeral Homes*), an actual "rue Morgue" is listed but this is decades after Poe's story was published. And this street is not where Poe places it, but in the little area (now a park) behind the cathedral of Notre Dame on the Île de la Cité.

The original morgue, the room in the Châtelet prison, was moved in 1804 into a building on the banks of the Seine near the Pont St. Michel. When Haussmann razed and remade much of Paris in 1864, this morgue building was torn down and a new morgue was built behind Notre Dame cathedral, off the Quai de l'Archevêque. This morgue and the little street that bore its name did not exist when Poe wrote his story.

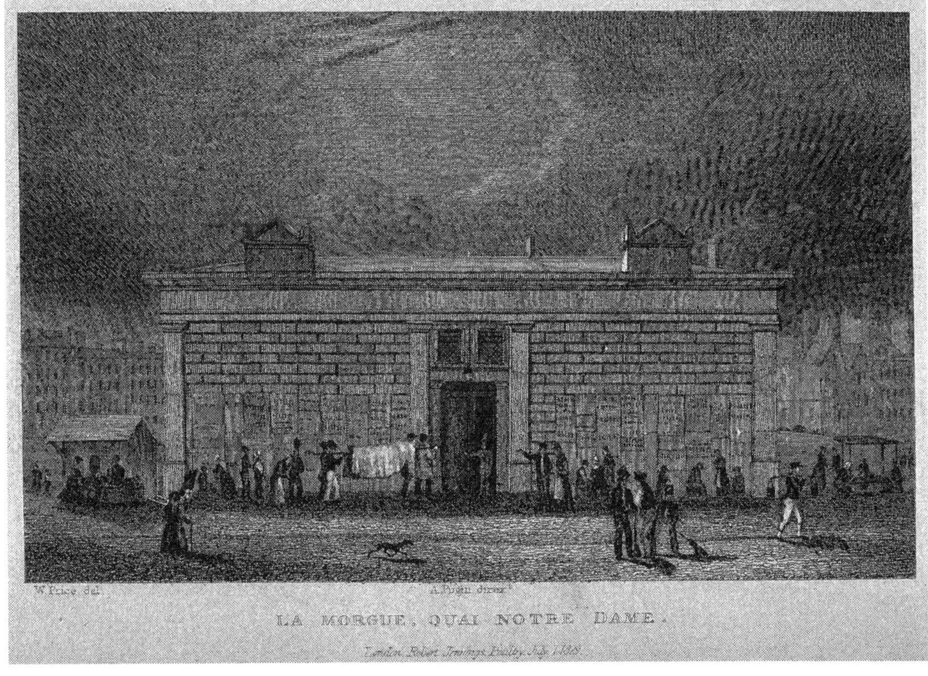


*Fig. 34 - The Morgue, Paris: by Nôtre Dame.*
*Etching (1829), after W. Price after A. Pugin.*
*(photo courtesy of Wikimedia,*
*licensed under the Creative Common License)*

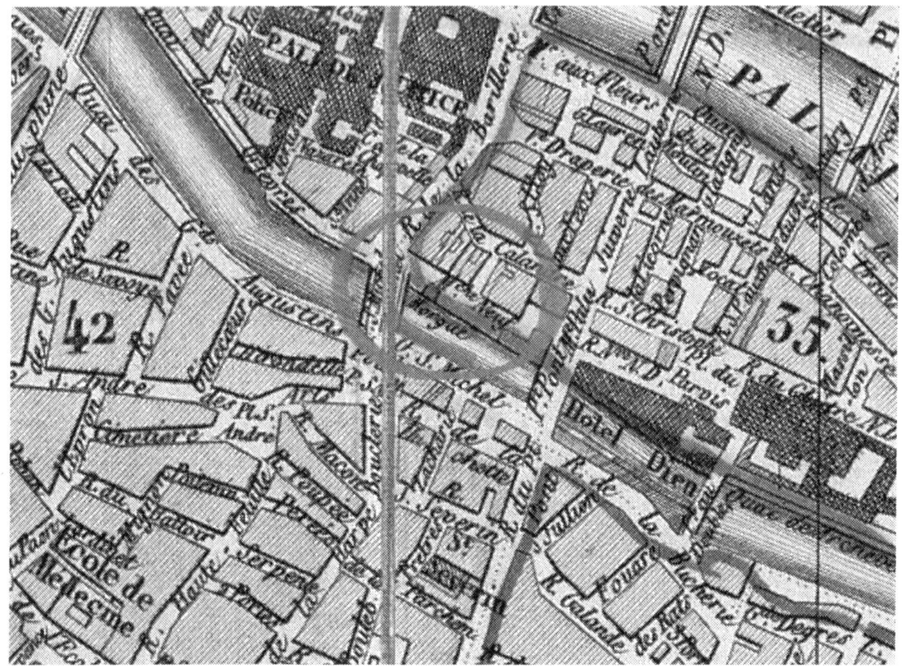


*Fig. 35 - Map Showing the Old Morgue*

However, an 1814 map, created for Emperor Napoleon, has a *rue des Morts* (Street of the Dead) in an area near St. Lazare, in the cemetery adjacent to the Hospital for Incurables. Perhaps Poe found this map and used it as inspiration for his story. Or perhaps Poe took the name from a contemporary map of his time (1832), which shows the location of the 1804 morgue.

Here, then are possibilities for the origin of Poe's rue Morgue. Poe merely relocates it to an area in Paris well known for close quarters and cramped streets, with the still lingering aura of the cholera epidemic from just a decade before.

Even if Poe had no inkling of these maps, he would likely have heard of the Paris morgue, which was already a popular tourist attraction. (See Chapter 1: The Unknown Girl of the Seine). The word "morgue" wouldn't be much of a stretch for an imagination like Poe's to come up with for the title of a murder mystery. He certainly had the imagination to create a mood with his penchant for resonate and mournful sounds. In his essay "The Philosophy of Composition" published in *Graham's Magazine* in April 1846, Poe discusses how he set the mood of his poem, "The Raven":

> Having made up my mind to a refrain...to have force, [it] must be sonorous and susceptible of protracted emphasis...these considerations inevitably led me to the long "O" as the most sonorous vowel, in connection with "R" as the most producible consonant.
>
> The sound of the refrain being thus determined, it became necessary to select a word embodying this sound, and at the same time in the fullest possible keeping with that melancholy which I had predetermined as the tone of the poem. In such a search it would have been absolutely impossible to overlook the word "Nevermore."

Poe uses the word "nevermore" as a starting point to build the drama of his poem. He is on record that at least in this instance, he starts with a sound, a tone to create a mood. It is not a stretch to imagine that perhaps Poe invented a "rue Morgue" solely for its sonorous sound—and for its connotation and relationship to death and the macabre.

That would suggest there was no need for Poe to be in Paris, to walk its streets for inspiration, to craft his murder mystery and set it there. Yet there is evidence, mostly circumstantial, that Poe knew Paris, and had connections there. Can someone write intimately about a city to which they have never been, especially in the days when there was no easy way to research a place?

Yes, it is well-known that Bram Stoker wrote his chilling novel *Dracula* having never been to Transylvania, so Poe could have written about Paris without ever having visited it.

But, if Poe had been to Paris, how did he get there? When did he go? How did he pay for the trip? We know Poe traveled abroad at least once, in 1815, when he was just six years old. In that year, he was taken by his foster family, the Allans, to Scotland and then London, where he briefly attended a grammar school before being enrolled in the Manor House School in Stoke Newington, London. As a student who boarded there from 1817-1820, he would have studied French. Most Poe scholars believe, however, that there is no evidence he visited the Continent or Paris during these years.

However, some assert that Edgar Allan Poe spent some time in Paris at another point in his life. In March 1831, right after he was drummed out of West Point, Poe wrote a letter to its superintendent, Colonel Sylvanus Thayer. Poe wrote, "I intend by the first opportunity to proceed to Paris with the view of obtaining, thro' the interest of the Marquis de La Fayette, an appointment (if possible) in the Polish Army."

What could lead Poe to believe that the Marquis de Lafayette would take any interest in him, a young struggling ex-soldier who had recently been kicked out of a prestigious institution such as West Point? And furthermore, does this mean Poe did go to Paris?

The evidence of Poe's travels to Paris rests on two legs. First, there is this authentic West Point letter, wherein he states his intention to travel to Paris to secure an appointment through the great General Lafayette. Scholars believe that young Poe *was* known to the French General through Poe's paternal grandfather, David Poe, who had served in the Continental Army as a deputy quartermaster. Lafayette knew Poe's grandfather very well. David Poe, as quartermaster, provided Lafayette's regiments with needed supplies and uniforms during the American Revolution.

When Lafayette returned to the United States for a nostalgic reunion tour in 1824, he visited all twenty-four states and was warmly received as a true hero. There were many parades, parties, and reunions with old friends during his fourteen months in the US. He loved the United States, a nation which he had helped create. Its people adored and celebrated him as much as they did heroes like Washington, Jefferson, and Franklin.

While visiting Baltimore, Lafayette made it a point to seek out his old friend and compatriot, David Poe, only to be dismayed to learn his good friend had died. Records show he made it a point to visit the gravesite.

Lest we think the friendship between Lafayette and David Poe was just casual, it is important to consider the circumstances Major General Lafayette and the Continental Army faced in the uncertain years of the Revolution. At the time, victory against the British Empire seemed nearly impossible. Lafayette was barely twenty. He had gone through a grueling process to get permission from Louis XVI to leave France and join General Washington. He so impressed the commander-in-chief that Washington commissioned him as a major general. Then he had to prove his mettle.

Supplies and supply lines for the troops were skimpy, insufficient, and provisional at best. Lafayette could do virtually nothing if his troops were ill-clothed, ill-fed, and short on weapons and ammunition. As quartermaster, David Poe was Lafayette's lifeline, and he came through. He used his own money to equip Lafayette's units. David Poe's wife is said to have sewn some 500 uniforms herself for Lafayette's soldiers.

The marquis' affection for Poe's grandfather would have been strong. They forged a real bond in the life and death struggle for American independence, so when Lafayette visited the United States, his stop in Baltimore was, at least in part, to see his old friend, young Edgar Allan's grandfather David Poe, once again.

After Baltimore, Lafayette headed south to Richmond, Virginia, where a fourteen-year-old Edgar Allan Poe was a lieutenant in Richmond's Junior Morgan Riflemen student cadet corps. Young Poe was present at the official ceremonies welcoming General Lafayette, who inspected the young troops dressed in their full uniforms. Poe was particularly proud of his role that day. A family friend chronicled the event, saying, "Poe, dressed in uniform...walked in front of the marquee erected on the Capitol Square, under which the old general held a grand reception." It is highly likely that Poe and Lafayette met. Lafayette would have known this young man was his dear friend's grandson.

When Poe was drummed out of West Point and declared his intentions to seek a commission, his great confidence that the Marquis de Lafayette would help him is entirely understandable. His letter of resignation to West Point brims with confidence. Evidently, the scheme he proposes was not only believable, but possible.

Another bit of evidence that Poe may have visited Paris is one that has ignited some controversy. It is the existence of a letter purportedly from the great writer Alexandre Dumas, author of *The Count of Monte Cristo*, *The Three Musketeers*, and *The Man in the Iron Mask,* among many other classics. The letter, which some say is a forgery, turned up after Poe's death.

Dumas' letter said:

> It was about the year 1832. One day, an American presented himself at my house, with an introduction from...James Fenimore Cooper. Needless to say, I welcomed him with open arms. His name was Edgar Poe. From the outset, I realized that I had to deal with a remarkable man.

The letter would put Poe in Paris, and the date is in line with Poe's dismissal from West Point and his stated intention to seek out the Marquis de Lafayette, who was in France at that time. Most of what is written about this remarkable letter points to it being a forgery. Yet what reason could someone have for creating it? If actually from Dumas, was the letter a true account of Poe's arrival with an introduction from the famous American author? Or would Dumas, not known for pranks, write it as a hoax or a joke?

If Dumas did write the letter, and it is a factual account, Poe could have had a letter of introduction from James Fenimore Cooper. Letters of introduction were common in those days, something to vouch for your character as you traveled away from home or to foreign lands. A letter from a well-known person would help secure assistance and entry into social and business circles.

Cooper, having arrived in Paris in 1826, was a celebrity in Parisian society and one of the most successful authors of his day. His years in Paris with his family are well documented. Of the many Americans who came to Paris at the time, he was easily the most famous. Cooper and Poe knew each other, but did Cooper help Poe in this way?

And what other circumstantial evidence could help solve the mystery of Poe in Paris?

Consider Poe's fictional character, the amateur sleuth C. Auguste Dupin. Dupin first appears in "The Murders in the Rue Morgue," the short story universally acclaimed as the first detective story. With this tale, Poe created a whole new genre of fiction. Dupin appears again in two other stories, both set in Paris: "The Mystery of Marie Rogêt" (1842) and "The Purloined Letter" (1844). Dupin, it is widely agreed, becomes the model for his more famous literary brother, Sherlock Holmes.

Sir Arthur Conan Doyle, a huge admirer of Poe's, said, "Where was the detective story until Poe breathed the breath of life into it?" In his first Sherlock Holmes story, *A Study in Scarlet*, Conan Doyle pays a sort of backhanded homage to both Poe and Dupin:

> Sherlock rose and lit his pipe. "No doubt you think you are complimenting me in comparing me to Dupin," he observed. "Now in my opinion, Dupin was a very inferior fellow. That trick of his of breaking in on his friends' thoughts with an apropos remark after a quarter of an hour's silence is really very showy and superficial. He had some analytical genius, no doubt; but he was by no means such a phenomenon as Poe appeared to imagine."

Written in 1887, Conan Doyle harkens back in classic fashion to Poe and Auguste Dupin, while at the same time deriding both. However, he is just emulating the master, Poe, who in that same spirit made a direct reference (and backhanded homage) to *his* inspiration, the inspiration for Poe's character Dupin: Eugéne François Vidocq.

Vidocq lived from 1775 until 1857. He was a French con artist, one of the best, and at the time one of the most notorious criminals in all of France. Eventually, he gave up his life of crime to become a police officer, rising through the ranks to become the founder and the first director of the French national police force, the Sûreté Nationale. Later in 1812, he created what is considered the first known private detective agency, *Le bureau des renseignements Universels pour le commerce et l'Industrie* (The Office of Universal Information for Commerce and Industry), which inspired Scotland Yard to create a criminal investigation department. In the US, Allen Pinkerton would not set up his detective agency until decades later. On top of this, with his methods of investigation, Vidocq is heralded the world over as the father of modern criminology.

*Fig. 36 - Eugéne François Vidocq (1775 - 1857)*
*by Achille Devéria (public domain)*

Vidocq's methods were unique, at once extremely sophisticated and novel for the times, sometimes brazen and even bizarre. He initiated the practice of enlisting other criminals to be spies and informants, and he invented the idea of the plainclothes officer. He first had the idea to dig a bullet out of a body and compare the slug to the gun from which it was fired. He also first conceived of the technique of taking fingerprints and of making plaster footprints and matching them with those found at the crime scene. A master of disguise, he would appear as a beggar, an old woman, or even hide for days at a time in a pile of debris to stake out and catch criminals.

When Poe wrote his Dupin mysteries, Vidocq was still alive, and Poe would undoubtedly have been familiar with him. Julian Symons, famed mystery writer and Poe biographer, said, "He had read Vidocq, and it is right to say that if the *Mémoires* had never been published, Poe would never have created his amateur detective." Vidocq's life story inspired many others beyond Poe, such as Victor Hugo and Balzac.

Vidocq's *Memoirs* were a swashbuckling tale of his exploits published in 1828. They were popular and made their way across the Atlantic as a four-volume translation published in 1829 in England by Whittaker, Treacher, and Arnot. Poe got his hands on a copy sometime between then and 1841 and created his fictional detective based on these memoirs.

Vidocq inspired Poe, no doubt. Vidocq's memoirs gave Poe a treasure trove of information on detective work, murder, crime solving, and Paris. In "The Murders in the Rue Morgue," Poe has Dupin exclaim:

> "We must not judge of the means," said Dupin, "by this shell of an examination. The Parisian police, so much extolled for acumen, are cunning, but no more. There is no method in their proceedings, beyond the method of the moment. They make a vast parade of measures; but, not unfrequently, these are so ill

> adapted to the objects proposed.... The results attained by them are not unfrequently surprising, but, for the most part, are brought about by simple diligence and activity. When these qualities are unavailing, their schemes fail. Vidocq, for example, was a good guesser and a persevering man. But, without educated thought, he erred continually by the very intensity of his investigations. He impaired his vision by holding the object too close. He might see, perhaps, one or two points with unusual clearness, but in so doing he, necessarily, lost sight of the matter as a whole. Thus there is such a thing as being too profound.

The direct thread of Poe's connections to Paris runs from the Marquis de Lafayette, through Vidocq and Poe's inspired stories, possibly to Dumas and long-term Paris expatriate James Fenimore Cooper and beyond, to a French writer who was strongly influenced by Poe: Charles Baudelaire. Baudelaire so admired Poe that for well over a decade, from 1852 until 1865, he read and studied Poe's work and then translated Poe into French.

Baudelaire's strong affinity for Poe was that of someone who was more than just an admirer; he was drawn to Poe's vision, and he saw Poe as a brother—a kindred spirit in their shared circumstances. Each knew poverty, each dealt with addictions, and both were well known to have severe depression. Each struggled with their writing and had difficulties getting published, coming up against a staid and often unyielding literary establishment that did not comprehend their genius.

What's more, at their core, both had as a fundamental foundation in their writings a search for deeper meaning and truth. Each was extraordinarily drawn to the macabre and the mystical. Images both fantastical and grotesque emerged from their pens to the delight and horror of the public.

**Travelers' Tips**

 **Métro Station Tuileries, Line 1 — rue de Richelieu, rue Saint-Roch, Avenue de l'Opera (1st arr.)**

 **Métro Cité, Line 4 — Quai de l'Archevêché (4th arr.)**

Poe's Paris. Is there such a thing? Perhaps one day Poe scholars will come across irrefutable evidence that the master storyteller, genius of horror and the macabre, and inventor of the modern detective story actually set foot in Paris. Until then, there are a few Poe-related places to visit. Wander the *quartier* between the rue du Rivoli and the Opera. At No. 202 rue de Rivoli, the Hôtel Saint James and Albany was for a time the home of the Marquis de Lafayette. A plaque in the courtyard marks the marquis' meeting with Marie Antoinette in 1779.

A walk up the rue Saint Roch or the rue Richelieu is a step back in time to a Paris that has largely disappeared. On the rue Saint-Honoré at the Place du Marché Saint-Honoré is the site of the *Couvent des Jacobins*, the place where Danton, Maximillian Robespierre, and other supporters of a constitutional monarchy met. Known as the "Society of Friends of the Constitution," their ranks also briefly included the Marquis de Lafayette, until he broke with them over their increasingly radical ideas.

The church of Saint Roch stands at No. 286 rue Saint-Honoré. Its cornerstone was laid by King Louis XIV, the Sun King himself, in 1653. The face of the church bears the battle scars, cannon shot, and bullet holes from street battles before and during the revolution, especially when, on October 5, 1795, Napoleon's troops slaughtered

200 royalist sympathizers who were determined to overthrow the Convention. With this "whiff of grapeshot," the young (age twenty-six) army general went from being unknown to a fast-rising celebrity.

Here, too, the infamous Marquis de Sade was married in 1763, as was the Marquis de Lafayette himself in 1774.

*Fig. 37 - Saint-Roch Church (photo by the author)*

Home to many Polish exiles, the church was known as the "Polish Church" for a time in the 1830s. Frédéric Chopin was a regular attendee at Mass.

Janet Morgan's book *The Secrets of Rue St Roch: Intelligence Operations behind Enemy Lines in the First World War* details the activities of British Intelligence, which operated out of a secret location at No. 41 Rue Saint Roch.

Running parallel to the rue Saint Roch is the rue de la Soudière. Robespierre escaped an angry mob by fleeing into the church Saint Roch and taking a secret tunnel that exits at No. 10.

The other street bordering Poe's rue Morgue is the rue Richelieu. This fascinating street has several interesting sights, including the Palais Royale, the statue of Molière, and the Bibliothèque Nationale de France (the French National Library). Once one of the most fashionable streets in Paris, it is named for Cardinal Richelieu, who built and resided in the Palais Royale before it was given to Louis XIV's brother, Philippe Duc d'Orleans.

Completed in 1639, the Palais Royale became the social center of Paris while the Duc d'Orleans and his wife lived there. Notoriously gay, the Duc d'Orleans made the Palais Royale a place where all types of amusements, parties, and wares could be found. A profligate spender, he rented out the ground floor spaces to taverns, brothels, gambling houses, shops, and other establishments, which financed his lavish lifestyle while he lived on the upper floors.

Today, the Palais houses the Comédie Française at No. 2 rue Richelieu, beautiful gardens, several restaurants, including one of Paris' most famous, Le Grand Vefour, and a plaque at No. 9 rue de Beaujolais where Colette lived in her final years.

Sidonie-Gabrielle Colette was an acclaimed French author and journalist who led a scandalous life. She is the author of several books, including her most famous works, *Gigi* and *Paris From My Window*, about her years living in Paris during the Nazi occupation. She died in 1954 and was refused a religious funeral by the Catholic Church because of her divorces. She was, however, the first woman of letters to be given a state funeral by the French government.

Nearby, you can visit the Bibliothèque Nationale, which dates back to 1368, when King Charles V amassed a collection of manuscripts, books, and other items at the Louvre Palace. After being housed in several locations over the centuries, it moved to No. 58 rue Richelieu in 1868. Subsequently, three other locations in addition to this one house its vast collections.

## How Paris Shaped Our World

Edgar Allan Poe may or may not have visited Paris, yet he set three of his most memorable and important stories there. His choice of Paris for his world-shaking, groundbreaking crime/mystery genre was no accident.

Poe seems to have been familiar with Paris streets. Although any evidence of an actual rue Morgue doesn't show up on maps until the 1860s, *the* Morgue is clearly marked on earlier maps. Poe also was familiar with the contemporary father of modern detective work, Vidocq of the French police department. Although the word *detective* did not exist at the time Poe wrote "The Murders in the Rue Morgue," Vidocq had started what would become known as the world's first detective agency in 1833. And Poe certainly knew about the Paris cholera epidemic of 1832, which inspired his story, "The Mask of the Red Death."

Poe was well acquainted with French literature. As a critic, he reviewed (and strongly denounced) an English translation of Eugène Sue's sensationally lurid tale *The Mysteries of Paris*, written in 1842.

We could imagine that Poe gathered this knowledge in the earliest years of his life, in an eclectic fashion, then somehow wove the elements into stories which just happened to create an entire genre of fiction hitherto unknown. Or is something else at work here, hidden in plain sight? Was Poe ever in Paris? Like most of Poe's life, events, and circumstances, reality and fiction are shrouded in mystery and uncertainty, lost in the mists of time and fading memory.

Poe invented the genre that became one of the most popular types of literature ever created, one that has churned out thousands of short stories and novels, not to mention plays and movies: the detective story. A mystery to be solved, clues to be followed. "The Murders in the Rue Morgue" as well as "The Purloined Letter," "The Mystery of Marie Rogêt," and "The Gold-Bug" all written during the 1840s, were the headwaters of a stream that turned into a torrent, one that continues to amaze and delight to this day.

Most regard "The Murders in the Rue Morgue," first published in 1841 in *Graham's Magazine*, as the world's first detective fiction. That Dupin was featured in two of Poe's other stories firmly cements Poe as the creator of detective fiction. Poe's C. Auguste Dupin is the direct ancestor of Sir Arthur Conan Doyle's Sherlock Holmes and Agatha Christie's Hercule Poirot. It could even be said Dupin prefigures *Star Trek's* Mr. Spock because Dupin relies on a technique Poe dubbed "ratiocination" in which a precise, careful, logical, and unemotional examination of the facts will solve any mystery no matter how bizarre the conclusion might appear to be.

Poe even gives Dupin a fictional Paris address, "au troisième, no. 33 Rue Dunôt, Faubourg St. Germain." There is no rue Dunôt in Paris today, if there ever was one. There is a rue Dunois in the 13th arrondissement (Paris is divided up into twenty districts, known as "arrondissements") and a rue Dutot in the 15th, and a rue Duphot near la Madeleine, on early nineteenth-century maps, which still exists today (and on which, coincidentally, is the restaurant le Baudelaire). Any of these streets could have easily been reworked by Poe to create a place for Dupin to call home.

Poe is directly connected to one of France's greatest poets, Charles Baudelaire. Each influenced the other's work, and through Baudelaire, Poe strongly influenced other French and European writers, both writing at a time of an intense clash between Romanticism and modern society. Poe also inspired artists like the French Impressionist Edouard Manet who fashioned a portrait of Poe in 1876.

Baudelaire began translating Poe's work in the mid-1840s. The Decadents movement, which Baudelaire helped start, owed much of its ambiance to Poe and his Gothic, macabre, and horrific stories. Poe's fiction was also influential among the Surrealists and Symbolists. In Poe, Baudelaire felt he had found his literary soulmate.

Baudelaire's seminal work, *Les Fleurs du Mal (The Flowers of Evil*), dealt with subjects—much like Poe's work—which were startling for the time: death, sex, loss of innocence, and urban modernization, which was encroaching on people's homes, lives, and psyches. The way he approached these topics was considered scandalous, and highlighted the growing feeling of impending destruction that marked the age. He was writing at a time when Baron Haussmann was upending Paris, razing neighborhood after neighborhood, destroying much of the old ways and the ancient cityscapes to create a more functional and modern city.

*Les Fleurs du Mal* was an instant hit and an instant scandal. The images were too raw, the expressions too intense, the sexual energy too obvious. Baudelaire and his publisher were successfully prosecuted and fined for "an insult to public decency." Baudelaire wrote of his book:

> But this book, whose title (*Fleurs du mal*) says everything, is clad, as you will see, in a cold and sinister beauty. It was created with rage and patience. Besides, the proof of its positive worth is in all the ill that they speak of it. The book enrages people. Moreover, since I was terrified myself of the horror that I should inspire, I cut out a third from the proofs.

Without Charles Baudelaire's affinity for him, Edgar Allan Poe would have likely remained a minor writer and certainly would not have influenced European literary thinking and styles as he did.

From a spare and tiny cottage in the Bronx where his beloved wife lay dying, to the mysterious and possibly imaginary streets of Paris, from West Point to a Baltimore street where he was found delirious and disoriented, wearing someone else's clothes and crying out the name, "Reynolds,"—which meant nothing to anyone—and finally, to his death and burial at the back of Baltimore's Westminster Hall and Burying Ground without a headstone, Edgar Allan Poe's life has been shrouded in mystery. Rumor, scandal, gossip, good friends, and malicious enemies all weave themselves in and around the story of his life and death.

*Fig. 38 - Portrait of Poe by Manet*
*(public domain)*

Was Poe ever in Paris, France? Did he visit Alexandre Dumas and the Marquis de Lafayette? Did he find the real rue Morgue to use in his story? We may one day know for certain. Or perhaps it is better that we don't. That way we are given the gift of mystery to tease and enthrall us, just as Poe did for us in his stories. Perhaps as we wander

Paris streets we will be caught up in a mystery, an intrigue, a swirl of events that propels us into places unknown from which we will return changed forever.

Paris is like that....

# Chapter 5
# Tear It Down!

(Nineteenth and Twentieth Centuries)

*"I like The Eiffel Tower because it looks like steel and lace. Sometimes it looks like a needle, poking silver stars against the sky. Sometimes it looks like an iron corset (Fact: The Eiffel Tower was steampunk before steampunk was cool). Sometimes it looks like a scrawny giant. Sometimes it looks like the skeleton of a castle."*
— Natalie Lloyd, Author

*"It is the wind that determined the basic shape of my tower."*
— Gustave Eiffel

WINTER IS A dreary time in Paris. It gets dark quite early, and it is often cloudy, rainy, cold, and damp. The Parisian mood often reflects this palpable sense of melancholy, of *ennui*, of the futility of life—in music, literature, poetry, art, and philosophy. French sensibilities are a paradox—existential and fatalistic, while infused with a *joie de vivre.* This is a well-known, celebrated, and yet rarely understood fact.

Existentialism takes its root from the words "exist" and "existence." An existentialist philosophy is also a paradox, brooding and introspective while emphasizing experience—not mere thinking, but acting, feeling, living fully as a human being. Existence, once called into question, creates what has been called "the existential angst": an attitude of dread, a sense of disorientation, confusion, or anxiety when one is alone and faced with confronting a world that is apparently meaningless and absurd.

*La Tour Eiffel*, its history and mystery...its very *existence* as the *new* heart of Paris, answers these existential questions. It is the result of a marriage between the paradoxes: thinking, feeling, *and* action, a *crie de coeur* that shouts against the futility of life, raising a fist to the gods and saying, "I am here!"

La Tour Eiffel represents the paradox of existence, meaning, and meaninglessness, as it stands wrought in solid physical form: iron, fire, and gossamer air....

It was close to midnight on a typical dreary winter's night in the days after the New Year of 1908. A light still burned in the office of the *maître ingénieur*, the master engineer. From the ground the light was not visible. A thousand feet above the Champ de Mars, clouds had rolled in, shrouding the top of the tower in wraiths of mist and drizzle. Yet any Parisian who walked by and looked up knew *he* was up there, working....

There, Gustav Eiffel sat, head in hand, still as stone. It was late, he was tired, but he couldn't quit. They couldn't be serious. They wouldn't, couldn't hold him to the contract he had signed nearly twenty years earlier, a foolish agreement which said that his tower, his beloved masterpiece, must be torn down.

Hadn't it proved itself a success many times over? Why, the Exhibition of 1889 and the Universal Exhibition of 1900 alone saw more than two million people visit her. And what about all the visitors in all the years in between? Eiffel had made himself a fortune, it is true, but the city had profited as well.

He bolted up and began pacing his small office. Yes, there was controversy. Of course, all genius invites ridicule and scorn from those who cannot see with true vision. Yes, the ironwork was arresting, jarring, some might say. Fools called her ugly.

But then again, the public had never seen the skeleton of a building before. The underlying structure was beautiful by itself. Why couldn't they see that? This new building material, iron, was the reason. And it *was* jarring, the conflict, the contrast between what the old aesthetic said was "supposed to be," and the actuality, the daring, bold, and audacious vision, exposing what held everything together—*that* was what made the tower both beautiful and necessary for a modern world. Why should the organizing framework be clothed and hidden away? Bah! That was how everyone erected a building, wrapping it in metal or stone. Here was something no one had ever seen before.

They couldn't be serious...but they were. The tower sat on land owned by and leased from the City of Paris, marshy land at the edge of the Champ de Mars. Worse, from a legal perspective, the competition Eiffel had entered—to build the grand entryway for the Exposition of 1889—contained language that was crystal clear: one of the criteria for the winning structure was that it had to be easily dismantled. And, once the twenty-year lease was up, the structure had to come down.

He would not let that happen. Gustav Eiffel would find a way to save the tower—his tower—the Eiffel Tower. He would find a way, somehow, to make it so that they couldn't tear her down.

## Travelers' Tips

### Métro Station Trocadéro, Lines 6 and 9 (16th arr.)

Take Métro line six or nine and get off at Métro station Trocadéro. The tourist guides (and the Line 6 Métro signs) will tell you to get off at station Bir-Hakeim, but they are wrong, because the tower is a truly arresting sight when seen from the Trocadéro hill. You will emerge from Trocadéro station and see the tower in the middle distance across the river.

Stand at the edge of the Trocadéro, at the spot where Hitler once stood on his one and only visit to the city he loved, envied, and almost completely destroyed. Look across the expanse and gaze at *La Tour Eiffel*—the Iron Lady. Look past her to the field beyond, to the *Champ de Mars*, the Field of War. Let your mind drift; take yourself back in time to the Paris *Exposition Universalle* of 1889, held to commemorate the one-hundredth anniversary of the French Revolution.

From this vantage point, one can visit several interesting places that are close by. The name Trocadéro commemorates a battle in southern Spain, which French forces won in 1832. Built on the hill of Chaillot, the old Palais du Trocadéro was demolished in 1937, replaced by the current Palais de Chaillot, which is home to the *Musée national de la Marine* (naval museum) and the *Musée de l'Homme the Cité de l'Architecture et du Patrimoine*, including the *Musée national des Monuments Français* and the *Théâtre national de Chaillot*.

Off to the right of the Trocadéro is the rue Benjamin Franklin and the statue of the great man commemorating Franklin's nine years in France (1776-1785) as the emissary from the fledgling American colonial government, which was trying to gain French support in their fight for independence from Great Britain. Franklin's fame preceded him across the Atlantic, and France received him warmly as a genius, scientist, philosopher, and statesman.

One French account of his arrival noted:

> The celebrated Franklin arrived at Paris the twenty-first of December and has fixed the eyes of every one upon his slightest proceeding.... He was not given the title Monsieur; he was addressed simply as Doctor Franklin, as one would have addressed Plato or Socrates. If it is true that Prometheus was only a man, may one not believe that he was a natural philosopher like Franklin?

Franklin lived on an estate in this area of Paris, which was then the small rural village of Passy. A good walk down the rue Benjamin Franklin and into the village will take you to the Clemenceau Museum, home of George Clemenceau, French Prime Minister during World War I. Clemenceau also figured prominently in a major event in French history: the Dreyfus Affair. It was Clemenceau who, on January 13, 1898, published Émile Zola's *J'Accuse...!* a highly controversial open letter to the president of France, on the front page of *L'Aurore*, a newspaper that he owned and edited.

Farther down along the rue Rayounard is the home of Honoré de Balzac, famous writer, novelist, and playwright, who wrote *The Human Comedy* and the historical novel *Catherine de Medici*. A stroll past the Balzac Museum, on the right a sharp-eyed observer will notice a stone plaque high on an apartment building. On the spot where the estate stood where Dr. Franklin made his home, the plaque commemorates the first lightning rod in France, which Franklin installed here.

*Fig. 40 - Benjamin Franklin plaque commemorating the installation of the first lightning rod in France, at the estate where Franklin stayed in Passy (photo by the author)*

*Fig. 41 - The statue of Benjamin Franklin off of the Trocadéro (photo by the author)*

*Fig. 42 - Street sign—rue Benjamin Franklin*
*(photo by the author)*

Back to the tower…

Eiffel's entry won out against the other 107 competitors, all vying to build the grand entryway to the fair. Most entries were tossed without a second thought; they were so uninspired. Some were simply impractical, like the giant guillotine which did more than commemorate the French Revolution. It proposed to celebrate The Terror that had left some 17,000 French men and women headless.

Besides the generally weak competition, records show that Eiffel's design won out thanks to a change in the contest criteria that "coincidentally" mirrored his plan, guaranteeing his success. A last-minute clause was inserted into the competition criteria:

> Competitors will have to study the possibility of raising on the Champ de Mars a square base iron tower, 125 meters wide at the base and 300 meters high. They will include this tower on the plan of the Champ de Mars....

On January 8, 1887, Eiffel himself signed the agreement in which he personally committed to build his *Tour en Fer de Trois Cents Mètres* (Iron Tower of 300 Meters) and to operate the tower, which was to be up and running by the opening of the Exhibition. He received a subsidy of 1,500,000 francs, less than one-fifth the eventual cost of more than 7,800,000 francs. The remainder came out of Eiffel's own pocket.

*Fig. 43 - Eiffel and his team during construction of the Eiffel Tower—Maurice Koechlin, Stephen Sauvestre, Gustave Eiffel, Emile Nouguier, and Adolphe Salles. (Wikipedia—licensed under the Creative Commons Attribution-Share Alike 4.0 International license)*

*Fig. 44 - Illustration of caisson for making foundations (c. 1887, print published in 1892). Watson, William. Paris Universal Exposition: Civil Engineering, Public Works, and Architecture. Washington [DC], Government Printing Office (public domain)*

The agreement, however, gave Eiffel the exclusive rights to operate the tower for the duration of the Exhibition, including the "public ascension and from the point of view of the installation of restaurants, cafes, or other similar establishments," and the "continuation of enjoyment for twenty years from January 1, 1890." This proved to be an astute business move on his part. The tower became profitable almost immediately upon opening, and it remains so to this day.

A pause here is appropriate to honor three men whose names have been nearly forgotten and lost to history. While clearly Gustave Eiffel was a visionary and a shrewd entrepreneur without whom the tower would never have existed, he did not come up with the idea. Two extraordinary engineers, Maurice Koechlin and Emile Nouguier, and an equally remarkable architect, Stephen Sauvestre, actually conceived of the idea and sketched rough plans for the "Eiffel" Tower, which they showed to their employer. Eiffel liked them and purchased the rights to their idea.

From that point, the tower belonged to Eiffel. Besides having the financial resources to build the tower from his own funds, Eiffel had the professional reputation, not to mention the political connections, to win the competition and carry out the project successfully.

Once the contracts were signed, Eiffel's team went to work. Sauvestre, Koechlin, and Nouguier led a cadre of fifty engineers and draftsmen who drew up more than 5,300 plans and drawings for the tower's design and construction. Prior to starting any work on the site, a complete in-depth soil analysis had to be done to understand the consistency and durability of the soil. The engineers found solid earth in the area where the east and south legs would be situated, but in the places where the north and west legs would stand, the soil was soft, not well-suited to support such a massive structure. These sections, closer to the river, were actually in an area that was in ancient times the Seine's actual riverbed. This area was prone to flooding, making the soil in that area even weaker.

Construction began almost immediately at the end of January 1887. Eiffel and his company started making pieces of the tower at his factory in Levallois-Perret, just outside of Paris. Meanwhile on site, crews began pouring the foundations to support the footings for the four legs of the tower, which took five months to complete. Exact placement was crucial; otherwise the tower would be unstable. Perfectly level footings with virtually zero tolerance were necessary for the tower's safety. The foundations for the four legs must be able to successfully support the weight of 10,000 tons and endure for decades, lasting without any deterioration. Any flaw, no matter how minor, would eventually cause major problems for the structure's integrity: the tower could fall, list, or pieces could fall off.

Eiffel's construction crews dug four foundations, fifty feet down, to specifications provided by these visionary engineers. Then they poured twenty feet of concrete, onto which they placed massive limestone blocks, and they topped it off with layers and layers of cut stone.

For the twin problems of soil instability and periodic flooding at the sites closest to the river Seine, Eiffel fashioned an ingenious solution—a two-system foundation: a "dry" foundation coupled with a compressed air foundation, an innovative technique that had recently been used in underwater construction.

Each of the legs of the tower's base has two twenty-six-foot-long anchor bolts, each one four inches in diameter. Once the legs were anchored in place, Eiffel used another ingenious technique to make the foundations and legs perfectly level: a hydraulic jack. The jack enabled the crew to raise or lower the platforms to level each one.

It took just over two years for more than 300 onsite employees, plus another 100-150 workers at the Eiffel factory, to erect the nearly 1,000-foot tower. Upon completion, it became the tallest structure in the world, surpassing the tallest at that time: the Washington Monument in Washington, DC. The Eiffel Tower would remain the tallest until 1930 when the Chrysler Building in New York City was completed.

Eiffel had already been instrumental in creating another iron framework, a structure designed to support the massive sheets of copper that were to become Frédéric Auguste Bartholdi's sculpture *Liberty Enlightening the World*, better known as the Statue of Liberty. Built in Paris between 1879 and 1884, Eiffel's innovative iron skeleton for the Statue of Liberty was a revolution in engineering, architecture, and construction. Along with Eiffel's Tower, replicas of the head and shoulders of Bartholdi's statue would be exhibited at the world's Fair of 1889.

After the foundations for the footings were completed, the tower began to rise. Prefabricated pieces of the structure were brought to the site from Eiffel's *atelier* (workshop). French journalist Émile Goudeau wrote an article describing his visit to the construction site, just as work was beginning in 1889:

> A thick cloud of tar and coal smoke seized the throat, and we were deafened by the din of metal screaming beneath the hammer. Over there they were still working on the bolts: workmen with their iron bludgeons, perched on a ledge just a few centimetres wide, took turns at striking the bolts [these in fact were

> the rivets]. One could have taken them for blacksmiths contentedly beating out a rhythm on an anvil in some village forge, except that these smiths were not striking up and down vertically, but horizontally, and as with each blow came a shower of sparks, these black figures, appearing larger than life against the background of the open sky, looked as if they were reaping lightning bolts in the clouds.

Eiffel used his cutting-edge knowledge of the metal arch and truss forms, which were superior to conventional forms. This was especially important because of the tower's height. He needed to account for stresses never before encountered in building construction, including the tower's unheard-of weight and the wind. His work initiated a revolution in civil engineering and architectural design.

In fact, the tower had to be flexible, moving to accommodate winds that could reach speeds of more than a hundred miles per hour at the top. The tower is closed during high winds, but at other times, visitors can actually feel the tower swaying gently—about six inches in any direction. Regardless, it is safe. It is designed to withstand movement caused by up to five times the highest winds ever recorded. Today, a laser alignment system monitors the tower's movements due to wind but also because the tower leans slightly in bright sunlight. Incredibly, one side expands when heated by the sun.

The tower's construction was a marvel of modern engineering. While critics saw an ugly, exposed skeleton, the frame of a building that ought to be hidden away behind a beautiful façade, Eiffel recognized the beauty and harmony inherent in the design and construction of his masterpiece.

The innovative use of the truss design coupled with the relatively new building material, puddled iron, allowed the tower to be far taller than anything built before, strong, *and* lightweight. Indeed, the tower is mostly empty space, with some iron bars interlaced within. Mathematicians can prove that if all the material in the tower were melted down, it would comprise a ball of iron less than forty feet in diameter. They can also prove that the column of air enclosing the tower weighs more than the tower itself.

The construction of the tower was as innovative as anything at the time. Engineers had contemplated building taller structures, but stone and wood would not allow anything close to the height of the Eiffel Tower. The preliminary design work, the preparation of the construction site, the design and laying the foundations for the four legs, and the actual organization of the work at the site were all extremely new and innovative for the late nineteenth century. Eiffel's design using latticed iron demonstrated something that up until that time was hotly debated—that iron could be as strong as stone while being lighter.

***Construction Facts***

18,038 metallic parts

5,300 workshop designs

50 engineers and designers

150 workers in the Levallois-Perret factory

150 to 300 workers on the construction site

2,500,000 rivets

7,300 metric tons of iron

60 metric tons of paint

5 elevator lifts

2 years, 2 months, and 5 days of construction

1 fatality

As if the practical difficulties of weather, wind, water, soil, materials, labor, politics, and other logistical factors of design and construction weren't enough to keep Eiffel busy, a growing chorus, a howl really, of disapproval, disgust, and disdain arose and grew louder within Paris. The first beams that would become the four legs of the tower had not even begun to rise off their pedestals when a protest erupted: 300 prominent artists, one for each meter of the tower's height, lent their names to a petition calling on the government to halt work and cease any further construction on the tower.

The controversy divided the protesters between those who thought the design unfeasible and dangerous (i.e., it would collapse) and those who objected on purely aesthetic grounds (i.e., it was an ugly eyesore). The petition was signed by such important figures as Charles Garnier (designer and architect of the Paris Opera House that bears his name) and writers Guy de Maupassant, Alexandre Dumas the Younger, and Sully Prudhomme.

Paul Verlaine called it a "belfry skeleton." Others said it was a "truly tragic streetlamp" or "mast of iron gymnasium apparatus." One observer said the growing structure was, "incomplete, confused, and deformed." Guy de Maupassant called it "this high and skinny pyramid of iron ladders, this giant ungainly skeleton upon a base that looks built to carry a colossal monument of Cyclops, but which just peters out into a ridiculous thin shape like a factory chimney."

Opinion went from discontent to amazing feats of invective, with one of the 300 artists saying the tower was, "a half-built factory pipe, a carcass waiting to be fleshed out with freestone or brick, a funnel-shaped grill, a hole-riddled suppository."

The protest against the tower reached a climax when a letter signed by forty-seven members of the committee was sent to the minister of works and commissioner for the exhibition and a copy was published in *Le Temps* on February 14, 1887:

> We, writers, painters, sculptors, architects, and passionate devotees of the hitherto untouched beauty of Paris, protest with all our strength, with all our indignation in the name of slighted French taste, against the erection...of this useless and monstrous Eiffel Tower.... To bring our arguments home, imagine for a moment a giddy, ridiculous tower dominating Paris like a gigantic black smokestack, crushing under its barbaric bulk Notre Dame, the Tour de Saint-Jacques, the Louvre, the Dome of les Invalides, the Arc de Triomphe, all of our humiliated monuments will disappear in this ghastly dream. And for twenty years...we shall see stretching like a blot of ink the hateful shadow of the hateful column of bolted sheet metal.

Later that year in the newspaper *Le Monde*, Eiffel replied to the artists' protest:

> For my part I believe that the Tower will possess its own beauty. Are we to believe that because one is an engineer, one is not preoccupied by beauty in one's constructions, or that one does not seek to create elegance as well as solidity and durability? Is it not true that the very conditions which give strength also conform to the hidden rules of harmony?
>
> Now to what phenomenon did I have to give primary concern in designing the Tower? It was wind resistance. Well then! I hold that the curvature of the monument's

> four outer edges, which is as mathematical calculation dictated it should be...will give a great impression of strength and beauty, for it will reveal to the eyes of the observer the boldness of the design as a whole. Likewise the many empty spaces built into the very elements of construction will clearly display the constant concern not to submit any unnecessary surfaces to the violent action of hurricanes, which could threaten the stability of the edifice. Moreover there is an attraction in the colossal, and a singular delight to which ordinary theories of art are scarcely applicable.

Besides Eiffel's eloquent defense, another strike against the artists' protest was that Garnier himself had been one of the Tower Commission members. When he and the commission judged the 107 competing proposals, he did not voice any objections. This fact did much to blunt the protestations of the Committee of Three Hundred.

Afterward, many of those who objected so vehemently changed their minds. Some even apologized to Eiffel. Guy de Maupassant was not one of them. It is said that he ate lunch every day at the Eiffel Tower restaurant. When asked why he ate there since he hated the Eiffel Tower so much, he supposedly replied that since the restaurant was *in* the tower, he could eat in peace and not have to look at the tower.

All in all, the tower took two years, two months, and five days to complete, finishing on March 31, 1889, when Eiffel led a group of dignitaries and journalists to the top of the tower. Because the lifts were not operating yet, they walked the entire way, with Eiffel stopping often to point out features and explain how and why things were done the way they were done.

The elevators, engineering marvels in and of themselves, were not operational until May 26. Before then, patrons had to climb the 1,710 steps to the top. The attraction was so popular that 30,000 people paid to make the climb before the elevators were in operation. By the end of the Exposition, nearly 1.9 million people had paid to ascend the tower!

*Fig. 45 - Drawing rendering of the Eiffel Tower's elevators—Originally published in La Nature, (Paris) May 4, 1889, Unknown author (signed as "Poyet") (courtesy Wikimedia, public domain)*

*Fig. 46 - Neurdein Frères postcard, Le Globe Celèste, View of the Eiffel Tower and of the Globe during the 1900 Paris World Fair. The globe was decorated with images of constellations, and the pillars on which it stood were decorated with mythological sculptures. Paris Exposition of 1900 Published in: Neurdein frères and Maurice Baschet. Le panorama, Exposition universelle. Paris: Librairie d'Art Ludovic Baschet, 1900. (Courtesy Wikimedia, public domain)*

The contract with the Exposition required all parts of the tower be made in France. However, no French elevator company could be persuaded to design and build the elevators, which had to swoop up the legs of the tower rather than make a straight vertical ascent. Finally, the bid was awarded to the Otis Elevator Company, which confidently had already started designing the lifts even before the contract was awarded. The north and south pillars contained the original Otis elevators.

The elevators' ascent to the first floor was simple enough. The journey between levels one and two was more difficult, because it was not straight up and down. The design had to overcome the curvature of the legs. Otis' engineers came up with an ingenious solution: hydraulic cable lifts running on rail tracks. In fact, these are not traditional elevators, but are a hybrid cross between an elevator, a funicular, and perhaps even a cable car, climbing up a sloping fifty-four-degree inclined track to the first floor, and then adjusting to seventy-four degrees up to the second floor.

In 1889, the tower opened to the public on May 6, nine days after the official opening of the *Exposition Universalle*. It was immediately a hit with the crowds attending the Exhibition. Although the elevators were still being readied, tens of thousands made their way up the Eiffel Tower, as it was already being called. At night, the tower was illuminated by hundreds of gas lamps. A beacon sent out the red, white, and blue beams of light—the tricolors of the French flag.

Excitement and activity surrounded the tower's opening. An observer at the time, Monsieur G. Le Notre, wrote:

> All Parisians, lifelong or temporary, are now possessed of a magical carpet. This carpet, a simple

> ticket of entrance, is the talisman that admits them to the country of dreams. Here you are transported, according to your caprice, from Cairo to the Americas, from the Congo to Cochinchina, from Tunisia to Java, from Annam to Algeria.

The French newspaper, *Le Figaro*, began producing a special *Tour Eiffel* daily edition of the newspaper onsite from offices on the second floor. A post office opened, where one could send postcards—by balloon. The Neurdein Brothers, successful commercial photographers in Paris, produced exclusive images of the tower for patrons of the exposition. In 1899, they would go on to win a gold medal for photography at the *Exposition Universalle*.

Eiffel delighted in giving famous visitors a personal tour. Thomas Edison, the Prince of Wales, Czar Alexander III of Russia, Sarah Bernhardt, and the Archduke Ferdinand of Austria toured the tower with Eiffel. Buffalo Bill, whose Wild West Show was part of the American exhibit, hitched his horse to the Eiffel Tower as he toured the exposition. The allure continues today, with the famous and near famous drawn to the tower. Tom Cruise proposed to Katie Holmes on the tower.

Through the heady activity of both the 1889 and the 1900 *Expositions Universalle*, the impending destruction of the tower was barely a thought. The throngs passing through the gateway and the thousands upon thousands heading up the stairs or later piling into the lifts were able to gaze at Paris in a new way: an ariel view without the hazards of a hot air balloon.

Then there was the praise, the speeches by politicians, the articles and editorials in the papers, the comments from friends and foes alike. All of this kept Monsieur Gustave Eiffel whirling in a state of constant euphoria at the positive reception of his monumental and unique achievement.

But now the fairs and the expositions were over. Things quieted down considerably. The tower still attracted visitors, but hundreds a day, not thousands. Time was growing short. The city had made it clear Eiffel must honor the original agreement. They insisted the gateway arch was a *temporary* structure and *would* be dismantled in 1909. In any case, the lease on the land would be up by then, and Eiffel would have no rights to the land or the structure.

Eiffel spent the intervening years wracking his brain for ways to save his masterpiece. He worked diligently on atmospherics research. He had a wind tunnel built at the foot of the tower. He reasoned if the tower were seen as a unique place to perform experiments and discover new ideas and phenomena about the climate, weather, and atmosphere, it would become indispensable to science, something the French revered. That usefulness, he thought, would engage the scientific community and surely sway officials.

Other experiments followed, investigations on the nature of gravity and on the uses and power of electricity. Eiffel invited scientists from everywhere to use the tower's top floor offices to run their experiments and test their theories. This is why the names of the seventy-three mostly French "savants" or scientists are engraved on the four sides of the Eiffel Tower, luminaries including Daguerre, Poisson, Ampere, Foucault, and Coriolis.

While experiments in, around, and on the tower proved to be interesting and somewhat useful to scientists, nothing earth-shaking came from the work being done there, nothing that could not have been done just as well on the ground as 990 feet in the air. Astronomy, Eiffel thought, was a distinct possibility. He proposed using the tower as an observatory, and this too proved interesting but not a particularly unique place for star-gazing. Any mountaintop would do as well or better, given the Parisian lights.

By 1907, Eiffel's lease would end before long, and with it, his hopes for saving the tower. Soon they would tear her down, and he seemed powerless to stop it. Making the tower indispensable was proving elusive. His intuition told him the structure, higher than any built before, *must* have some scientific utility—but what remained unclear. His goal of preserving the tower seemed wholly out of reach.

Although electrical telegraphs using wire to transmit signals had been around since the early 1830s, the 1880s and '90s saw the beginnings of wireless and radio transmission technology. In 1897, Guglielmo Marconi was in England demonstrating advances in the wireless transmission of Morse Code signals across a distance.

Eiffel had already seen this technology and conducted experiments in wireless transmission on the tower, including a transmission of Morse Code signals between the tower and the Panthéon in 1898. So this avenue of investigation seemed a dead end until a French Army Captain, Gustave Ferrié, approached Eiffel with a novel idea. What if the tower could be used militarily? With this stroke of genius, Ferrié opened a new avenue of possibility for saving the tower.

*Fig. 47 - Monument on the Champ de Mars to Captain Gustave Ferrié, the man who helped save the Eiffel Tower (photo by the author)*

Ferrié was already in charge of studying military applications for wireless radio transmissions. So, in 1908, he set up a demonstration, financed by Eiffel, in which they transmitted a signal to an army unit some 400 kilometers (248 miles) away. Later, more powerful transmitters allowed Ferrié to communicate with the naval base in Tunisia. By 1909, a permanent station was built underneath the Champ de Mars, and the tower's strategic value was confirmed. Now the Eiffel Tower had important military and strategic application. Once it became a significant part of national security, city officials could not evict Eiffel or tear down his tower.

Eiffel's concession was renewed on January 1, 1910—for seventy years.

### How Paris Shaped Our World

Arguably, while the military importance of the tower was limited, it did prove useful in directing troop movements around Paris during World War I. The tower did not fall into enemy hands in the Great War as it was in World War II, when the Nazis occupied Paris. Soon after its fall, Hitler made his one and only visit to Paris in late June 1940. In honor of his visit, the German high command wanted to hoist a huge Nazi flag high atop the Eiffel Tower. Unfortunately for them, the French Resistance had anticipated their move, and cut the cables to all of the tower's elevators. The German soldiers, undeterred, climbed the 1,710 steps to the top and hoisted their flag—only to have it blow away in the high winds within a few hours.

The tower's elevators remained inoperable until 1946. When Allied forces neared Paris in August 1944, a French Resistance fighter scaled the tower and hung the *tricolore* French flag once more as the German army retreated.

During World War I, the Battle of the Marne was decisive in keeping the Germans from overrunning Paris. When the tower's staff received word the Germans had halted due to problems organizing divisions, this pause enabled the French troops to be redirected to the area.

*Fig. 48 - On the Trocadéro, Hitler and his entourage visit the Eiffel Tower, June 23, 1940. (courtesy Wikimedia via The German Federal Archive)*

In the famous (and successful) defense of Paris, an event known to all French schoolchildren as *Les Taxis de la Marne*, hundreds of Parisian taxis ferried the French soldiers to the front lines.

Since it was first built, the tower has made its way into the highest levels of iconography, recognized by virtually anyone on the planet. Who can see the Eiffel Tower and not think of Paris? And would Paris be Paris without the Eiffel Tower? Certainly, it would not be the same.

As an aside, did you know that certain images of the Eiffel Tower are protected from commercial use? Images of the tower when it is lit up at night cannot be taken and sold without express permission. The lighting scheme dates back to the year 2000 millennium celebration. The lighting scheme, not the tower itself, is a protected image for commercial purposes. Tourists are free to take as many pictures as they want, day or night; they just cannot sell the illuminated shots.

The Eiffel Tower holds the distinctive honor of being the most visited monument in the world, in the most visited city in the world. It annually receives between six and seven million visitors. It is also the most valuable monument in the world, with an estimated price tag (counting revenues, radio transmission antennas, materials, etc.) at €435 *billion*, dwarfing the next most valuable monument, the Roman Coliseum, which is valued at a mere €91 billion.

By luck or by Providence, somehow Eiffel saved his tower from being demolished. Trying to imagine the City of Paris and the world without it is difficult, it has so ingrained itself into our consciousness. It is not a static hunk of metal, but a living, breathing monument. Its testimony to genius, innovation, vision, the breathtaking and the beautiful is beyond doubt today.

Quite a feat for something that was almost torn down.

# Chapter 6
# The First and Last Meters

## (Eighteenth and Nineteenth Centuries)

*Fig. 49 - Drawing, design for a monument commemorating systematization of weights and measures in France (continued, see figure credits, public domain)*

*"The most lasting and universal consequence of the French Revolution is the metric system."*
— Eric Hobsbawn, British Historian

VIRTUALLY, THE ENTIRE world uses the metric system of measurement. Indeed, only three countries currently do not: Liberia, Myanmar, and the United States. Britain still uses a mix of the old, often illogical "Imperial System" of measurement along with the metric system. How did this revolutionary *Measurement Universalle* come to be? And how did this, one of the most important inventions in modern history, gain nearly universal acceptance?

Clearly, the metric system affects every aspect of modern life: science, engineering, international trade, politics, the world economy, etc. A uniform system of measurement that touches people in their daily lives is something most take for granted, using it with little thought for its origins, or the difficult road it took to achieve. Yet clearly this convenience, which makes life easier and more predictable, did not always exist, nor was its success guaranteed.

Of course, the story of the metric system and how it was created begins here in Paris And it is here in Paris that we will find "The First and the Last Meters."

Throughout the countries of medieval Europe, and from region to region and town to town, the measurements people used to weigh and determined length and size varied—sometimes considerably. Consistent and reliable measurements which are necessary for science, commerce, and trade, and to levy taxes were non-existent. Often, the length of a measure was determined by the current sovereign, sometimes literally using the dimensions of the monarch's body. So, the measurement would change when the throne changed hands. "Standards" were flexible and made and enforced by decree.

For example, the "foot" dates back to early Greek and Roman civilization. While other ancient peoples in countries such as Egypt used the "cubit" as a measurement, the foot, as the name implies, was based roughly on the size of a man's foot and could vary wildly—anywhere from 9.6 to 13.2 inches. Today, the United States is the only industrialized nation still exclusively employing the foot (technically known as the "international foot") in daily life and for commercial, engineering, and other activities, rather than the meter. Others, like British Commonwealth countries, use both imperial and metric measures.

At one time in France alone, hundreds, if not thousands, of different forms of measurement were in use. These vague, random ways of measurement caused considerable confusion. Disagreements frequently arose between merchants and customers and between traders and merchants. Disputes arose between neighboring cities and towns and between nations.

This lack of a uniform system disrupted the free and easy movement of goods across regions and borders: How's a "foot" in this city different from a "foot" in the next city? What does a "pound" actually weigh? How do you know you're getting a fair measure? The answers varied depending on who you were dealing with and what town, region, or country you were in.

In addition to everyday business and commercial needs, the growing scientific community required more accurate ways to measure their observational and experimental data. Random systems based on royal decree or physical prototypes no longer served scientists and inventors and their increasingly rigorous scientific and mathematical calculations.

In an essay titled "The Measure of Enlightenment," J. L. Heilbronn writes:

> The existence of French men and women around 1790 was made miserable by, among other things, 700 or 800 differently named measures and untold units of the same name but different sizes. A "pinte" in Paris came to 0.93 litre; in Saint-Denis, to 1.46; in Seine-en-Montagne, to 1.99; in Précy-sous-Thil, to 3.33.

The aune, a unit of length, was still more prolific: Paris had three, each for a different sort of cloth; Rouen had two; and France as a whole no fewer than seventeen, all in common use and all different, the smallest amounting to just under 300 lignes, royal measure, the largest to almost 600.

France possessed non-uniform measures in law as well as by custom. Their multiplicity went with other relics of the feudal system, which maintained arbitrary rents and duties usually to the disadvantage of the peasant.

A landlord wanted his bushels of grain or hogsheads of beer in the biggest measures in use in the neighborhood, and he preferred to sell according to the smallest. Nor were all seigneurs above enlarging the vessel in which they collected their rents; and since in many cases they possessed the only exemplars of their patrimonial bushel, no one could be certain that it did not grow in time. But one suspected.

A frequent complaint in the cahiers, or notebooks of desiderata brought by representatives of the people to the meeting of the Estates General in 1789, was that 'the nobles' measure waxes larger year by year. These same representatives castigated the oppressive confusion of customary measures as barbaric, ridiculous, obscurantist, gothic, and revolting, and demanded an end to them, and the establishment of a system of unchanging and verifiable weights and measures throughout the country, or at least throughout their region. Many urged that the King's measure, the royal foot, be made the law of the land.

> Sharpers and crooks whose practices were not sanctioned by ancient rights and wrongs and middlemen acting in analogy to money changers opposed the rationalization that menaced their livelihood.

For centuries, nothing was done, despite these obvious problems. As far back as the fifteenth century, proposals were made in England, France, Germany, and elsewhere to unify measurement standards. Attempts were made, but nobody seemed to have the power to create the standards, much less enforce compliance. In England, the philosopher John Wilkins, a founding member of the Royal Society of London, proposed a system, a "Universal Measure," or "meter" in "An Essay Towards a Real Character, And a Philosophical Language," written in 1668.

Sir Isaac Newton, a student at the same time Wilkins was the head of Trinity College in Cambridge, used the French foot for a standard measurement in all his writings and descriptions of his experiments, which was at the time the closest thing Europe had to an international standard.

To set up a rational system *and* to make everyone adhere to it, a government that prized logical and scientific reasoning was needed, with the political power to implement and enforce its new standards. Furthermore, any rational, logical, and mathematically-sound approach needed approval from the scientific *and* political classes. Once that herculean feat was accomplished, then the people would need to be educated in the new system, shopkeepers, tradespeople, and customers alike.

What finally caused the change? The French Revolution. And given Heilbron's description of the state of things in France at the time, is it any wonder a major upheaval was necessary to upend an ad hoc system that rewarded cheats, crooks, and those in power at the expense of the powerless?

When the French king was overthrown in the Revolution of 1789, the revolutionaries did not just seek to change their monarchist system of government—they were intent on remaking all of society. After two centuries, the Age of Enlightenment had reached its full flowering. The Enlightenment's political philosophers, especially French thinkers like Voltaire and Rousseau, saw the ultimate goal of the Enlightenment as a new awakening, not just scientifically or philosophically, but in politics and government as well; they envisioned a civil society based on rationality, equality, and "natural" law and rights.

The Renaissance and the Scientific Revolution had already awakened and remade nearly every aspect of life and society, the sciences, the arts, philosophy, religion, economics, the law and more. New, more enlightened theories of governance and the "inalienable" rights of people were beginning to move from theoretical to practical application, with an inevitable and immense struggle waged by the old order.

The recently created United States of America was the world's first attempt at a system of governance by the consent of the governed, rather than by the "divine right" of a monarchy. The government created out of the American Revolution was enshrined in the US Constitution. This miracle of republican democracy was made possible only because of the French Enlightenment philosophers and their ideas of liberty and justice (as well as French warships, soldiers, military supplies, and weapons).

The French Revolution came just a decade later, inspired by the Americans' success and spurred on by France's own corrupt system, with its two tiers of justice and its grinding poverty and taxation. In the decades leading up to the Revolution of 1789, the average French citizen suffered while the nobles, the wealthy, and the clergy lived lavish lifestyles. The revolutionaries believed that their government would perfect the ideals of enlightened governance that had been only just started in the United States. They attempted to approach the practicalities of governance logically, scientifically, and pragmatically. Liberty and kinship were to be its cornerstones, along with (and above all) equality, as much as was humanly possible, in every aspect of life.

The French Revolutionary government held power for just ten years. Yet for its short duration, it had worldwide influence, far surpassing its brief moment in history. Enshrined in the Revolution's DNA—and still today in modern France—are the ideals of *liberté*, *égalité*, *fraternité* (liberty, equality, and fraternity), as espoused in the 1789 Declaration of the Rights of Man and of the Citizen (*Déclaration des droits de l'homme et du citoyen de 1789*).

The Declaration is a human civil rights document, drafted by the Abbé Sieyès and the Marquis de Lafayette, in close consultation with Thomas Jefferson. Building on Enlightenment ideas of "natural rights," these "rights of man" were seen to be universal, applying to everyone, everywhere. The Declaration was the foundation for a free nation, made up of free citizens, equal in law and in every other way. As such, the Declaration declares that the law:

> Must be the same for all, whether it protects or punishes. All citizens, being equal in its eyes, shall be equally eligible to all high offices, public positions and employments, according to their ability, and without other distinction than that of their virtues and talents.

The Declaration of Rights serves as a sort of a preamble to the French Constitution, reaffirming the indivisibility and the great principles of the French nation: freedom of the press, equality, the right to public assistance, work, education, insurrection, and resistance to oppression.

To achieve these goals, the French National Convention moved to implement vast changes in the lives of the French citizens. Every aspect of daily existence was examined and changed if possible. One experiment that failed miserably was the new French Revolutionary Calendar (also known as the French Republican Calendar). It lasted only about twelve years, until the rise of Emperor Napoleon. It was briefly revived in 1870, for a grand total of eighteen days, during the short and tragic reign of the Paris Commune.

Many notable people of the time were involved in creating the French Republican Calendar: mathematicians, astronomers, geographers, playwrights, poets, and the gardener of the Jardin des Plantes. Its creators looked to ideas of nature and the Enlightenment, to rationality and uniformity. They also looked back to the republics of Rome and ancient Greece to organize their new system to measure the year.

As with the metric system, multiples of ten were the key. The twelve months of the current Gregorian calendar were divided into three weeks, each with ten days. A ten-day "week" was called a "*décade*" with the tenth day replacing Sunday as a day of rest. This scheme left five or six extra days to round out the year. These were named, "Complimentary Days" and were placed at the end of each year.

They invented new names for the months, names like *Prairial* and *Floréal* (meadow and flower) in the spring, *Thermador* and

*Fig. 50 - The sinking of the Vengeur, dated by the new Revolutionary Calendar as 13 Prairial, An 2 during the Glorious First of June 1794 (Third Ushant Battle). By Leopold Morice, 1883. Pedestal of the Monument to the Republic. (Statue of Marianne at the Place de la Republique (photo by the author)*

*Fructidor* (heat and fruit) in the summer, *Frimaire* and *Brumaire* (frost and mist) in fall, and *Ventôse* and *Nivôse* (windy and snowy) for the winter months, names with mostly French, Latin, or Greek roots.

Even with eminent scholars and scientists doing their best, the calendar caused widespread debate and met with resistance and even scorn. A British satirist of the time poked fun at the newly unveiled calendar, renaming some of the months Wheezy, Sneezy, Slippy, Drippy, Flowery, Hoppy, and Poppy.

Inevitably, controversy in France erupted even before the calendar was unveiled. The calendar's starting date was a primary point of contention: When would Year One begin, relative to the current Gregorian calendar? Consistency with the calendar widely used in the rest of the world was vital and yet caused much confusion. Should the starting date fall on the date of liberty, which was July 14, 1789? Or September 22, 1792, the date the Republic was created? The debate raged on.

These practical problems were compounded by other questions: How to conform financial transactions between the old and new calendar? How to fix the date of leap years? etc. There were also problems interpreting the language of the establishing decree written by the Revolutionary National Convention.

But for all of these technical problems, one real-world difficulty proved insurmountable: people liked (and insisted on having) their Sundays and holidays. The Revolution, which was determined to abolish all connections to religion and the Catholic Church, removed any references to saints and religious feast days. On the old French calendar, *every* day was devoted to one or another Catholic saint—a common tradition still in use on French calendars today.

The loss of the major religious holidays, Christmas and Easter, the many minor ones, *and* the abolition of Sundays—which was no longer to be celebrated or even acknowledged on the official state calendar—went too far. Most people insisted on resting every seventh day, regardless of what the new calendar said. This was the final blow that caused the demise of the Republican Calendar, which died soon after the French Republic officially ended with the rise of Emperor Napoleon I.

However badly the French Revolution's calendar experiment went, their plan to adopt a new system to measure weight, length, volume, and temperature proved to be a success. The system had its French origins in a proposal made by Gabriel Mouton, vicar of St. Paul's church in Lyon in 1670. Mouton's idea was similar to Wilkins' idea in Britain and was as simple: a base-ten, aka a "decimal system," to measure distances and lengths, weights, volume, and other things like cloth and wood, with the goal of creating a universal standard of measurement based upon reason and on naturally occurring and consistent criteria.

The National Convention adopted the idea and took steps to implement it throughout revolutionary France and in all of the areas under French control. The best minds in the scientific establishment were tasked with the job of creating the system. In 1790, a panel was appointed by the *Académie des sciences* to begin work on the new system of weights and measures. Five of the most important French scientists of the time, including Jean-Antoine Nicolas de Caritat (aka Nicolas, Marquis de Condorcet) were charged with the task.

An idealist and true son of Revolutionary France, the Marquis of Condorcet was a philosopher, mathematician, and visionary champion for liberal ideas, such as free public education for every child and equal rights for women and all races. Among his voluminous writings are pamphlets denouncing slavery and supporting universal women's suffrage. In line with the Revolution's beliefs in universal equality, Condorcet declared this new system of measurements was intended to be "for all people, for all time."

Condorcet had some important friends overseas in the newly created United States. Benjamin Franklin, scientist and diplomat, was the fledgling nation's first ambassador to France, serving in

*Fig. 51 - The Marquis de Condorcet—passionate promoter of the metric system by an unknown painter (courtesy Wikimedia, public domain)*

the eight years before the French Revolution (1776-1784). Thomas Jefferson, himself a scientist, inventor, and political philosopher succeeded Franklin as ambassador in 1784, remaining in Paris until

1789. Condorcet and Jefferson were close friends and maintained correspondence after Jefferson returned to the US.

Both Franklin and Jefferson had strong ideas about money in the colonies. The state of currency in the colonies was chaotic and needed to be reformed. Before the American Revolution, commerce was carried out using currencies from other lands, chiefly British pounds, but also Dutch guilders, Irish coppers, and Spanish reals (also known as dollars). Some colonies also minted their own coins from tin, brass, and even pewter.

Franklin, a shrewd businessperson and a printer by trade, wrote a tract as a young man, "A Modest Enquiry into the Nature and Necessity of a Paper Currency," promoting a new idea for currency as early as 1729—paper money. It was his goal to establish a national paper currency to replace the haphazard system in the colonies. People were used to hard currency (silver and gold coins) because its value was apparent, existing in the metal itself. But hard currency was also scarce. The entrepreneur in Franklin saw an opportunity to do good *and* make a profit. He even printed paper money for the colony of New Jersey for a time.

Jefferson and Franklin championed a "decimal currency" for the United States, in addition to a decimal system for measurement. They laid the foundations for this new monetary system, securing agreement among the thirteen states in 1785. Two years later, Franklin designed and began minting the "Fugio Cent," the first official currency of the United States, the first to use the decimal system, where one hundred cents equals one dollar.

By 1790, Jefferson, then the nation's first Secretary of State, offered his "Plan for Establishing Uniformity in the Coinage, Weights, and Measures of the United States" to Congress. Jefferson highlighted the international efforts then underway in England and France. The principle of a decimal dollar had already been agreed upon back in 1785, with the Mint Act of 1792 codifying that decimal system.

*Fig. 52 - Fugio Cent Franklin Fugio Cent,*
*probably produced at the Scovill Mint in Waterbury, Connecticut*
*(courtesy Wikimedia, public domain)*

The American success with a decimal currency surely influenced Condorcet and the panel to press on with a decimal system of measurements. After more than a year studying various alternatives, the panel made a series of recommendations for new standards for weight, length, liquid volume, and other measures. For length and distance, many scientists had believed for some time that a naturally derived, accurate, and consistent measure of length could be achieved by measuring the length produced by the motion of a "seconds pendulum"—a pendulum with a half-period of one second. Ultimately, this idea was rejected after it was discovered that the movement of a pendulum could vary depending on the force of gravity in a given location.

Other alternatives were explored, and the panel eventually determined that the basic unit of length would be called a "meter," and the commission proposed a method to set the length of the basic unit of distance. They defined it as "one ten-millionth of the distance between the north pole and the equator" along a line of longitude that would need to be carefully surveyed. The kilogram, in turn, was defined as the mass of a cubic decimeter of rainwater at four degrees Celsius. This quantity of mass was translated for practical reasons into a platinum cylinder. The French eighteenth-century prototype became an international prototype still in use today.

The proposed method for determining the meter certainly used a naturally occurring phenomenon—namely the size of the earth itself. But it involved tremendous study and research. To accurately determine the meridian's length, first the very circumference of the Earth had to be precisely determined. Since France was establishing this new measurement, they used the "Paris Meridian"—the line of longitude that runs through Paris.

Two teams of scientists, under the direction of Pierre-Francois-Andre Mechain and Jean-Baptiste-Joseph Delambre, were sent out to survey the arc of longitude of the Paris Meridian. They headed off in opposite directions from Paris, one team north toward Dunkirk and the other south toward Barcelona, measuring how far they had gone along the meridian using basic trigonometry, triangulating using prominent features found on the landscape like hills, castles, and church spires.

Because war had broken out between Revolutionary France and other countries in Europe, the team was frequently thought to be a group of spies, so they were arrested and imprisoned multiple times. The survey took seven years, much longer than anticipated, but the results were impressive, even if not quite accurate. (They failed to account for the earth's flatness, but this was not discovered until much later.)

After the survey was completed and the distance from pole to equator determined, it was just a matter of calculating one ten-millionth of the distance, and *voilà*! They had found The First Meter.

*Fig. 53 - One of the 135 medallions from the "Hommage à Arago" monument scattered along the Paris meridian in the 1st, 2nd, 6th, 9th, 14th and 18th arrondissements. This one is located near the Senate in the Jardin du Luxembourg (photo by the author)*

The French Assembly accepted the proposals on March 30, 1791. Following acceptance, the *Académie des sciences* began the implementation process, with separate groups focusing on different tasks. One group was given the assignment of surveying and measuring distances along the meridian to determine the exact latitudes and lengths of the arc. For the system of weights, another group was tasked with determining the weight in a vacuum of a given volume of distilled water. Still another working group was asked to draw up and publish conversion tables, correlating the new units of measure to existing measures.

The metric system was officially adopted on December 10, 1799—or by the French Revolutionary calendar, *19 frimaire in the Year VIII*. In 1801, it became the sole legal system of weights and measures in France. Once the length of the "standard meter" was fixed, the commission had a physical model made—a platinum bar to be kept in Paris.

Many asked, why go to such lengths? (Pun intended.) Why not just fashion a bar of some approximate length and call it "a meter"? Actually, they could have done just that. For all of their pains and years of effort, subsequent calculations showed that the standard meter bar was off—by two-tenths of a millimeter (or one eight-thousandth of an inch for any Americans reading this).

The great diplomat Charles Maurice de Talleyrand, French political leader and later on Napoleon's chief diplomat, championed the new system. He had corresponded with Jefferson and Franklin, and it was he who made the initial proposal to the French National Assembly to develop the system in 1790. Talleyrand's goal, however, was more than just uniformity in measurements in the new French Republic. He had a much larger vision.

Talleyrand saw that such a standardized system would eventually be embraced by other countries, to the glory of France and the Revolution. It was a diplomatic and geo-political masterstroke that would help make the Republic of France the preeminent power that it aspired to be. Before work even started on conceiving and developing the system, other countries were offered the opportunity to help fashion it. Great Britain, France's arch-rival, immediately refused to cooperate. Other countries demurred as well. Eventually, the French Academy of Sciences decided to go it alone, creating the commission to explore what such a system would look like and how best to introduce it to the French people.

The metric system soon became popular in much of the world, both because of its uniformity and especially because it lent itself to scientific, engineering, industrial, and commercial pursuits, giving everyone a common language to discuss and determine actual dimensions, distances, weights, and measures. But at its start in 1799, how was the ordinary shopkeeper, artisan, or tradesperson to know what this so-called "meter" actually looked like? How could they determine if the cloth they were buying was a meter long? They surely couldn't measure the arc of the Paris Meridian to get an accurate idea.

Before the government introduced the metric system, it made a five-year effort to familiarize citizens with the new system. The French Revolutionary government handed out thousands of pamphlets to educate the public. Businesses chipped in, creating educational games, instructional guides, almanacs, devices, and charts to help people convert measures to the upcoming system.

Paris, was slated to be the first region of the country to phase in the metric system. The government planned to distribute meter rulers to the Parisian population. Estimating that they would need some 500,000 rulers just for Paris, they produced only 25,000 in the month after the meter became the official measurement. The government eventually was forced to provide incentives to businesses to mass-produce enough rulers.

Despite the best efforts to roll out the new system and enforce compliance, the Parisian police reported widespread defiance of the law mandating use of the metric system by merchants and citizens alike. Shopkeepers routinely abused the system, taking advantage of their customers' ignorance, rounding prices up and giving smaller measures.

In addition to supplying Paris with meter rulers, the French Revolutionary government had standard meter bars (*mètre étalons*) placed in the busiest corners of the city of Paris. Between February 1796 and December 1797, sixteen marble markers with a horizontal line and the word "METRE" engraved on it were installed around the city to help people get a feel for the new system of length measurement.

Two of those markers survive today. The Last Meters!

*Fig. 54 - One of only two plaques left in Paris to help citizens determine the correct length of a meter. This one is located in Place Vendôme, underneath a window at the Palais de Justice. The other is across from the Senate on the rue de Vaugirard (photo by the author)*

**Travelers' Tips**

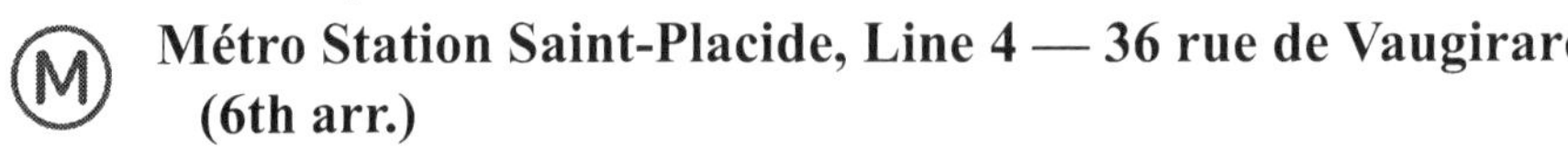

**Métro Station Saint-Placide, Line 4 — 36 rue de Vaugirard (6th arr.)**

**Métro Station Saint-Jacques, Line 6 — Paris Observatory, 61 Ave. de l'Observatoire (14th arr.)**

**On the Left Bank:** The rue de Vaugirard borders the northern end of the Jardin du Luxembourg. Walk west along the rue until you come to No. 36. You will find the meter under the arcade of the building across the street.

Afterwards, head into the Jardin du Luxembourg, one of the most beautiful parks in the world. The gardens and palace were built by Queen Marie de Medici, second wife of King Henri IV. Homesick for her childhood home in Florence, Italy, she had this palace and garden built to resemble the Pitt Palace in Florence, Italy.

Today, Queen Marie's palace is the seat of the French Senate. In the garden, all of the statues except one are of notable French women, *les Reines de France et Femmes Illustres* (Queens of France and Famous Women), which were installed in 1848. The unwritten (but strictly followed) rule in the garden for the chairs is that everyone is entitled to two—and no more: one chair to sit on and another for your feet or to place bags and packages.

For little children, or kids at heart, you can rent a boat to sail in the *Grande Bassin*, the duck pond in the center of the garden. This is a tradition that is approaching its one hundredth year. The original boats came from a man named Clément Paudeau. He carved the handmade wooden boats (his wife sewed the sails). They began renting them to children in the Luxembourg Gardens. The original price was two sous. Today, you can rent the *P'tits Voilier* (and a stick to guide the boat), which are the same boats carved by Paudeau (with new sails). Kids can choose a flag from various countries or even a pirate flag.

The park has several beautiful fountains, including *La fontaine Medicis* (*Medici Fountain*), which dates from around 1630. The grotto fountain, the *Fontaine de Leda* representing the mythical story of Leda and the Swan, and the *Fountain of the Observatory* at the southern end, which dates from around 1867, are among the other fountains.

The Paris Observatory, in the fourteenth arrondissement (*61 avenue de l'Observatoire*), sits directly on the Meridian. Founded in 1667, a hundred years before the Revolution, the *Observatoire* is one of the largest astronomical centers in the world. Inside, the Meridian line is marked by a strip of brass along the floor of the Meridian Room.

Outside of the observatory, the invisible line of the Paris Meridian is marked by 135 bronze medallions set into the pavement, placed throughout Paris by Dutch artist Jan Dibbets. In 1994, Dibbets installed these markers along the Meridian line. The word "Arago" is his homage to the French astronomer François Arago. A number of these markers still exist, although many have been pried up and stolen or paved over.

### Ⓜ Métro Station Concorde or Tuileries, Line 1 — Ministry of Justice, Place Vendôme (1st arr.)

**On the Right Bank:** Head from the rue de Rivoli up the rue de Castiglione and into the fashionable Place Vendôme. This magnificent square, one of the most fashionable addresses in all of Paris, was a quiet cul-de-sac until Napoleon I opened up the northern end to through traffic when he ordered the creation of the Rue de la Paix.

Head to your left on the western side of the Place to the Ministry of Justice. Look for the meter there.

Afterward, circle the Place Vendôme to see what is on offer in the many high-end shops. The Ritz Hôtel is here at No. 15. The Swiss hotelier César Ritz founded the Ritz in 1898 with his partner, the famous French chef, Auguste Escoffier. In the latter half of the twentieth century, it was owned by Saudi Prince Al-Fayed. His son, Dodi Al-Fayed, dined here with Princess Diana in the Imperial Suite before getting in their car for their fatal last ride through Paris. At No. 12, you will see the last residence of Frédéric Chopin, who died here in 1849.

At the center of it all stands the majestic Vendôme Column, which was erected by Napoleon I in 1810 to commemorate his victory at the Battle of Austerlitz. The column is made out of cannon captured by Napoleon's armies.

In May of 1871, the column was toppled during the heady days of the Paris Commune, but subsequently re-erected. A painter, Gustave Courbet, president of the Federation of Artists and elected member of the Commune, proposed the demolition of the column, which came back to haunt him. After the Paris Commune was suppressed, Courbet was ordered to pay the cost to rebuild the column, estimated at about 323,000 francs. Not able to pay such a sum, Courbet went into exile in Switzerland. With his paintings and property seized and sold, Courbet died in exile in December 1877.

***

Today, people pass the plaques in the Place Vendôme and nearby the Senate without even a glance. Yet these modest plaques, placed during the French Revolution, mark the start of another kind of revolution—one that changed the world by making everyday activities fairer and more universal. Of the sixteen shelves originally installed, only two survive: one underneath a window at the Ministry of Justice, in the Place Vendôme in the first arrondissement, and the other at 36 rue de Vaugirard, just off the Jardin du Luxembourg, under the arched walkway across from the French Senate building.

When you see these first and last meters, put yourself in the shoes of an eighteenth-century Parisian living in the midst of historic and tumultuous times, whose daily concerns are for bread, work, children, health, and maybe a little happiness along the way. You have gotten by under the old system, and like most of us, don't relish changing your ways.

Then some bureaucrats tell you that you must learn this new-fangled system. The shopkeepers don't get it, your friends don't get it, you don't get it. This so-called "METRE" seems arbitrary and difficult to remember. But over time, society will adapt and soon it will become ordinary and commonplace. you're standing in front of a revolutionary idea that will change how things are done for billions around the world.

And here is one of only two remaining, left to tell the tale of The First and the Last Meters.

## How Paris Shaped Our World

The metric system almost landed on the dust heap of history. Like the Revolutionary Calendar, the metric system was mostly unpopular. After the Revolution and the First French Republic, after only twelve short years, Napoleon I became emperor. He disliked the new metric system. He found it greatly inconvenient and preferred the use of the traditional measures. He also recognized the difficulty in gaining acceptance from the French people.

Napoleon, by imperial decree on February 12, 1812, introduced *les mesures usuelles* (usual or customary measurements), solely for use by the retail trades, while government, legal, and other work continued under the metric system, which also remained as a required subject in schools.

These measurements were a hybrid, a compromise between the metric system and the traditional measurements that the population was used to. The system stayed as the method for measurements until 1840, when the metric system, the one that was first enacted through the laws of measurement from 1795 and 1799 in Revolutionary France, was revived.

The metric system is without question one of the greatest innovations in modern history, ushering in an age of uniformity to the benefit and the increased prosperity of all. The modern development of a standardized mathematics of measurement is today known as the International System of Units (SI). Since the nineteenth century, there has been a steady movement toward greater standardization using clearer, more rational, and more consistent units. Adoption has been widespread by governments, business and industry, and the general public.

The practical problems of nonstandard units of measurement were evident in many areas of industrialization. Screw thread sizes, fastener sizes, lightbulbs and sockets that didn't mate, unnecessary difficulties in the maintenance of steam engines (until 1841, the rail companies had all used different sized screw threads, causing predictable frustration) needed to be addressed.

Sir Joseph Whitworth, First Baronet and Fellow of the Royal Society—the same Royal Society founded by John Wilkins—was an English engineer and inventor. In 1841, he devised the British Standard Whitworth system, which to this day is an accepted standard for screw threads. The "British Standard Whitworth" (BSW) was the world's first national screw thread standard, and was adopted by the Royal Navy and soon after by British railway companies.

Standardization is not a sexy topic, but it is a cornerstone of any scientifically based, modern civilization. In the age of space travel, molecular biology, medicine, nuclear physics, and modern engineering, it has only become more important. Much of what we take for granted as "normal" and mundane today was once revolutionary and difficult to conceive. To bring into existence this modern system of measurement, one needed Enlightenment thinkers in science and politics, a revolution, and the meridian of the Earth that runs through Paris to create a revolution in measurement.

*Fig. 55 - Salle Méridienne (dite salle Cassini), l'Observatoire de Paris, 14th arrondissement, file licensed under the Creative Commons Attribution-Share Alike 3.0 Unported license Date 14 July 2000 (FredA — courtesy Wikimedia)*

# Chapter 7
# The First Shot Fired in World War II

(Twentieth Century)

*Mob law ruled in Berlin throughout the afternoon and evening and hordes of hooligans indulged in an orgy of destruction. I have seen several anti-Jewish outbreaks in Germany during the last five years, but never anything as nauseating as this. Racial hatred and hysteria seemed to have taken complete hold of otherwise decent people. I saw fashionably dressed women clapping their hands and screaming with glee, while respectable middle-class mothers held up their babies to see the "fun."*

— Hugh Carleton Greene, *Daily Telegraph* correspondent on the events of November 9-10, 1938

To say young Herschel Grynszpan was distraught would be putting it mildly. Out of money, out of work, running out of time—he felt like an animal who had been cornered. At least his mind was made up. What he needed to do in his desperate situation was clear. He stood on a Paris sidewalk just outside of No. 78 rue de Lille, fingered the gun in his pocket and waited....

*"With God's help.*
*My dear parents, I could not do otherwise,*
*may God forgive me, the heart bleeds when I hear of your tragedy and that of the 12,000 Jews.*
*I must protest so that the whole world hears my protest, and that I will do.*
*Forgive me."*

— Postcard message found on Herschel Grynszpan

Citizenship, a sense of place, of belonging had always been an issue for Herschel and his family, the Grynszpans, Polish Jews who had immigrated to Germany. They arrived before World War I and settled in Hanover. Even though Herschel was born there, he could never be German, because German law operated under the principle of *jus sanguinis* (right of blood). This means that a child's nationality is the result of the parents' blood, their nationality. This principle contrasts with *jus soli* (right of soil), which says a child's nationality is based on where the child was born. This German law is one of several crucial factors necessary to understanding the circumstances young Herschel faced.

A sense of displacement, of disconnection from the nation where they lived, was typical for many Jews, especially those the Germans called, *Ostjuden* (Eastern Jews). These Eastern European Jews often considered themselves Jews first and *then* citizens of the nation or regime they lived under, which were often changed by war, as borders shifted.

At the start of the twentieth century, some six million Jews lived in Eastern Europe in communities large and small. Bigger cities, such as Warsaw, had Jewish populations in the hundreds of thousands. Countless small towns across Poland, Ukraine, Belarus, Latvia, Lithuania, Estonia, Russia, Romania, Hungary, and Bessarabia (a part of Russia that is today Moldova) held a few score or maybe a few hundred Jewish folk.

France, however, was different. French Jews usually thought of themselves as French first, then Jewish—or the two statuses felt equally important in their minds. Like elsewhere, anti-Semitism was a part of the Jewish experience in France, with many instances of exile or persecution over the centuries. But the French Revolution changed things for Jews in France. In 1791, France officially "emancipated" the Jews living there. Only two other countries were known to have done this. One was the newly created United States of America, where religious freedom was ratified in the US Constitution. It was further affirmed specifically for Jews in 1790 by George Washington, who penned a letter to the Jewish congregation in Newport, Rhode Island, confirming his personal (and the United States' official) position on religious freedom and citizenship for Jews.

The other country, the first to officially emancipate the Jews living within its borders, was Poland—some 500 years earlier.

Throughout the centuries, all European countries had restrictions on Jews and Muslims living within their borders. These restrictions could range widely, from mandating that Jews wear special clothing to prohibitions on owning certain businesses or practicing certain trades. Countries often placed limits on their movements, enforced mass expulsions, created edicts stopping them from practicing their religion, enacted special taxes that applied only to Jews, forced baptisms, forced oaths, and forced renunciation of their religion under pain of torture and death.

Emancipation of the Jews in Poland occurred in 1264, when Prince Boleslaw the Pious issued the "Statute of Kalisz." This "General Charter of Jewish Liberties" in Poland allowed Jews personal and legal freedom with protections against official persecution. The charter stayed in effect and was ratified again and again by Polish monarchs over the centuries.

As a result, whenever Jews were expelled *en masse* from Western European countries, they often found safe haven in Poland, which eventually became home to the largest Jewish population in Europe. Jewish immigration brought with it a wealth of benefits to Poland because Jews were generally skilled and industrious workers. By the eighteenth century, Jews made up 7 percent of the Polish population.

Following Jewish emancipation during the French Revolution, the Emperor Napoleon went several steps further, officially recognizing Jews as full citizens of the empire. what's more, he liberated the Jewish communities in every area he conquered. In 1806, Napoleon enacted measures supporting Jews throughout the empire. He abolished laws that restricted Jews to ghettos, and included Judaism as one of the official religions of France (Roman Catholicism, Lutheranism, and Calvinism were the others). By the turn of the century, French Jews, the majority of who lived in Paris, could take pride in their full participation as French citizens and felt themselves completely assimilated into French culture.

After World War I, the situation in France changed. A flood of Jewish refugees and immigrants came from Russia, and eastern and central Europe. The character of French Judaism underwent a marked change with these new arrivals who brought with them their culture, mores, and language. These Jews did not easily assimilate into French culture—nor were they necessarily willing to be. Moreover, in addition to their cultural differences, which seemed alien to the French Jews and non-Jews alike, these recent arrivals brought radical ideologies that were gaining currency among the extreme political left and the French intelligentsia—beliefs in things like Zionism, socialism, and communism.

The Popular Front was a potent alliance of left-wing thinkers and movements. It included the French Section of the Communist International (SFIC, also known as the French Communist Party), the socialist French Section of the Workers' International (SFIO), and the progressive Radical-Socialist Republican Party, during the frothy, turbulent period between the two world wars. The Spanish Popular Front won sweeping electoral victories in early 1936, defeating the right-wing parties. Soon after, the French Popular Front followed, winning legislative elections. A new government was formed headed by SFIO leader Léon Blum.

For ordinary people of all nationalities and ethnicities, this period of intense competition between extreme right- and left-wing factions played itself out with serious consequences. In Spain, the left-wing victory was soon followed by a right-wing *coup d'état,* which resulted in the brutal dictatorship of Generalissimo Francisco Franco. Franco's coup drew partisans from all over the world to fight against it in the Spanish Civil War, including a young Ernest Hemingway. Spain would live under a right-wing dictatorship that endured until Franco's death in 1975. This right- and left-wing backdrop is another crucial factor in understanding the life and circumstances of young Herschel Grynszpan.

The Grynszpan family was a tiny part of this great upheaval—this movement of people and of ideas—across Europe. As émigrés to Germany, Herschel's parents, Sendel (Zindel) and Rivka, had well-established Polish citizenship. Herschel too was considered a Polish citizen by the Germans, even though he was born in Germany in 1921. Just a minor detail in the 1920s, this fact would become consequential later on.

Besides lacking official recognition as citizens of Germany, the *Ostjuden* were generally more religious and observant than their German Jewish neighbors, who were similar to French Jews in that they often considered themselves Germans first, then Jewish. The Grynszpans, like many of these new arrivals, spoke Yiddish at home. Herschel was sent to study at a yeshiva in Frankfurt, where he was considered an intelligent, albeit somewhat lazy student. Eventually, he dropped out. Family finances being tight, he had to look for work. He tried to find an apprenticeship in some kind of trade, plumbing, for example, but he was unable to secure anything, at least in part because he was a Jew.

Herschel's future did not look secure in Germany, so his parents looked for other ways for their young son to gain a foothold in the world. They explored ways he might get permission to emigrate to British Palestine, but he was only thirteen at the time. He would have to wait at least a year.

Herschel's father had a brother in Belgium, Uncle Wolf, and another in France, Uncle Abraham, a tailor by trade, with a wife named Chawa. Belgium didn't appeal to Herschel, but Paris? Now, that sounded wonderful. For hundreds of years, the mystique of Paris had lured countless young people from all over. Music, art, beauty, a strong and vibrant Jewish community, lively nightlife, and heady political and intellectual conversations in the cafés...all this fired Herschel's imagination. He was clear on his choice and his parents agreed happily: he would go to live with Uncle Abraham in Paris.

Herschel obtained his Polish passport and his German residency card, and he received permission from the German government to leave Germany for Belgium. But there was just one problem. He had no legal entry papers for France because he could not show he had sufficient financial support. Because Jews were forbidden to take money out of Germany and without adequate funds to show the French government, France was officially closed to him. Despite this obstacle, early in the fall of 1936, fifteen-year-old Herschel Grynszpan made his way legally to Belgium where he crossed the border illegally into France. He made a beeline for Paris, where he would live increasingly on the margins for the next two years.

Herschel settled with his aunt and uncle in their apartment on the rue Martel, amidst the insulated community of Polish Orthodox Jews. He kept close to his people and the *quartier* in which they lived. He learned little to no French and found little to no work. At first, his life was similar to that of most young people newly arrived in Paris. He spent his days exploring the city, walking everywhere, and seeing all of Paris. Wandering the streets, venturing into the cafés and cinemas was like a dream for the youth coming from the poverty of dreary and dark Hanover.

The first flush of excitement eventually faded, and things slowly turned bad for Herschel. He tried without success to get papers to legalize his status in France, without which he could neither work nor go to school legally. To make matters worse, his German reentry papers expired in April of 1937 and then his Polish passport at the beginning of 1938. He was *sans papiers* at that point. With his applications for legal status in France rejected, he was ordered to leave the country by the Prefecture of Police.

Lonely, without skills, unable to speak French, and living illegally, Herschel grew desperate. He depended on his uncle for support and that, too, was becoming untenable. Abraham and

Chawa were poor themselves and could not support their nephew indefinitely. Moreover, his status as an illegal immigrant jeopardized their position with the authorities. The stress on everyone in the household grew.

Without a reentry permit for Germany, Herschel was stuck—a man without a country. And unbeknownst to this poor teenager, he was becoming caught up in the growing, swelling political and economic tides of history. Larger and ominous forces were moving.

As pressure mounted in Paris, suddenly Herschel's parents situation become precarious as well. News from Germany was not good: the family's business was failing, and Herschel's brothers were out of work. At the same moment, the forces of prejudice and persecution were rising. In August 1938, the Polish government revoked citizenship for all Jews living outside of Poland. Germany took advantage of this move and cancelled all of its residence permits for foreigners living in Germany. They would have to be renewed if the Grynszpans were to continue to live there.

Herschel had always been acutely aware of Jewish suffering. Although friends and contemporaries described him as a shy young man, he would become quite agitated when he spoke about the plight of the Jews in Eastern Europe, which often did at length. Their plight moved him to tears.

And now he had personal reasons. The recent changes affecting his family added fuel to his already strong and strident passion. His close-knit and loving family was in trouble and he was hundreds of miles away. He missed them greatly and felt powerless to help them in the face of this move by the German government.

Soon after this order, the Nazis pulled the rug out from under all Polish Jews. In October of 1938, the Gestapo ordered the immediate arrest and deportation of all Polish Jews in Germany. The "Polish Action" or *Polenaktion* affected many thousands of people. Stripped of personal property and money, they were put on trains bound for the border with Poland.

At first, Poland was caught off guard by the expulsion and allowed Polish Jews to reenter the country. But soon they began refusing entry. Now, thousands of homeless Jews were caught at the border, stranded in refugee camps. The Polish Red Cross provided some relief, food, and shelter, but living conditions were horrendous. An account of a British Red Cross worker is quoted in *The Holocaust: The Human Tragedy* by Martin Gilbert. "I found thousands crowded together in pigsties. The old, the sick, and children herded together in the most inhumane conditions...some actually tried to escape back to Germany and were shot."

Herschel Grynszpan's parents were among the deported. Ordered to report to the police station with their Polish passports, they were taken forcibly to the train station and herded into boxcars. In Paris, Herschel was unaware of this until his sister Berta sent a postcard with the grim news. The postcard dated October 31 reached Herschel on November 3.

Herschel was beside himself with worry, helplessness, and rage. What could he do to aid his family? He asked his uncle to send them money, but his uncle had none to spare. A fight ensued and Herschel left, stealing what money he could. He spent the night in a cheap pensioner's hotel.

The next day, Herschel formulated a hasty plan. He wrote a farewell postcard to his parents, which he put in his pocket. It read: "With God's help. My dear parents, I could not do otherwise, may God forgive me. The heart bleeds when I hear of your tragedy and that of the 12,000 Jews. I must protest so that the whole world hears my protest, and that I will do. Forgive me."

On the morning of November 7, 1938, he went to a store on the rue de Faubourg Saint-Martin where he bought a 6.35mm revolver and some bullets. He then caught the Métro at the Gare de l'Est, changing to Line 12, which he rode to Métro station Solferino. Exiting the station, he walked the few blocks to the German embassy on the Rue de Lille.

Arriving outside the embassy, Herschel passed right by Count Johannes von Welczeck, never realizing that this man was the German ambassador leaving at 9:45 a.m. for his daily morning walk. They exchanged a quick "Good morning," and Herschel entered the embassy. Approaching the receptionist, he asked to see the ambassador. He was a German citizen and a spy with very important information, he said. He needed to talk to someone high up in the ranks.

The ambassador was not available. Was there anyone he could speak with, Herschel asked. The clerk summoned a junior officer, Ernst vom Rath. When Herschel entered vom Rath's office, he pulled out his gun and shot vom Rath five times in the stomach. As he fired, according to police accounts, he screamed, "You are a filthy kraut, and here, in the name of 12,000 persecuted Jews, is your document!" Vom Rath collapsed as people from the embassy rushed in. Vom Rath was rushed to the nearby Alma Clinic where he underwent emergency surgery.

Herschel Grynszpan dropped the gun on the floor. It still had its 250-franc price tag attached. He was arrested without a struggle and held until the police arrived.

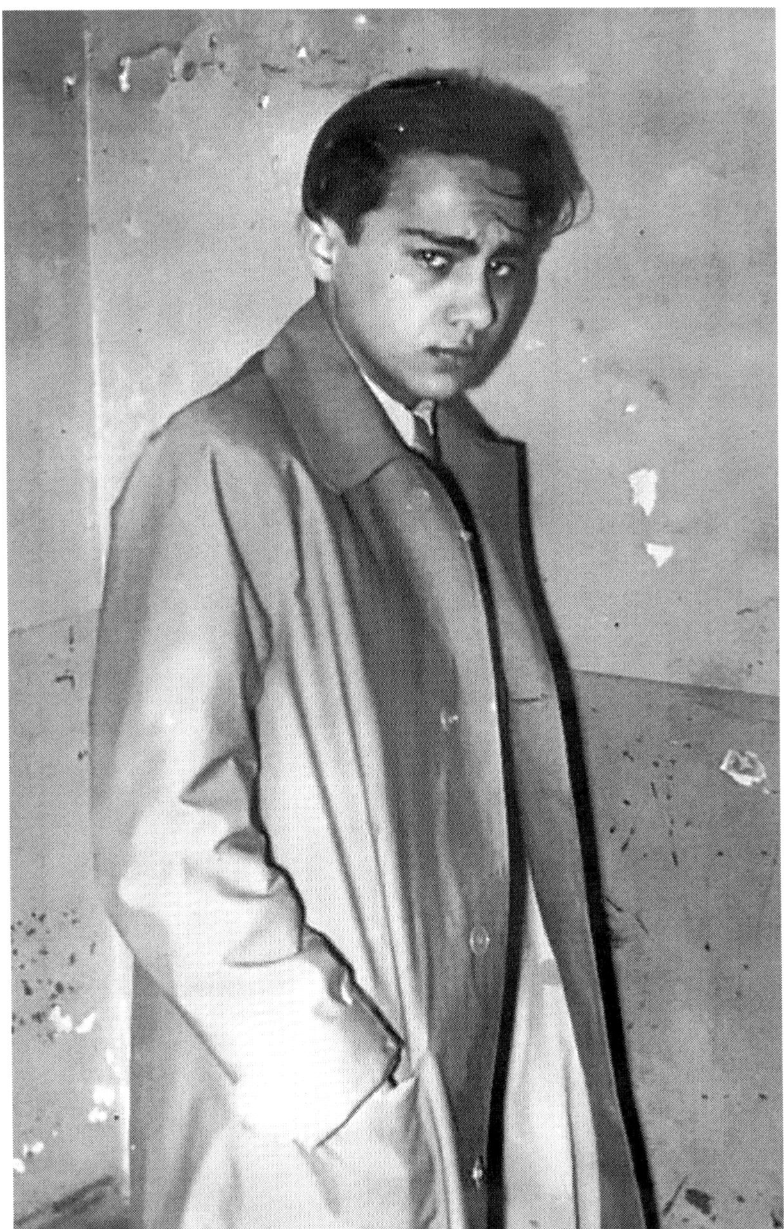

*Fig. 56 - Arrest photo of Herschel Grynszpan in Paris, November 1938, Image provided to Wikimedia Commons by the German Federal Archive (Deutsches Bundesarchiv) as part of a cooperation project. This file is licensed under the Creative Commons Attribution-Share Alike 3.0 Germany license.*

*Fig. 57 - Ernst Eduard vom Rath*
*(courtesy Wikimedia, public domain, photographer unknown)*

**Travelers' Tips**

**Métro Station Assemblée Nationale or Solferino, Line 12 — 78 rue de Lille (7th arr.)**

The Hôtel Beauharnais at 78 rue de Lille is today the official residence of the German ambassador in France. This historic building was built for the French foreign minister to Louis XIV, Colbert de Torcy. Completed in 1714, it is considered one of the most beautiful examples of Empire architecture in Paris.

The Hôtel survived the French Revolution, although it was ransacked and stripped of its furnishings. It was later acquired by Eugène de Beauharnais, the Emperor Napoleon's stepson.

*Fig. 58 - The Hôtel Beauharnais at 78 rue de Lille by Jospe (courtesy of Wikimedia, This file is licensed under the Creative Commons Attribution-Share Alike 3.0 Unported license)*

After Napoleon's defeat, the grand mansion was purchased by Prussia's King Frederick William III, and it became his Paris residence and the seat of the Prussian Legation, and later the German embassy. After World War II, the building was confiscated by the French government, which it held until it was returned to the West German Republic in 1962.

In this Left Bank quartier of Paris, there are quite a few other things to see and do. Nearby is the Boulevard Saint-Germain, one of the most fashionable streets for strolling and window shopping. Here you can practice the art of being *un flâneur.* The Boulevard Saint-Germain is the perfect street to practice this leisurely art.

Another wonderful street to stroll in the opposite direction is the rue Saint Dominique with its quaint shops and, farther down, past Les Invalides, there is a magnificent view of the Eiffel Tower.

A quick walk toward the Seine brings you to the Musée d'Orsay, the former train station turned museum that holds some of the most iconic and beautiful Impressionist masterpieces: works by Monet, Manet, Degas, Renoir, Lautrec, and Van Gogh and other pieces of art created between 1848 and 1914.

Les Invalides (Hôtel national des Invalides) is, of course, where Emperor Napoleon is interred. Entering the Church of the Dome to see his sarcophagus is a prime tourist stop. But there much more to this complex, including a fascinating military museum. Stroll the Esplanade with its displays of cannon and its moat before going inside. Look for the rabbits who live on the grounds and down in the moat.

The history of les Invalides is also worth mentioning. Opened in 1670 by Louis XIV to house and care for homeless war veterans, it is still a hospital and shelter today, housing a small number of veterans. When Louis was building Versailles, many injuries and deaths occurred on the massive construction site. The workers, most of whom had served in one of King Louis' many wars, went on strike. Rather than arrest, torture, and kill the ringleaders, the king was persuaded by his councilors to negotiate with the workers—which was unheard of.

But, they reasoned, Versailles would remain half-finished unless the men went back to work. The idea for a home and hospital for wounded war veterans arose from the talks, and Louis started the first homeless shelter for injured war vets. Later, it was expanded, including adding a chapel, known as the church of Saint-Louis-des-Invalides, for the soldiers to hear Mass. The veterans were required to attend services each day. The king wanted to attend Mass with his troops, but (of course) he could not be expected to mingle among them, so a separate royal church was built for the king: the Church of the Dome. Completed in 1706, this is the large, gold dome that marks les Invalides and can be seen far and wide. The priest serving Mass stood on the altar, which is located between the two churches, the king in his church and the men on the other side.

Napoleon, who died in 1821, was interred here in an opulent ceremony in 1840 after his body was returned from St. Helena.

The infamous Dreyfus affair, one of the most controversial and polarizing political dramas in French history, played out behind these walls and on these grounds with reverberations felt throughout Europe and still felt today. Captain Alfred Dreyfus was a French artillery officer of Jewish ancestry who was accused of treason, tried, and convicted. In December 1894, Dreyfus was stripped of his rank and degraded publicly in front of troops assembled in front of the main building. In 1906, he was exonerated of the trumped-up charges and his rank was restored, the ceremony taking place in the courtyard of the complex.

## How Paris Shaped Our World

Today, Ernst vom Rath and Herschel Grynszpan are not household names. Yet the little drama in which they starred, the tragedy that unfolded in Paris on the rue de Lille, had far-reaching, worldwide, earthshaking consequences.

The caption of Herschel's mug shot is pure Nazi propaganda. It reads: "The Jewish murderer. The Polish Jew Herschel Seibel Grynszpan, who yesterday in Paris seriously injured Legation Secretary vom Rath from the German Embassy with revolver shots, after his arrest." (*Der jüdische Mordschütze. Der polnische Jude Herschel Seibel Grynszpan, der gestern in Paris den Legationssekretär vom Rath von der Deutschen Botschaft durch Revolverschüsse schwer verletzte, nach seiner Verhaftung.*)

Despite their best efforts, vom Rath lingered in agony before dying two days later, on November 9. German doctors, including Hitler's two personal physicians, did their utmost to save him.

As Fate would have it, vom Rath died on the fifteenth anniversary of the Nazi "Beer Hall Putsch," the date in 1923 when the Nazi Party attempted a failed *coup d'état* in Munich. The event brought attention to the Nazis throughout Germany and the world; they were little known before then. Hitler was arrested, tried, and convicted of treason. He spent only nine months of his five-year sentence in jail, where he made use of his time by writing *Mein Kampf*. The event also redirected his political philosophies away from revolution and toward taking power by legal means.

So this assassination in Paris could not have been timed better for the Nazis' nefarious purposes. Rather than celebrating the Beer Hall Putsch anniversary, Hitler and his leadership were consumed by vom Rath's murder. Ironically, vom Rath was not a Nazi, but a professional diplomat who was suspected of holding anti-Nazi sympathies. In fact, he was under investigation by the Gestapo for being "politically unreliable."

This did not matter to the Nazi propagandists who immediately lauded vom Rath as a loyal member of the Nazi party, killed by a Jew in cold blood. The Nazis saw the murder as a welcome excuse to launch a pogrom against the German Jews. Up until then, boycotts, deportations, and other indignities were the limits of Nazi persecution.

"The shots in Paris will not go unpunished," were the headlines the next day in German newspapers. German anger was great, as was the Nazis' cunning. They gave vom Rath a state funeral in Düsseldorf, which Hitler himself attended. There was much publicity, with a eulogy given by Joachim von Ribbentrop, Germany's Foreign Minister, who railed against the attack by Jews against the German people.

Later that evening, Minister of Propaganda Josef Goebbels made a rousing and violence-inciting speech at the very beer hall in Munich where the "Putsch" was organized. Goebbels said the German people were right to be angry at this attack by the Jews. They demanded justice and they would have it. "We understand the challenge, and accept it," he thundered to great applause in the Hall. He "imagined" that the good people of Germany would likely rise up against the murderers and avenge this noble young man's death. It was a public call for mob violence, and those Germans who had been primed for years to blame the Jews for all manner of ills heard the call.

Goebbels' own journal entries outline the plan formulated directly with Hitler. The Jews should feel the people's fury. That night, within hours of his speech, all across Germany, and in Austria too, mobs of people poured out into the streets and began looting, attacking, and destroying Jewish property.

*Fig. 59 - Synagogue in Hanover, Germany, set ablaze during the Kristallnacht pogrom of November 9-10, 1938 (public domain)*

*Fig. 60 - Frankfurt Synagogue; Burning on Kristallnacht; November 9, 1938, (photo courtesy Center for Jewish History, NYC, Photographer Unknown, Repository: Leo Baeck Institute, Parent Collection, National Socialism Collection, Call Number: AR 119, No known copyright restrictions)*

Times.

THREE CENTS

NAZIS SMASH, LOOT AND BURN JEWISH SHOPS AND TEMPLES UNTIL GOEBBELS CALLS HALT

*All Vienna's Synagogues Attacked; Fires and Bombs Wreck 18 of 21*

*Jews Are Beaten, Furniture and Goods Flung From Homes and Shops — 15,000 Are Jailed During Day—20 Are Suicides*

BANDS ROVE CITIES

Thousands Arrested for 'Protection' as Gangs Avenge Paris Death

EXPULSIONS ARE IN VIEW

Plunderers Trail Wreckers in Berlin—Police Stand Idle —Two Deaths Reported

*Fig. 61* - The New York Times *following the Kristallnacht pogrom of November 9-10, 1938 (public domain)*

Goebbels had, in fact, cooked up an orchestrated reaction to the assassination, sending messages to police headquarters by teletype, instructing them to organize and carry out "spontaneous" attacks on Jews, their homes, businesses, and houses of worship. He ordered them to loot and burn and to arrest as many Jews as they could, especially the rich. Fire companies were given strict orders to stand by as the fires blazed, unless, of course, the fires threatened non-Jewish properties.

Goebbel's telegram read:

> SECRET!
>
> Copy of Most Urgent Telegram from Munich on November 8, 1938, 1-20 a.m.
>
> To all
>
> Headquarters and Stations of the State (Political) Police
>
> To all

Local and Regional Offices of the Security Service (SD)

Urgent! For immediate attention of Chief and his deputy!

Re- Measures Against the Jews Tonight.

Because of the assassination of Legation Secretary vom Rath in Paris, demonstrations throughout the Reich are to be expected tonight—November 9 to 10, 1938. The following orders are issued for dealing with these occurrences.

1) Upon receipt of this telegram, the chiefs of the political police [Gestapo] stations or their deputies must immediately contact the appropriate political authorities for their district [the local Nazi Party leaders]...by telephone to arrange a discussion about the conduct of the demonstrations. This discussion should include the competent Inspector or Commander of the Order Police....

[The local] political authorities are to be informed that the German police have received from the Reichsführer SS and the Chief of the German police the following orders to which the actions of the political authorities should be correspondingly adjusted—

a) Only such actions may be carried out which do not threaten German lives or property (e.g., burning of synagogues only when there is no threat of fire to the surroundings).

b) Stores and residences of Jews may only be destroyed but not looted. The police are instructed to supervise compliance with this order and to arrest looters.

c) Special care is to be taken on commercial streets

> that non-Jewish businesses are completely secured against damage.
>
> d) Foreign citizens, even if they are Jewish, may not be molested.
>
> 2) ...demonstrations in progress should not be prevented by the police but only supervised for compliance with the guidelines.
>
> 3) ...existing archival material is to be impounded by the police in all synagogues and offices of the Jewish community centers to prevent its destruction in the course of the demonstrations.... [This material] is to be turned over to the...offices of the SD.

The terror began late on the night of November 9. Mob violence raged on throughout that night and the next day. Nearly one hundred Jews were killed in this officially inspired violence. Tens of thousands were arrested. Thousands upon thousands of Jewish shops, homes, offices, and synagogues were vandalized, smashed up, or torched. The mobs were left unchecked to roam the streets and terrorize Jewish families while the police stood by and did nothing or even participated in the violence.

Klaus Langer, whose diary is one of the few contemporary accounts by a teenager of the early period of Nazi persecution before the war, recorded his experiences in an entry dated November 11, 1938:

> The past three days brought significant changes in our lives. On November 7 a German legation member was assassinated in Paris. He died two days later. The day following, on November 10 [sic], came the consequences. At three o'clock the synagogue and the

> Jewish youth center were put on fire. Then they began to destroy Jewish businesses. During the morning, private homes also were being demolished. Fires were started at single homes belonging to Jews. At six-thirty in the morning the Gestapo came to our home and arrested Father and Mother [. . .] Mother returned after about one and a half hours. Dad remained and was put in prison. In the morning I went to the Ferse home. Bobby was at the synagogue and at the youth center in the morning and saw how they burned. Later we went to the day care center where the children had been brought from the community home, which they had to flee during the night.
>
> We [. . .] returned to our neighborhood by two o'clock. Not far from us we saw a gang vandalizing a home, throwing things out of the window. When I went around the corner and looked up my street there was nothing to see. It looked peaceful. I, therefore, returned directly to our house. When I turned into the front yard I saw that the house was damaged. I walked on glass splinters. In the hallway I met Frau Baum, who lived upstairs. I ran into our apartment and found unbelievable destruction in every room. It was the same in the apartment of the caretaker below us. Mother and Grandmother were there. My parents' instruments were destroyed, the dishes were broken, the windows were broken, furniture upturned, the desk was turned over, drawers and mirrors were broken, and the radio smashed.

*The New York Times* reported on the events in Germany the next day with a headline screaming:

JEWS ARE ORDERED TO LEAVE MUNICH

Some Told They Must Get Out of Germany Despite Fact They Lack Passports

FINE SHOPS ARE WRECKED

Four Synagogues Set On Fire in Frankfort on the Main, Many Jews Arrested

MUNICH, Germany, Nov. 10—All Jewish families were ordered this morning to leave Munich within forty-eight hours and were instructed to inform the political police by 6 P.M. when they would hand over the keys to their dwellings and garages.

Instructions were issued to confiscate all Jewish-owned cars and the sale of gasoline to Jews was forbidden. In some cases Jews were told that they must leave Germany and they were forced to sign a statement to this effect. No notice was taken of the objection that most Jews were without passports. The only Jews with passports are those who have already made preparations to emigrate.

The news of the death of Ernst vom Rath in Paris was the signal for a reign of terror for the Jewish community in Munich, which began with the wrecking of shops during the night and continued with incendiarism during the morning and wholesale arrests and notices of expulsions during the day.

Crowds Fill Main Streets

Large crowds filled the main streets this morning to gaze on the destruction wrought in last night's riots, the full extent of which was visible only by daylight. Kauffingerstrasse, one of Munich's main streets, looked as if it had been raided by a bombing lane. A half-

> dozen of the best shops were converted into wreckage overnight with plate-glass windows splintered on the pavement, shelves torn down and goods lying broken and trampled on the floor.
>
> So far as can be gathered every Jewish-owned shop in town was completely or partly wrecked as well as several "Aryan" businesses, which shared the general fate for having previously belonged to Jews.

The events of November 9 and 10, 1938, the horror that came to be known as *Kristallnacht* or the "Night of Broken Glass," stunned the world, bringing an end to British and American policies of appeasement and resulting in a tremendous wave of Jewish emigration out of Germany. No longer could the Nazis hide their evil intent, although the full extent of their plans to invade their European neighbors and exterminate the Jewish people were yet to be revealed.

The United States immediately recalled its ambassador. Other countries went further, severing diplomatic ties with Germany. One swift reaction of the British government was to approve the *Kindertransport* program, admitting Jewish refugee children into England. In the following year, Britain admitted 10,000 unaccompanied Jewish children.

Sadly, many reactions were cautious and muted. The US did not break off diplomatic relations, nor did Roosevelt offer any assistance to German Jews. American public sentiment on a response was mixed and weak. In 1939, a Gallup poll asked Americans if the government should permit 10,000 children to come to the US. A majority, 61 percent, said no. The lack of a firmer reaction, it has been argued, likely encouraged the Nazis to move from a policy of expelling Jews (while stealing their property and wealth) toward the more horrific "Final Solution" of genocide.

Herschel Grynszpan's fate has never been accurately determined. In the immediate months following the assassination and subsequent violence, Herschel was a celebrity, interviewed by journalists while awaiting trial. Money was raised for his defense and legal maneuvers ensued. When Germany invaded in June 1940, he was sent south to Orléans along with other prisoners. In July, the Vichy government agreed to the German government's request that Grynszpan be turned over to them, and he was transferred into German custody.

Herschel Grynszpan was likely executed, but that has never been confirmed. The record gets sketchy after September 1942. It is known that he was moved several times between Moabit Prison in Berlin and the concentration camps at Sachsenhausen and Flossenbürg. At Sachsenhausen, he shared a cell with Kurt Schuschnigg, the last chancellor of Austria.

Goebbels' plan was to put on a show trial and blame "international Jewry." But in a further twist of fate, Goebbels had trouble trying Grynszpan. Although the evidence was clear and he was indicted in October 1941 with a trial date set for January 1942, as the date got closer the Nazi high command grew nervous. Goebbels had "grave doubts," about putting Herschel on trial, doubts which he communicated to Hitler.

Why? Some historians credit an unproven theory that Herschel and his lawyer, Vincent de Moro-Giafferi, cooked up a fiendish ploy to save his skin: vom Rath and Herschel Grynszpan had a love affair. The allegation is probably false, but his defense quite possibly rested on this tactic. Vincent de Moro-Giafferi was France's most successful defense attorney. He allegedly won every case he ever tried, save for one. His brilliance at legal strategy and his courtroom skills were so legendary that people would go to a trial just to watch him in action.

If the legend of Herschel's defense is true, then this explains why the Nazi propaganda machine never took advantage of this opportunity to publicly try a hated Jewish assassin. The defense may have asserted they would allege in open court that Grynszpan and vom Rath met at a known trysting place for gays and started an affair. After a short time, an ashamed Herschel tried to break it off but vom Rath persisted, stalking and harassing Herschel.

Herschel had no choice but to confront vom Rath, a confrontation which ended violently. Grynszpan may have used a vile tactic in modern hate crimes: the "gay panic defense." The Nazis could not hazard a public show trial where the "homosexuality" of a Nazi martyr was the defense's alibi.

Whatever the reason, the proceedings were postponed again and again, and Herschel was kept alive, even treated less harshly than most prisoners. Records show him still alive as late as early 1944 when he was interrogated by Adolf Eichmann in Berlin at Gestapo headquarters. Eichmann, at his trial at Nuremberg, recounted the meeting:

> I did then exchange a few words with Grynszpan. He was very brief and brusque, was indifferent and gave short replies to all the questions. I wanted to ask him, since I had no knowledge at all of the whole matter, where he had been and things of that kind.
>
> On the whole he looked well, he was small—he was a smallish lad…this is still preserved in my memory, and then he was again returned to custody in Prinz Albrechtstrasse 8.

*Fig. 62 - Herschel Grynszpan's lawyer, Vincent de Moro-Giafferi (1913 courtesy Wikimedia, public domain)*

Rumors later asserted that Herschel Grynszpan was still alive in Magdeburg Prison in January 1945.

Whatever his ultimate fate, Herschel was finally and officially declared dead by the West German government in 1960, at the request of his parents. Continued rumors of his survival persisted into the 1950s, and as late as 2016, a photo surfaced of a man resembling Grynszpan taken in Germany after the war.

Herschel's parents survived the war and the Holocaust and managed to make it to Israel, where they both lived until their deaths, she in 1963, he in 1976. Herschel's Aunt Chawa and Uncle Abraham were not as fortunate. Both died in the death camps at Auschwitz.

Certainly, many of the events of World War II would have occurred without Herschel Grynszpan. The invasions of Poland and Germany's neighboring countries, the Holocaust, Pearl Harbor, and the other major events that led up to the war, these would have happened all the same.

Yet Kristallnacht might have never happened. Certainly, the circumstances would have been different. Would the horror of the Night of Broken Glass have occurred without this precipitating event? If not, the world may have slept on a while longer, oblivious to the Nazi threat; that Hitler had no murderous intentions toward the Jews and other "undesirables" like gays, the mentally ill, and the developmentally disabled.

The events of the night of November 9-10 alerted the world to something they could no longer ignore—Germany's plans of official persecution of Jews, a fact not so conveniently dismissed after the world witnessed mob riots and looting intentionally instigated and officially sanctioned.

What young Herschel Grynszpan did that November day in Paris is not well known. Yet the results reverberated worldwide.

Today, you can exit the Solferino métro station and walk the few short blocks to the rue de Lille in Herschel's footsteps. Approach No. 78 and stand just across the street. Feel the intense despair of this seventeen-year-old boy for his family, for his people and their serious plight.

Those responsible for uprooting them from their home, for ruining their meager lives and stealing what little they possessed were here—just inside the walls of this embassy. Someone must be held accountable. The Americans, the French, the British were turning a blind eye; nobody was standing up for the Polish Jews being persecuted by Germany.

Herschel Grynszpan would stand up for them, and the world would hear the sound of his rage—here in Paris, the sound of the first shot fired in World War II.

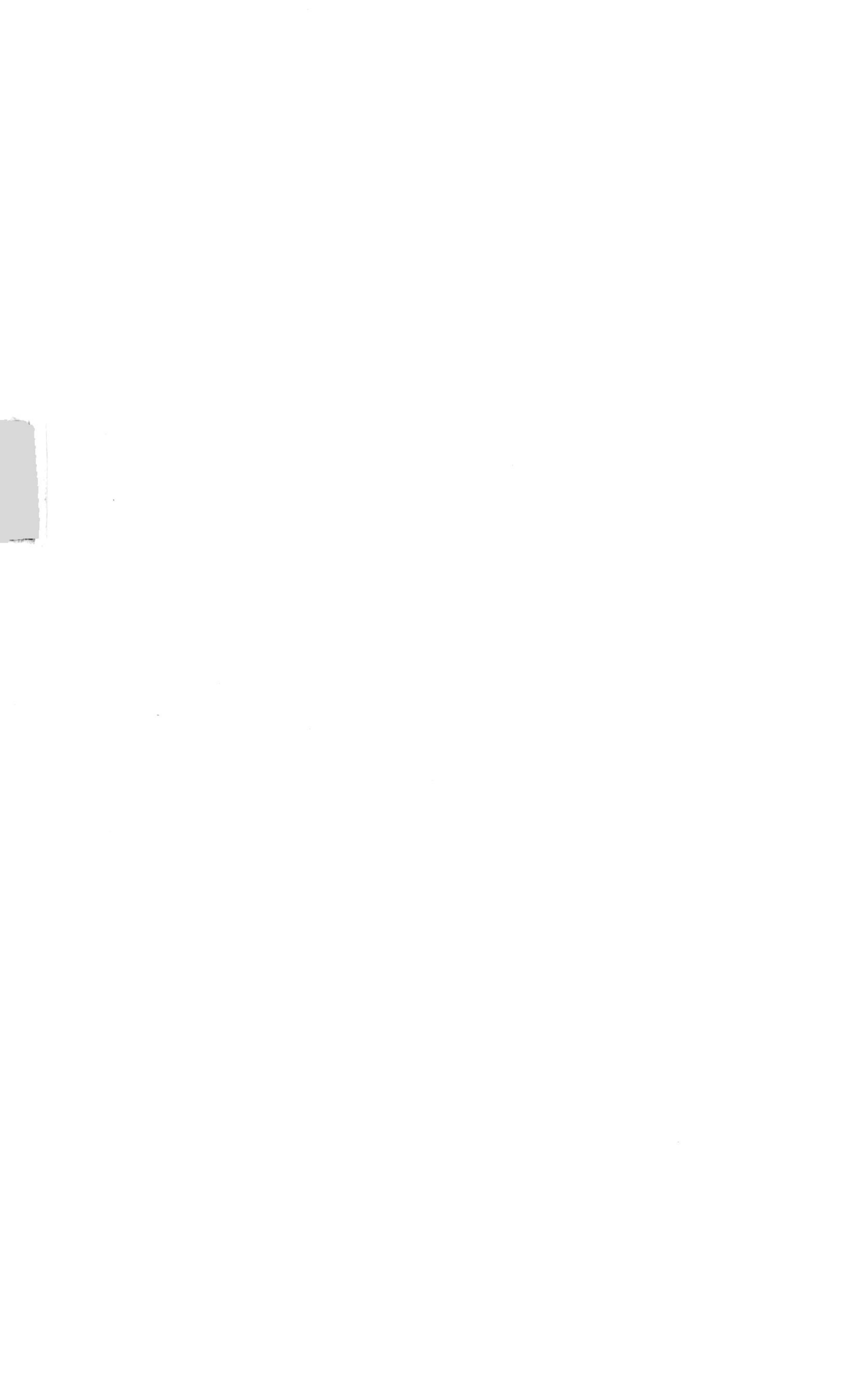

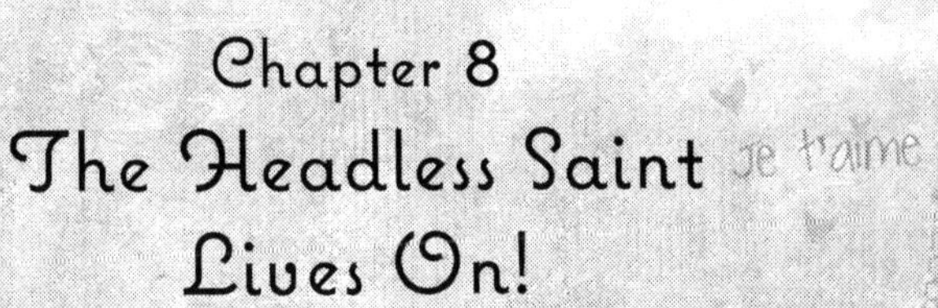


# Chapter 8
# The Headless Saint Lives On!

(Third Century)

*"Saint Denis and companions, you died in the mission fields*
*of the Church's eldest daughter, France.*
*Your blood spilled long ago so that our blood would not spill today.*
*We thank you for your witness and ask your intercession to make us fearless like you."*
— Prayer to Saint Denis

THE CHRISTIAN MISSIONARIES knew that they were in trouble. Dionysus, Rusticus, and Éleuthèrius were surrounded by hostile Parisii tribe members, including their high priest who was doing a slow, menacing dance, shaking his talisman in their faces. Several Roman soldiers accompanying the tribesmen looked on amused. They would not intervene. Indeed, these *legionnaires* were sent to ensure the missionaries did not return back down the hill to the city the Romans called *Lutetia.*

History and legend tell us that the missionaries did not survive the encounter, but that's just the beginning of the story....

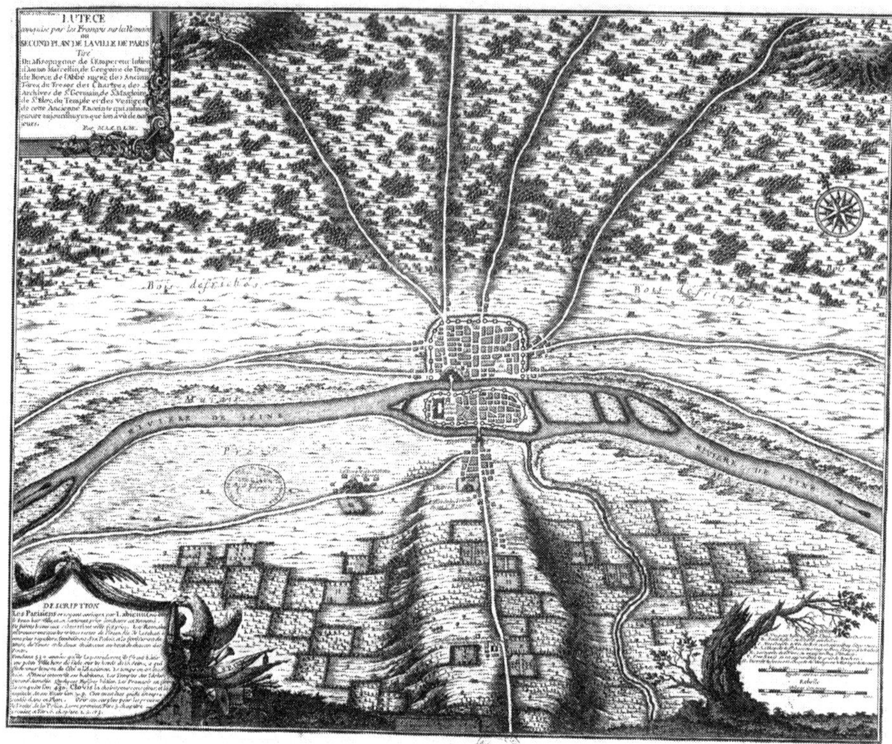


*Fig. 63 Plan of Lutèce/Paris in the year 508. Image from the National Library of France, courtesy of Wikimedia, public domain*

"*Lutetia*!" The romantic name echoes down through the centuries in names like *Lutèce,* the famous New York City restaurant. But in the Latin vernacular of ancient Rome, the name *Lutetia Parisiorum* means "the place of the Parisii near the swamp." The reality of this tiny backwater Roman outpost that became Paris today lies in stark contrast with some later mythologies that attempted to give Paris magical origins. One of the most popular myths about the city of Paris is that it takes its name from Paris, the fabled prince of Troy, who stole Helen of Sparta, causing the Trojan War. According to legend, exiles from Troy fled here after their defeat at the hands of the Greeks. But, alas, the Paris of Troy never made his way to Paris, France.

Romans did arrive, however, during the reign of Caesar Augustus, perhaps as early as 28 BCE. They found a simple native village nestled on an island and along the shores of a lazy river, which the Celtic tribes called "the Sequana," a river that wends its way through a rich and fertile valley. When the Romans appeared, the Parisii abandoned the island (today's *Île de la Cité*), destroying the river crossing and carrying away everything they could. Eventually they returned and rebuilt their village on the island.

Two hundred years later, the settlement was a Roman city with 8,000 inhabitants and growing. The Romans concentrated their settlement on the south side of the river, safe from the Seine's frequent floods, building their dwellings up the side of the *Mons Lucotitius* (today's Mont Sainte-Geneviève). The growing outpost featured the usual amenities of Roman life: hot and cold thermal baths, a large amphitheater for outdoor games and public executions, and an aqueduct to bring fresh water to homes and the public baths. The amphitheater, one of the largest in Gaul, was located just outside the city. Named the *Arènes de Lutèce*, it held up to 15,000 people.

Dionysus, Rusticus, and Éleuthèrius were sent to convert the Gauls by Pope Fabius, who named Dionysus "first Bishop of Lutetia." They headed north from Rome, and when they arrived, they found a cautious but friendly welcome among the natives. The Gauls were a tough lot, strong but prone to drinking too much wine. The missionaries spent several months living among the Parisii, bringing them the gospel (Good News)—at that time, nothing more than a disorganized collection of writings and oral retellings of the life, death, and resurrection of a virtually unknown prophet, Jesus.

The Roman soldiers and citizens looked on with indifference or amusement at the missionaries with their strange beliefs, who slowly began to gain the trust of the Parisii. Soon these "Apostles to the Gauls" began converting the natives to Christianity. They preached and taught every day except one, a day when they rested and fasted—from sunset on *diēs Veneris* until sunset on *diēs Saturnī* (sunset on Friday to sunset on Saturday). Eventually, a few of the Parisii consented to be baptized in the river, with the ceremony attended by a large number of curious onlookers.

Dionysus sent word to Pope Fabius of their success, unaware that Fabius had died, martyred by Emperor Decius. Decius had begun persecuting Christians, ordering all Roman citizens to perform an animal sacrifice. Refusal was punishable by death. Pope Fabius refused the order and was martyred in the Coliseum. The emperor's order eventually reached Lutetia while the missionaries continued their work unawares.

Early one morning, Dionysus and his two companions set out across the river and made their way north, climbing the steep hill the Romans called *Mons Martis*, the Mount of Mars, which had a shrine to the god of war near the summit. The tribesmen and some Roman soldiers, who had their orders, followed them along the narrow goat path winding up the butte. At some point, the troop confronted Dionysus and his companions. The soldiers insisted that they make the animal sacrifice required by the emperor's edict. When they refused, they were tortured and then beheaded on the spot on the side of the hill we today call "Montmartre."

The legend, story, and history of Dionysus—known in French as Saint Denis (pronounced Den-knee)—is completely interwoven into the history of the city of Paris. Once Christianity swept Europe, the Roman name for the *Mons Martis* easily became Montmarte, or *Mons Martyrs* (Mount of Martyrs) commemorating the martyrdom of Denis and his followers. The story of Denis became a powerful tale of early Christian faith and martyrdom.

The first written accounts of Denis' life and death appear around 500 CE, some 250 years after his death. Through oral tradition and retelling across the burgeoning Christian world, the legend became well known in Gaul and beyond, all the way to Rome. Over time, the facts of Denis' life and death were embellished, becoming a legend entering into the realm of the mystical:

> After he was beheaded on Montmartre, Denis did not die, but instead he calmly picked up his severed head and continued on his way up along the narrow goat path on which he had been traveling. The amazed onlookers, including his executioners, followed as he proceeded on, carrying his head.
>
> As if this wasn't miracle enough, Denis then began preaching a sermon, people following as Denis continued to walk and talk. He preached all the way up the summit of Montmartre and down the other side. Finally, some ten kilometers (six miles) from where he was decapitated, Denis finished his sermon, laid down, and died.

The story of Denis' miraculous walk and sermon converted more people than he could have ever hoped to in a lifetime. Saint Gregory of Tours, in his sixth century *History of the Franks*, wrote:

> Under the emperor Decius many persecutions arose against the name of Christ, and there was such a slaughter of believers that they could not be numbered.... And of these the blessed Dionisius, bishop of Paris, after suffering divers pains in Christ's name, ended the present life by the threatening sword.

Dionysus was buried on the spot where he fell, and his legend grew. One of three patron saints of Paris, Denis is known throughout France, although the rest of the world has largely forgotten him. Soon after his death, a small shrine was erected on the spot where he fell and the town of Saint Denis grew up around the holy site.

Matters might have ended there but for the intercession of another powerful holy figure and patron saint of Paris: Sainte Geneviève. Two-hundred years after Denis' death, around the year 475, Sainte Geneviève dedicated a small chapel in Montmartre on the site where Denis was beheaded. Geneviève, especially devoted to Denis, wanted to ensure that the place on Mont of Martyrs became a place of pilgrimage and worship for the people of Paris and for Christians from all over the world.

*Fig. 64 - Site of the chapel, first dedicated by Sainte Geneviève on the spot where St. Denis was beheaded, 11 rue Yvonne le Trac (photos by the author)*

*Fig. 65 - Chapel where St. Denis was beheaded, 11 rue Yvonne le Trac (photos by the author)*

*Fig. 66 - St. Geneviève, patroness of Paris, Musée Carnavalet. Unknown painter, sometime between circa 1615 and 1625 (public domain)*

Sainte Geneviève also holds a very special place in Paris history. Besides bringing Saint Denis to prominence, she is credited with saving Paris and its citizens numerous times, both during her life and after her death. Geneviève was peasant girl, born in Nanterre. Her parents died when she was young, and she went to live with her aunt, who happened to be named Lutetia. In 429, Geneviève began her life of devotion when Saint Germanus (Saint Germain), Bishop of Auxerre, came to Nanterre. During his sermon, he saw the young Geneviève and told her parents that she should serve God and that people would follow her example. Germain gave Geneviève a brass medal engraved with a cross, which she wore all her life.

After becoming a nun, Geneviève went to Paris where her visions, her prophecies, and her piety brought her to the attention of King Childeric and his successor King Clovis I. In 451, Attila the Hun and his Mongol warriors were fast approaching Paris from the north, after having sacked many cities in Gaul. Word arrived they would soon be at the gates of Paris. Attila's ferocity and mercilessness were well known, and the populace was ready to evacuate. Geneviève persuaded the people to stay, fast and pray.

What happened next was deemed a miracle. Inexplicably, the horde veered away from Paris and attacked farther south at Orléans where Attila's army was defeated at the Battle of the Catalaunian Plains. Geneviève's prayers, her courage, and her powerfully persuasive appeal to the Parisian people were credited with saving Paris.

Many years later, when Paris was besieged by another hostile army, Geneviève led a secret mission to bring in food and supplies, which helped Paris hold out. This event, and her other acts of care for the poor and hungry, led to Geneviève often being depicted holding a shaft of wheat or a loaf of bread.

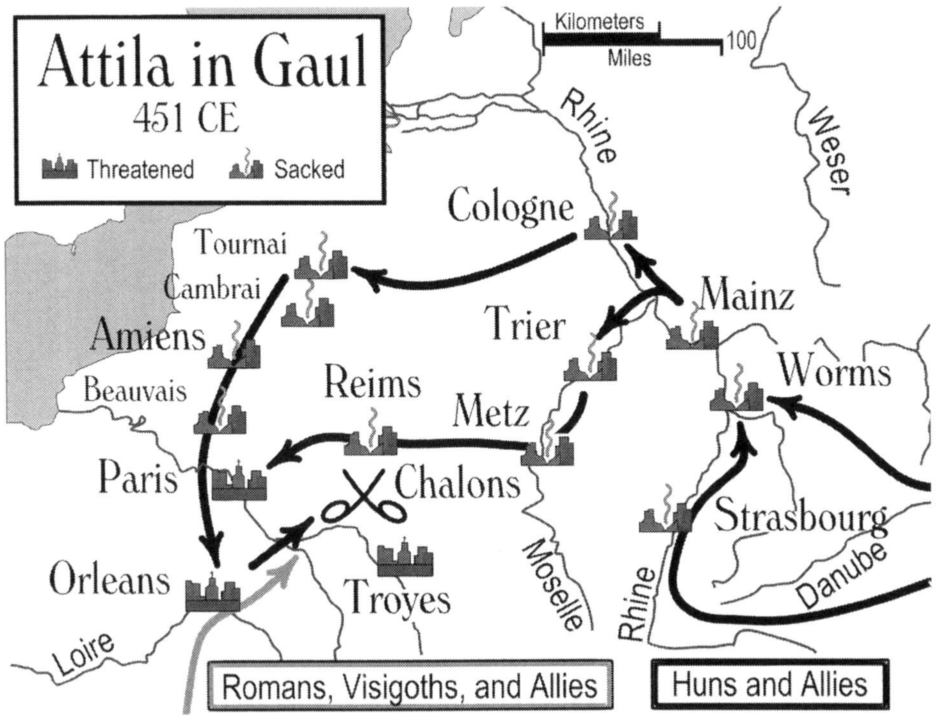


*Fig. 67 - Map of the Hun invasion of Gaul in 451 CE (courtesy Wikipedia, licensed under the Creative Commons Attribution-Share Alike 3.0 Unported license)*

After Geneviève's death in 512 CE, miracles continued to be credited to her, most famously when Paris experienced a mass epidemic of "Burning Fever" (likely ergot poisoning) in the twelfth century. It ended, many believed, thanks to her intercession.

In 1129, with the sickness raging throughout Paris, the Bishop of Paris ordered Geneviève's casket to be carried through the streets in a procession. Reportedly, thousands were cured when they saw or touched her relics, and the epidemic subsided. On a subsequent visit to Paris, Pope Innocent II ordered the date of the miracle (November 26) and her feast day (January 3) to be celebrated to commemorate the miraculous healing. To this day, Parisian churches still celebrate these holy days.

Sainte Geneviève built the martyrium in Montmartre, and she also had a larger shrine erected where St. Denis died. That little chapel that eventually became the Basilica at Saint Denis is also steeped in legend. According to the story, Sainte Geneviève bought the plot of land where Saint Denis was buried and told the local priests to build a chapel there. They replied that they didn't have the resources to build it, so she directed them to travel into Paris and go to the only bridge crossing the Seine. There they would be told what to do.

Doing as she asked, the priests overheard a conversation between two peasants discussing where a large quantity of fine stone could be had. They went and discovered a stone quarry with enough stone to build a chapel dedicated to the memory of Saint Denis. By the mid-700s, this chapel was replaced by a larger church. The site has been expanded over the centuries, the church growing in size, stature, and importance into the basilica it is today.

Construction of the present basilica began in 1135 by the Abbot Suger, Abbot of St. Denis, and was dedicated on June 11, 1144, with the completion of its choir. The basilica is the first example of early Gothic architecture, using all of the elements of the style that afterwards became known as the "French Style." From the eighth century until the end of the monarchy in 1789, almost every king and queen of France has been buried in the great Basilica of Saint Denis.

Sainte Geneviève also built the church on the Mont Geneviève in which she was buried. She was given the blessing and support of King Clovis, who was also buried there with his wife Clotilde.

This Church of the Apostles Peter and Paul was later rededicated as the Abbey of Sainte-Geneviève. The Abbey's collection of books and manuscripts eventually became the seeds of the Sainte-Genevieve library, whose origins go back to the year 831.

*Fig. 68 - Abbey church of Saint-Denis, west façade (photo by Thomas Clouet, Courtesy Wikimedia. This file is licensed under the Creative Commons Attribution-Share Alike 4.0 International license.)*

*Fig. 69 - Tombs of Henri II and Catherine de Medici in the Basilica of Saint-Denis (photo by the author)*

The library in turn grew into a school of theology. By 1108, the Abbey's theology school joined two other emerging religious schools—the School of Notre Dame Cathedral and the school of the Royal Palace—to form what would become known as the University of Paris, "la Sorbonne." The Sorbonne today is among the greatest educational institutions in the world, another legacy of Saint Geneviève. The founding of the Sorbonne heralded the start of the university system as we know it today. From 1108 to 1113, the great scholar and famous theologian Peter Abelard taught at the Abbey school. The story of Heloise and Abelard is one of the great love stories of all time.

**Travelers' Tips**

**Métro Station Saint-Michel Line 4 or Métro Station Cluny-Sorbonne — Musée de Cluny (5th arr.) Line 10**

***The Roman Ruins***

The ruins of the Roman baths and amphitheater can be seen today at the Cluny Museum, located off the Boulevard Saint-Michel. Also known as *la Musée national du Moyen Âge—Thermes et hôtel de Cluny* (National Museum of the Middle Ages—Cluny thermal baths and mansion), the museum houses the baths and other ancient artifacts, such as the first century "Boatman Pillar," given to Emperor Tiberius by Paris' guild of boatmen. It contains both Celtic and Roman carvings, including ones of the god Jupiter, showing a rare example of two cultures living side-by-side.

The ruins of some of the rooms that made up the Roman baths, some of which are visible to passersby on the street, are included as part of the museum. The frigidarium is the best preserved of the ruins uncovered so far, and this ongoing archeological dig promises more treasures in years to come.

**Métro Station Cardinal Lemoine, Line 10, Métro Station Jussieu, Lines 7 or 10 or Métro Station Place Monge, Line 7 — Roman Arena (5th arr.)**

The first century Roman arena, the Arènes de Lutèce, is located in the eastern end of the fifth arrondissement. If you don't know where to look, you could walk right by, never knowing this archeological treasure is here. Lost for centuries, even though the quartier retained the name *les Arènes*, the ruins were discovered by Théodore Vaquer when the Rue Monge was built in 1860. Almost destroyed in the urban renewal, Victor Hugo and others formed *la Société des Amis des Arènes,* determined to save the arena.

Turning from Métro Jussieu on to the Rue des Arènes, look almost immediately for Square Capitan through a gate to a children's playground and garden named L'illusion. From Métro Place Monge, walk along the Rue de Navarre. A gate on the street leads down a path to the arena.

**Métro Station Hôtel de Ville or Cité, Lines 1 or 5 — Facade of Notre Dame (1st arr.)**

***Façade of Notre Dame Cathedral***

Tourists at the Cathedral of Notre Dame de Paris often spend time contemplating the façade, rich in detail, artistry, and majesty. The intricate carvings of gargoyles and chimeras and the stories told in stone above the portals are mesmerizing. Look closely at the center portal, the door of the Last Judgment. Notice the chain that keeps the sinners in line as their souls are weighed on the scales. The chain, you will notice, is not attached to anything; they voluntarily hold onto the chain! Also, look for the mischievous demon putting a thumb on the scales, determining the next poor soul's fate.

Along the left-hand doorway, the Portal of the Virgin, look closely at the row of large statues. You will see a saint with his head cradled lovingly in his hands. You know who this is, of course: Saint Denis, first Bishop of Paris, and one of the three patron saints of Paris, along with Sainte Geneviève and Sainte Joan of Arc.

*Fig. 70 - Statue of St. Denis on the façade of Notre Dame (photo by the author)*

The fire that almost destroyed the cathedral in 2019 rocked Paris and the world with the realization that the Gothic icon could have been lost forever. Only the quick and heroic action of the Parisian *sapeurs-pompiers* (firefighters) saved the building. They did this by preventing the fire from reaching the twin belltowers.

Notre Dame has ten bells housed in the two towers. The two largest, the Emmanuel and the Marie, are both housed in the south tower. Together, they weigh nearly twenty-eight tons. Had the fire weakened the bells' supports, the weight of the falling bells would have doomed the entire building.

## Ⓜ Métro Station Basilique de Saint Denis, Line 13 — Basilique de Saint Denis

### *Basilica of Saint Denis*

The basilica of Saint Denis, in the town of Saint Denis, is the burial place of most of the kings and queens of France from the tenth century onward. This historic church is the first example of the early Gothic architecture that was soon to sweep Europe. The basilica is just outside of Paris (on Métro Line 13), so the trip is not on most travelers' itineraries. The beauty and history surrounding the basilica is the history of the French monarchy and the mystery surrounding the legend of Saint Denis.

The basilica has developed its own legends. One story is told of a leper who fell asleep in the nearly completed basilica. He awoke to find Christ, Saint Denis, and a host of saints and angels performing a ceremony to consecrate the church, their spirits appearing in a blaze of light. The legend holds that the leper was cured. A large, mottled patch on one of the columns in the church is said to be the skin of the leper, removed and washed clean by the Christ Himself.

A trip here is well worth the time. For a small entrance fee, one can explore the crypts and see the interesting carved stone tombs, including the resting places of Catherine de Medici and Henri II, Henri IV, Clovis, Louis XIV, Louis XVI, and Marie Antoinette.

### Travelers' Tips

**Métro Station Abbesses, Line 12 — 11 Rue Yvonne le Tac (18th arr.) or**

**Métro Station Pigalle, Lines 2 or 12 — Rue des Martyrs (9th - 18th arr.)**

### *The Rue des Martyrs and Montmartre*

Montmartre, once a separate village and now an arrondissement of Paris, is well known as a place that has attracted artists, painters, and musicians who lived, loved, drank, and worked there. Thanks to cheap rents and cheap wine, the area became famous and is infused with the spirit of this early saint, the first Bishop of Paris.

To the south of Montmartre, in the ninth arrondissement across the Boulevard Clichy, is the beginning of the street known as the rue des Martyrs. Legend has it that this street traces roughly the same goat path that Denis walked. It winds its way up the butte to the place near the top of the street where he was beheaded. The street starts at the church of Notre-Dame-de-Lorette, with its tall columns. Georges Bizet, composer of the wildly popular opera *Carmen*, was baptized here in 1840, as was painter Claude Monet in 1841. The street was treated (with some scandal) by Émile Zola in his novel *Nana*.

As the rue des Martyrs continues its upward climb into the 18th arrondissement, you will find the neighborhood of Pigalle, the notorious (now relatively tame) "red-light district" of Paris. In this area, you will find *le Divan du Monde* at No. 75 rue des Martyrs, hosting music and dance performances from around the world. Next door at No. 75 bis (No. 75½) is *Madame Arthur*, famous for its revues featuring transsexual and transgendered performers.

A nightclub has been on this spot since the early 1800s. Charles Baudelaire and Edgar Degas patronized the 1861 club *Brasserie des Martyrs*. Later called *le Divan Japonais*, this historic nightclub was made famous by an 1893 poster by Henri de Toulouse-Lautrec. He and Pablo Picasso were frequent visitors. In 1894, a notorious musical pantomime called *The Bride Going to Bed (La Couchée de la Mariée*) scandalized audiences with the performer appearing "naked" (actually wearing a gauzy, transparent blouse). Yvette Guilbert became famous singing there in 1901. One of her best-known songs was "Madame Arthur."

A wonderful book, *The Only Street in Paris: Life on the Rue des Martyrs* by Elaine Sciolino, chronicles life on the street, recalling a time in Paris that is rapidly fading. Here is a street largely without chain stores and full of the small businesses that are the backbone of a Parisian neighborhood: the *fromagerie* (the cheese shop), the *boulangerie* (the bakery), the *patisserie* (the pastry shop), the *poissonnière* (the fish store), the *quincaillerie* (the hardware store). Her book paints a picture of a Parisian life that is disappearing, but still exists in the quotidian activities of the people who live on this amazing street that follows a 2,000-year-old goat path.

## How Paris Shaped Our World

Over the past 2,000 years, Lutetia—the Roman city that became Paris—has affected the world at large in more ways than can be counted. Even today, the ancient Roman name "Lutetia" rings out, synonymous with beauty, light, and creative inspiration. Lutetia lends its name to Lutetium (Lu), the seventy-first element in the periodic table of elements, discovered in Paris by Georges Urbain, a French chemist, professor of the Sorbonne, and a member of the Institut de France.

The Roman influence on Gaul, the rise of Christianity, missionaries and martyrs like Saint Denis and Sainte Geneviève, and the legends and miracles that grew from their lives, have without a doubt profoundly affected the entire world. Without these two, Paris would not be the same.

And they, in turn, inspired another would-be saint, whose life has affected many millions more.

### *The Society of Jesus (aka the Jesuits)*

Probably Saint Denis' most important legacy was born on August 15, 1534, in the chapel at No. 11 rue Yvonne de Tac, in an event that changed millions of lives the world over for centuries.

The first chapel, erected in 475, marked the place where Denis and his two companions were beheaded. For centuries, this has been a place of worship and pilgrimage, with thousands flocking there during the Middle Ages and occasional miracles being reported. The chapel has been rebuilt several times over the centuries, most recently at the beginning of the sixteenth century. Workers at that time rediscovered the remnants of three graves marked with crosses and ancient inscriptions, perhaps Saint Denis and his companions. The discovery prompted the abbesses of the Abbey of Montmartre to erect a new chapel and buildings around the crypt.

And it was here on this site that a Spanish soldier and his small band of followers took vows to start a new Catholic order. Calling themselves the "Society of Jesus," this small group would grow to become the largest Catholic order in the world, surpassing even the Franciscans. The Order of the Society of Jesus financed missionary expeditions across the globe and founded many educational institutions.

This Spanish soldier and his six friends were all students at the University of Paris. Their leader had been wounded in battle, and he spent his long convalescence reading religious books and pamphlets. His faith deepened until he knew he must dedicate his life to a higher calling. By 1532, this soldier had become devout. For seven years he studied, spending long hours with his classmates discussing how they could best serve the Church and all of humanity. One by one, he convinced his compatriots they should create an order, consecrate themselves to God, and become priests in the service of saving souls.

They gathered in the crypt of St. Denis early one morning to take vows of poverty, chastity, and obedience and became "a Company of Jesus," making a pact to devote the rest of their lives to God.

They chose August 15 as the date to take their vows, the Feast of Our Lady's Assumption. Only one of the group, Peter Faber, was a priest, so he could offer communion to the small group, guiding them through the ceremony to pronounce their vows.

*Photos 71 & 72 - Stone sculpture, dated 1253, likely from the early Benedictine abbey on the butte Montmartre (photos by the author)*

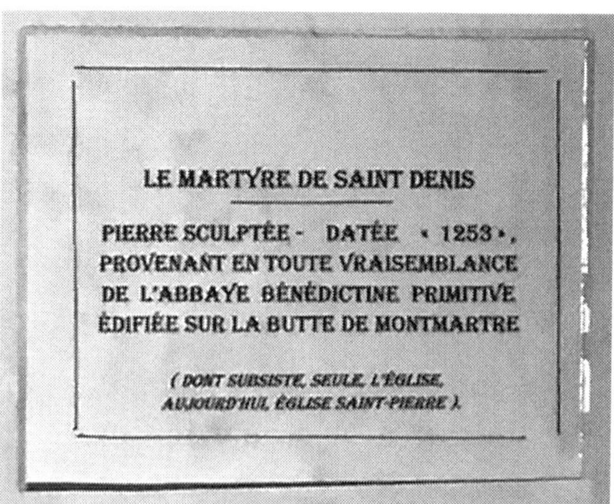


The soldier was Ignatius Loyola (1491-1556), founder of the Order of the Society of Jesus, better known as the Jesuits. The beginning of the Jesuit Order on the butte Montmartre, in the chapel of Saint Denis, has had world-changing implications. Loyola was beatified in July of 1609 and canonized as a saint in 1622.

The Jesuit Order has funded schools across the globe. Jesuit teachers, trained in both classics and theology, have educated millions of people. They also do missionary work throughout the world, often contributing to an understanding about the people and the cultures where they live, writing comprehensive books on native languages and dictionaries, translating native languages such as Japanese, and the many languages of the native tribes in the Americas.

The Jesuits played a significant role in the exploration and settlement of North and South America. Father Jacques Marquette, a Jesuit missionary, and Louis Joliet, a French explorer, mapped the northern reaches of the Mississippi River. John Carroll was the first Catholic bishop in the United States of America and went on to form Georgetown University in 1789, which remains a Jesuit school. The Association of Jesuit Colleges and Universities has twenty-eight Jesuit colleges and two theological centers active in the US, including Boston College, Fordham University, Le Moyne, Loyola Marymount, and Seattle University.

The Jesuits invented a method of teaching: the Ignatian Pedagogical Paradigm. Famous for its rigor and its practical effects, it emphasizes real-world application of theoretical principles—action being key—all in service to others. Jesuit students are expected to reflect on the concepts they have studied, but then they must go beyond learning into action for personal betterment and in service of a better world. Sound, conscious, and conscientious decision making and an active questioning of one's own beliefs are hallmarks of this 450-year-old method that has influenced countless millions throughout the ages.

The lives of Saint Denis and Sainte Geneviève infuse all of Montmartre, all of Paris, and much of the world, with stories, legends, and miracles. The aura and mystery of the village of Montmartre, its ancient religious and holy significance to Celts, Romans, early Christians, and modern-day pilgrims and tourists alike, all stem from the miraculous long walk Dionysus took that day, head in hand, preaching the Good News to all who gathered to witness his miracle. The town of Saint Denis and its unlikely basilica rising up out of the quiet suburbs of Paris, home to the many long dead kings and queens of France, is testament to their influence.

Head up the rue Des Martyrs to the rue Yvonne de Tac on a Friday afternoon when the crypt at No. 11 is open for a few hours (also the first weekend of every month). Enter with an open mind to hear what you might of Denis and Geneviève and their lives. Sit in one of the pews of rough chairs lashed together. Contemplate the thirteenth-century stone tableau of Denis and his followers at the moment of their martyrdom.

Some say Denis is still preaching his sermon, even today. Sit quietly in this place of miracles, a place of mystery and inspiration for two thousand years. And if you're quiet enough, you just might hear a voice preaching the Good News.

Truly, the headless saint lives on.

*Fig. 73 - St. Ignatius Loyola and his followers take their vows in the crypt of St. Denis (photo by the author)*

*Fig. 74 - The altar in the crypt of St. Denis*
*(photo by the author)*

*Fig. 75 - The Miracle of Saint Ignatius of Loyola, painting by Peter Paul Rubens, 1620, Kunsthistorisches Museum, Vienna (photo courtesy Wikimedia, public domain)*

# Chapter 9
# The Medici Column

je t'aime

PARIS

(Sixteenth Century)

*"It is the stars,*
*The stars above us, govern our conditions."*
— *King Lear*, Act IV, Scene 3

*"The perfect knowledge of events cannot be acquired without divine inspiration, since all prophetic inspiration receives its prime motivating force from God the creator, then from good fortune and nature.... So in conclusion, my son, take this gift from your father...who hopes you will understand each prophecy in every quatrain herein."*
— Michel de Nostradame
(Nostradamus)—Preface to *The Prophecies*,
Written to his son, César Nostradame,
Salon, France 1 March 1555

THE SKY WAS cloudy, starless, and moonless, and the wind howled as Queen Catherine ascended the secret staircase clad all in black, the only color she ever wore. The stairs wound around in tight concentric circles inside the Doric column that stood outside the Palace of the Queen. Passersby who paid attention would have noticed something strange. The column stood strangely, not supporting anything.

Catherine hastened, striding two steps at a time with great purpose, up and up to the platform encased in iron. She *must* see him, now! And he would be there. Clouds and darkness could not obscure his vision. The climb was arduous, but so eager was she for a report that she was barely winded as she reached the top and pushed open the hatch. The wind tore the door from her hands, slamming it hard upon the platform. The noise did not break the necromancer's concentration. Nearly one hundred feet in the air, he stood like a statue, his outline barely visible in the dark night.

The queen hauled herself up and tightly wrapped her cloak around herself. She made her way over to where a motionless Cosimo Ruggiero peered into a water-filled crystal bowl. Its surface, like a mirror, reflected the dark sky above. Though the winds whipped around, swirling in all directions, and the queen struggled to keep her cape about her, it barely rippled the hair on the old man's head. His cloak and hood were as still as his hypnotic gaze. Impatient as she was for news, she knew better than to break his concentration, so she waited.

The year was 1577. The woman was Queen Catherine Maria Romula di Lorenzo de' Medici, daughter of the great and wealthy Florentine banker, Lorenzo II de' Medici, great-granddaughter of Lorenzo the Magnificent, and niece of the former pope, Clement VII. The pope himself had arranged her marriage to the second son of the French King, promising King François I "three pearls" as her dowry—the cities of Genoa, Naples, and Milan. That night, she stood atop the *Colonne de l'Horoscope*, otherwise known as the *Medici Column.* Yet Queen Catherine had been standing at the precipice of great events for more than forty years. She had survived fierce and tumultuous times—driving, harsh, and unpredictable political winds that would have blown a lesser person clear off the edge and into oblivion.

In the whirlwind of intense historical forces, Catherine de Medici was not merely lucky. She was a sharp, shrewd political operator, a tactician, survivor, and fighter. Dealt a bad hand by fate, she played it exceedingly well. Much of her success in surviving the turbulent times in which she lived can be ascribed to her two occult advisors. One, an Italian like herself: Cosimo Ruggiero. The other a mysterious man from the south of France: Michel de Nostradame, known to the world today as Nostradamus.

Catherine trusted these two men and their powers to read the astrological signs, counting on their advice to confirm or refute what her counselors were telling her. Her goal was to ensure her survival and the survival of her children. Catherine even named Nostradamus *Counselor and Physician-in-Ordinary* to her son, the future King Charles IX.

Henri, Duke d'Orleans, was the second son and not destined to become king. So marrying Catherine, a commoner was acceptable. And yet fate made him king after the death of his older brother in 1536. Catherine, a foreigner from Italy in a strange land with strange customs and virtually no friends, was suddenly queen.

Catherine was fated to live in very troubled times, and her problems were many. Although she was queen, Henri never allowed her much power or authority, and this alone made her life difficult. Furthermore, she was a woman in an era when women were generally discounted, ignored, or abused. She was not considered beautiful in an age when beauty was often considered a woman's only asset.

Accounts describe her as having "protruding eyes," which apparently ran in the family.

As a de Medici, Catherine was immensely wealthy, but everyone knew she was a mere banker's daughter. Not being of noble birth was another strike against her in the eyes of many in and around the court of François I.

To add to Catherine's difficulties, her teenaged husband Henri showed no sexual or romantic interest in her. In fact before they were married, both at age fourteen, Henri had already taken a mistress: the thirty-six-year-old Diane de Poitiers, a courtier who'd had designs on young Henri for some time. While Diane de Poitiers usurped any influence Catherine might have had on Henri, she did prove, on occasion, to be a friend, even going so far as to encourage King François to arrange Henri's marriage to Catherine.

And later, Diane encouraged Henri to visit his wife's bed, so they would conceive children. For in addition to Catherine's many other troubles, she appeared to be barren. While the young couple showed "valor in the joust," according to the king, they remained childless for many years. Catherine's apparent inability to have children made her position in court even more precarious.

Eventually, Catherine was able to bear Henri a child—in fact, ten children altogether, five boys and five girls, with the last two (twin girls) dying in infancy. Three of her sons would become kings of France: François II, Charles IX, and Henri III. Her daughter, Margaret de Valois, would become queen to one of France's most revered kings, Henri of Navarre, crowned Henri IV.

But perhaps worst of all of her troubles, Catherine lived during the turbulent decades of religious strife that became known as the French Wars of Religion (1562–1598). The intense conflict between

Catholics and Protestants started with François I and his harsh treatment of the *Reformists*, as the Protestants were then called. His heir, Henri II, carried on this policy using even harsher measures, as did those who succeeded him.

The Wars of Religion were a long and violent period of strife and uncertainty. The new religion of Protestantism threatened the order established by the Catholic Church and a succession of popes stretching back nearly 1,500 years. The monarch's iron grip on power stemmed from his mutual interests with the Catholic Church, which the Protestant challenge put in jeopardy. After all, the Church crowned a new monarch, meaning God (in the guise of the Pope) had bestowed the crown. The new, radical Protestant sect (from the French word for "protester" *protestant*) threatened the divine right of kings because challenging the Church was challenging the sovereign.

Despite all these perils, Catherine had some advantages, not the least of which were considerable political shrewdness and a ruthless killer instinct. She was exceptionally intelligent. Records show she studied Latin, Greek, mathematics, natural history, astronomy, and astrology. As the mother of future kings and queens, she protected her children fiercely, stopping at nothing to keep them on the throne.

Catherine also employed an elaborate network of spies, as many as 300. Many were her ladies-in-waiting, who became known as her *l'escadron volant* (flying squadron). Catherine brought her Italian love for festivals and entertainments to France. And out of these came a new form of dance: the *ballet de cour.* Her ladies-in-waiting gave the first performance. Afterwards, the amazed French courtiers said the dancers in the spectacle looked "as though they were flying."

*Fig. 76 - Portrait of Catherine of Medici Attributed to Germain Le Mannier (courtesy Wikimedia, public domain)*

*Fig. 77 - Cosimo Ruggiero d. 1615 portrait by an unknown artist (public domain)*

Catherine's flying squadron mingled and circulated around the court, supplying her with tidbits of information, gossip, rumors, and news, which she and her advisors would sift through to discern the political winds, hoping to get ahead of any plots that might be brewing against her and her supporters. Tales of the squadron's use of seduction and wild sexual exploits are certainly grounded in some truth, but were just as likely wild exaggerations spread by her enemies to further diminish Catherine's reputation. Jeanne of Navarre, mother of the future king Henri IV, warned her son in a letter, "Although I knew it was bad, I find it even worse than I feared. Here women make advances to men rather than the other way around."

Catherine also kept close by her a number of dwarfs, believing they protected her from dark, occult forces. And she had her astrologers, Nostradamus and Ruggiero, who read the signs, the stars, and planets, and using whatever other supernatural means they could to decipher future courses of action.

> Two words explain this woman, so curiously interesting to study, a woman whose influence has left such deep impressions upon France. Those words are Power and Astrology. Exclusively ambitious, Catherine de' Medici had no other passion than that of power. Superstitious and fatalistic, like so many superior men, she had no sincere belief except in occult sciences. Unless this double mainspring is known, the conduct of Catherine de' Medici will remain forever misunderstood.
>
> — Honoré de Balzac, *Catherine de' Medici, Part II, The Secrets of the Ruggieri*

Cosimo Ruggiero (whom the French called "Côme Ruggieri" or "Roger") came from a family of mathematicians, seers, physicians, and astrologers. His appearance at the French court was first chronicled in 1571. Many myths, rumors, and legends swirled around him during his life and after his death.

Honoré de Balzac, author of *Catherine de' Medici*, dedicates a chapter to Ruggiero, Catherine's principal astrologer. In it, he writes:

> There lived a man for whom Catherine cared more than for any of her children; his name was Cosimo

> Ruggiero. He lived in a house belonging to her, the hotel de Soissons; she made him her supreme adviser. It was his duty to tell her whether the stars ratified the advice and judgment of her ordinary counsellors. Certain remarkable antecedents warranted the power which Cosimo Ruggiero retained over his mistress to her last hour.

Balzac describes the close link between the Ruggieros and the de Medici family, saying:

> Ruggiero the elder was so highly valued by the Medici that the two dukes, Cosimo and Lorenzo, stood godfathers to his two sons. He cast, in concert with the famous mathematician, Basilio, the horoscope of Catherine's nativity, in his official capacity as mathematician, astrologer, and physician to the house of Medici.

Catherine's faith in her astrologers was well founded. The horoscope that Ruggiero's father divined at her birth proved to be startlingly accurate.

Balzac also notes:

> Many other circumstances corroborated Catherine's faith in the occult sciences. The night before the tournament at which Henri II was killed, Catherine saw the fatal blow in a dream. Her astrological council, then composed of Nostradamus and the two Ruggieri, had already predicted to her the death of the king. History has recorded the efforts made by Catherine to persuade her husband not to enter the lists.

Henri II died in July 1559, in a tragic jousting accident at the Hôtel des Tournelles (the Little Towers, today's site of the Place des Voges). Catherine, queen for only twelve years, suddenly found herself a widow. Her already uncertain situation was even more perilous. In 1555, Nostradamus wrote this quatrain which is thought to have predicted the tragic death of Henri II:

XXXV.

*Le lyon ieune le vieux surmontera,*
*En champ bellique par singulier duelle:*
*Dans cage d'or les yeux luy creuera,*
*Deux classes vne, puis mourir, mort cruelle.*

The young lion will overcome the older one,
in a field of combat in single fight:
He will pierce his eyes in their golden cage;
two wounds in one, then he dies a cruel death.

Henri had ordered a feast to celebrate peace with the Habsburgs of Austria and the marriage of his daughter, Elisabeth of Valois, to King Philip II of Spain. The week-long celebration included a tournament. Historical records confirm Catherine tried to talk Henri out of competing in the joust.

On June 30, King Henry did well in the joust...at first. The crowd noted that he wore black and white, the colors of Diane de Poitier. After besting several opponents, Catherine tried to persuade the king to retire. The tournament was practically over. Henri insisted on one more go with his strongest opponent, Gabriel de Lorges, the first Earl of Montgomery, one of the King's Scottish Guards. Montgomery tried to refuse, but Henri insisted. In their first pass, Montgomery struck a glancing blow off of the king's helmet, his lance shattering.

A long wooden splinter broke off and found its way through the narrow visor of the King's helmet, piercing Henry's eye and into his brain.

*Fig. 78 - German print depicting the fatal joust between King Henri II and Lorges (courtesy Wikimedia, public domain)*

The king reeled, being helped off of his horse, lest he fall. His helmet was removed, revealing a splinter "of a good bigness" according to a contemporary account. The king was carried to his apartments in the Château des Tournelles. The English ambassador, Nicholas Throckmorton, later wrote: "I noted him to be very weak... as he lay all along, he moved neither hand nor foot, but lay as one amazed." Henri died after ten days of agony.

Poor Montgomery was imprisoned for a time in the tower that still bears his name while authorities investigated the accident. Montgomery was eventually beheaded on the Place de Grève—the large square in front of the Hôtel de Ville—but not for killing the king; he later became a leader of the Huguenot (Protestant) rebellion against Catholic rule.

*Fig. 79 - The Hôtel de Sens was the Paris home of Nostradamus and today houses the Forney Library dedicated to the decorative arts (photo by the author)*

Catherine's other principal astrologer was Michel de Nostradame, *Nostradamus*, who came into her service late in his life. Nostradamus was a simple local doctor, regionally known as a healer who helped stem a serious outbreak of the plague in Marseille, Aix-en-Provence, and in Salon-de-Provence, where his house still exists.

Nostradamus' reputation as a seer grew after he began to publish his almanacs—a mixture of prophecy, advice, significant dates for planting, moon phases, etc. These quickly brought him a wider reputation in France and Italy. In 1555, he published Les Prophéties, a book that has been enthralling and mystifying people for centuries. It is a compilation of 942 quatrains (four-line stanzas or poems). It initially received a mixed reaction, but many of the French elite began to give it credence, which drew the attention of Queen Catherine.

Catherine summoned Nostradamus to Paris in July 1556, where he had an audience with her that lasted more than two hours. She demanded that he explain some verses that seemed to imply threats to her and her family. Impressed by his manner and his abilities, she had Nostradamus cast horoscopes for her and her children. Finding favor, Nostradamus was installed as a trusted confidante and advisor to the queen.

Nostradamus' readings seemed to predict unfortunate ends for her seven children, troubling her greatly. He also predicted—quite accurately—that all of her sons would become king. Sadly, he also prophesied she would outlive them all, which also proved to be true. All of her sons died on the throne.

Nostradamus served Catherine until he died in June 1567. He would not be the household name he is today without Catherine de Medici, who elevated his reputation as an astrologer and prognosticator.

Nostradamus was barely brushed by scandal during his life, a time when many who practiced the arts of astrology earned imprisonment, torture, and death. Once, while living in Montpellier, he was accused of heresy, but he avoided prosecution by leaving the city rather than stand trial.

Catherine's other astrologer left much less of an impression. Few historical traces of Cosimo Ruggiero's life remain. He appears in Balzac's historical novel and is mentioned briefly in Alexandre Dumas' *Marguerite de Valois*. Otherwise, the record is scant. Unlike

Nostradamus, he left virtually no writings other than an almanac compiled in 1604 under the pen name, Jean Querberus.

*Fig. 80 - Portrait of Michel de Nostredame (Nostradamus), painted by his son César de Nostredame (courtesy Wikimedia, public domain)*

Ruggiero stood accused of treasonous plots several times, most notoriously in the death of Catherine's son, Charles IX. He was also accused several times of using sorcery. Wax figures stuck full of pins, said to have been created to cause illness and death to Catherine's enemies, were found in his chambers.

Dumas recounts in detail the death of Charles, implying that Catherine had Ruggiero poison him. Ruggiero was convicted and sentenced to nine years hard labor as a prisoner on a galley ship, a sentence which he never served. Catherine pardoned him, restoring him to her service and even allowing him to open a school for astrologers. Pardoning a man accused of murdering her own son led some to suspect her involvement in a plot against Charles.

Catherine was also suspected of giving a gift of poisoned gloves to Jeanne d'Albret, a key leader of the Protestant Huguenots and the mother of Henri of Navarre, the future King Henri IV. In *Marguerite de Valois*, Dumas writes:

> Moreover, Jeanne de Navarre...had died scarcely two months before, and singular reports had been spread abroad as to her sudden death. It was everywhere whispered, and in some places said aloud, that she had discovered some terrible secret; and that Catharine de Médicis, fearing its disclosure, had poisoned her with perfumed gloves, which had been made by a man named Réné, a Florentine deeply skilled in such matters.

The record shows that this was a rumor, contrived decades later. Jeanne of Navarre died in June 1572 from what an autopsy revealed as tuberculosis.

Ruggiero did make one prediction that rocked Catherine to her core. He told her she would "die near Saint Germain." At the time, Catherine was building the Tuileries Palace. But the Tuileries, adjacent to the Louvre, was situated within the parish of the church Saint-Germain de l'Auxerrois. In 1572, she halted construction of the Tuileries and commissioned a new palace to be built well away from Saint-Germain de l'Auxerrois. The new palace, the *Place de la Reine*, was near St. Eustache church. It would later be renamed the *Hôtel de Soissons*. Attached to the new palace was the mysterious Doric column, hollow inside with a winding staircase that led to a platform at the top.

The Tuileries was not completed in Catherine's lifetime. Staying as far away as possible from anything associated with the name Saint-Germain, she passed away in 1589, at her palace in Blois. A priest came to give her the last rites. His name—Julien de St. Germain.

After Catherine's death, Ruggiero continued to practice his magical arts in and around the court. Ruggiero survived Catherine by many years, dying in his bed on March 28, 1615, at a ripe old age, just as he had predicted. His corpse, however, did not fare well. History records that he refused the sacrament of the last rites, cursing the priests who came to his bedchamber. The account spread throughout Paris, and his body was dragged through the streets. The bishop denied him a Christian burial, and his corpse was left by the side of the road.

Catherine's life—the politics, the factionalism, the internecine power struggles between various camps, the shifting alliances, the intrigue—was perilous. Any misstep meant losing one's life. She was a young girl of fourteen when she arrived in France and was thrust into a sea of intrigue and a religious struggle for power. To stay alive, she had to be constantly on her guard, using every ounce of determination, strength, wit, cunning, and guile she possessed—and the help of her astrologers.

Queen Catherine de Medici played the awful hand she had been dealt exceedingly well. She kept her head and kept her children on the throne, first François II, who died in 1560, less than a year after his father; then Charles IX who ruled for fourteen years until his death in 1574; then Henri III who ruled until *his* death in 1589; then her daughter Margaret as queen to Henri IV.

Catherine has been vilified by many historians and novelists, while others see her as misunderstood, a victim of slander by her enemies. No one doubts she was a master tactician and strategist, a political genius who combined luck and skill with ruthlessness and intelligence. Many others add that she was aided by supernatural forces.

Which takes us back to where we started, on the windswept platform of the *Colonne de l'Horoscope*. The column is a mystery to most people if they notice it at all. Overlooked amid all the more famous monuments in Paris, its position near the Bourse de Commerce helps it blend into that building so, unless one knows what one is looking at, it is easily passed by.

Shrouded in mystery, its importance lost in the centuries, the *Colonne de l'Horoscope* stands as a silent witness to Queen Catherine de Medici and her astrologers. Looking up at the platform on a moonless night, you might catch a glimpse of Catherine with Ruggiero awaiting news....

## Travelers' Tips

**Métro Station Saint Paul, Line 1 — Place des Vosges/Hôtel de Sully, Montgomery Tower, Hôtel de Sens (4th arr.)**

Three of the important sites in this chapter can be found within a short walk of each other, all in the Marais district.

The magnificent *Place des Vosges*, built by Henri IV in 1605, is off the Rue Saint-Antoine. Look for No. 62 Rue Saint-Antoine, which is the Hôtel Sully-Béthune. Entering the Place des Voges here leads to a fine example of a seventeenth-century *hôtel particulier*, a free-standing mansion, a style of elegance that only the wealthiest could afford.

As you walk through the *cour d'honneur*, hear the clatter of horse hooves and carriage wheels on the cobblestones, echoes from a time gone by. Notice the allegorical Four-Seasons bas-relief statues.

Before the garden is a bookstore. Today, the hôtel is home to the *Centre des monuments nationaux* of the Ministry of Culture and Communication, which manages France's public historic buildings and monuments.

At the back of the garden, past the orangerie, is a door. Through this "secret doorway" you will find the Place des Vosges, an early example of urban planning. The site of the Hôtel des Tournelles, where Henri II died from wounds inflicted in his tragic jousting accident, it was a huge estate, bounded on the south by the rue Saint-Antoine, on the east by the rue des Tournelles, on the west by the rue de Turenne, and on the north by the rue Saint-Gilles. Here was a fourteenth-century collection of buildings, spread over some twenty acres, including twenty chapels, several English-style pleasure grounds, and twelve galleries.

During the English occupation of Paris (1420-1436), des Tournelles was home to John of Lancaster, Duke of Bedford. After Henri II's death, Catherine had the Gothic complex demolished and sold off. She moved to the Louvre Palace, using the proceeds to build the Tuileries Palace and gardens.

Henri IV planned construction of this square, calling it the Place Royale. Construction took seven years, and it was completed in 1612. Surrounding the Square Louis XIII, the Place des Voges embodies Italian and French Renaissance architecture and the era's growing wealth. The style was unique at the time: uniform houses and façades of red brick with strips of inlaid stone and pitched roofs. Two of the houses at the center of the north and south sections rise higher than the others. These are the "Pavilion of the King and of the Queen," although no royal has ever lived here, except Anne of Austria, who briefly lived in the Pavilion de la Reine.

The name was changed from Place Royale during the French Revolution, but the present name dates from Emperor Napoleon, who needed money to finance his armies. He held a contest: the first department that paid their taxes got naming rights. The Vosges, a small department in the east of France, won, and it has been known as Place des Vosges ever since.

At No. 6 is the Victor Hugo Museum, home of the great author, the man who saved Notre Dame with his novel, *Notre-Dame de Paris* (*The Hunchback of Notre Dame*). Hugo lived here from 1832 to 1848. Admission is free. The Place des Voges, considered by many to be the most beautiful outdoor space in Paris, is a wonderful place to relax, stroll, or have a picnic.

Back on the rue Saint-Antoine is the beautiful Saint-Paul-Saint-Louis church. Ordered built by Louis XIII and dedicated by Louis XIV, it replaced a church dedicated in 1125 to Paul the Hermit. In the rear, left-hand side of the church, you will see a painting by Eugène Delacroix, *Christ in Agony on the Mount of Olives*, which he painted for the church.

Leaving the church by the east-side doorway, you will step into a medieval *passage.* At the end is the rue Saint Paul. Turn south toward the river Seine and a few steps away you will find the rue Charlemagne. A few blocks west on this street is a schoolyard playground bordered by a portion of the twelfth-century wall of Philip II. One of the largest sections of this ancient wall only hints at what was once a massive fortification, eighteen to twenty-four feet high and as much as nine feet wide, with towers and a rampart strong and thick enough to drive a cart on top. The wall enclosed both right and left banks, and was anchored by Philip II's new fortress, the Louvre.

Here, too, you will see what remains of the Montgomery Tower, where the earl was held after his tragic jousting accident with the king.

Just past the tower, head south down the Rue du Fauconnier toward the Seine, and you will come upon one of the few remaining medieval residences in Paris: the Hôtel de Sens on the Rue du Figuier (street of the Fig Trees). Today's home of the Bibliothèque Forney (Forney Art Library) replaced a hôtel built here in 1345. The Archbishop of Sens resided here until the late 1500s.

Margaret of Valois, daughter of Catherine and Henri II and queen to Henri IV, lived here in 1605 after her return from exile. The street name relates to the story (perhaps true) that Queen Margaret had the fig trees cut down to accommodate her carriage, which was too wide for the narrow, little street. Perhaps the fig trees of today are descended from those very same trees.

High up on the front wall is a cannonball fired during the "Three Glorious Days" (*Trois Glorieuses*) of the July 1830 Revolution. With the date engraved below, it is still there, lodged in the wall.

Most importantly, this was the Paris home of Michel de Nostradamus when Queen Catherine summoned him. Lee McCann, in *Nostradamus: The Man Who Saw Through Time*, writes:

> In lodging Nostradamus in the residence of the Cardinal de Bourbon, Archbishop of Sens, the King had rather cleverly served notice on scoffers that the man of prophecy was under the approval and protection of both royalty and the Church. It was a tacit warning to skeptics to hold their opinions in leash.

*Fig. 81 - Montgomery's Tower (foreground) and wall of Philippe-Auguste (Courtesy Wikimedia, public domain)*

**Métro Station Louvre-Rivoli, Line 1, 2 Rue de Viarnes (1st. arr.)**

**Bourse de Commerce (l'Hôtel de la Reine) Pinault Collection of Modern Art**

Catherine's palace, *l'Hôtel de la Reine* (later the *Hôtel de Soissons*) was completed in 1584 on the spot where the Bourse de Commerce stands today. The Hôtel de Soissons was demolished in 1748, but the *Medici Column* or *Colonne de l'Horoscope*, was saved by the city of Paris. Originally the Corn Exchange, or *Halle aux blés*, the Bourse became France's commodities exchange in 1885.

The Bourse and the Column were declared historic landmarks in 1975. The dome is actually a separate historic monument from 1811. When the original Bourse was replaced in 1888, the dome was preserved. Today, the Bourse is a museum of contemporary art that houses the Pinault Collection. Its planned opening in 2021 was put on hold during the COVID-19 pandemic.

*Fig. 82 - The Medici Column (photo by the author)*

## How Paris Shaped Our World

How would the world be different had Catherine de Medici not kept herself in power and her children on the throne of France? Although it's hard to say, we can trace some significant historical trends and world-changing results to Catherine.

### *Persecution of the Protestants (Huguenots)*

The violent sectarian strife between Catholics and Protestants from 1562 until 1598 was the central destabilizing force of Catherine's era. Historians believe that Catherine tried to be a moderate in the struggle, attempting to balance the two sides' irreconcilable interests.

Henri II's accidental death in 1559 left a power vacuum, and the factions tried to take advantage of the instability. Catherine, somewhat friendless and powerless, found herself and her children in a perilous situation. Her son François was only fifteen when he became king. Catherine was the natural choice for regent.

But others hungry for power took advantage of the situation. A "quiet" coup d'etat took place the day after Henri died. With his widow powerless to stop them, the Cardinal de Lorraine and the Duke de Guise seized power, taking up residence in the Louvre Palace with young King François II and his wife Mary Stuart, Guise's niece, who would later become Mary, Queen of Scots.

But François II died after barely a year on the throne. Catherine then became regent to her second son, King Charles IX. She issued the Edict of St. Germain in 1562, granting limited tolerance to French Protestants, known as "Huguenots." This attempt at moderation did not work. A massacre of Protestants at Vassy further inflamed the religious strife. Catherine found herself forced to become more militant, if only to ensure survival for herself and her children.

"*Un roi, une loi, une foi* (one king, one law, one faith) became her slogan. By 1572, the struggle had reached its height.

*Fig. 83* - St. Bartholomew's Day Massacre, *by François Dubois, a Huguenot painter. Admiral Coligny is seen being thrown out of his bedroom window after having been brutally murdered. (courtesy Wikimedia, public domain)*

Although a significant minority, many French Protestants were nobles or wealthy members of the rising class of merchants, skilled tradesmen, and landowners, so their political and economic power—greater than their numbers—could not be easily ignored.

People have long debated Catherine's role in the Saint Bartholomew's Day massacre. Historical accounts of her role are mixed. The events began in Paris on the night of August 23, 1572, and quickly spread to other cities in the ensuing days of bloodshed when thousands of Huguenots were slaughtered in an orgy of violence. Those lucky enough to escape the massacre fled France by the tens of thousands.

History is muddled on the roles various people played. The marriage of Catherine's daughter, Margaret of Valois, to the Protestant Henri of Navarre (later King Henri IV) set the stage. The slaughter began in the days following their wedding, August 18, 1572. Henri of Navarre's rightful claim to the throne was strengthened by the marriage. Militant Catholics were incensed and afraid.

Henri's relatives and other notable Protestant guests came to Paris to attend the wedding. Prominent Catholics, meanwhile, fearing a plot against their own lives, decided to strike first. Allegedly, they plotted to kill only the few Protestant leaders, and one in particular, Admiral de Coligny. But events spun out of control—whether by design or force of mob rule.

So, on the evening of August 23, de Coligny's home was invaded. He was dragged out of bed and murdered, his body thrown out of his chamber window. The king's Swiss Guard had a list of leading Protestants to find and kill. They hunted them down and murdered them.

Then, sometime around midnight, the bells of the church Saint-Germain l'Auxerrois, the parish church directly behind the Louvre, began to peal wildly. This signaled the citizens of Paris, who began to hunt down and attack their Protestant neighbors. Neither man, woman, nor child was spared if they were found. Newly married Henri escaped with his life, by hiding in his bride's closet.

No one knows how many were slaughtered altogether. Estimates range from 2,000 to 3,000 in Paris and 3,000 to 7,000 elsewhere. Some estimated that upwards of 25,000 to 30,000 were murdered. A contemporary accounts ledger from the city of Paris lists payments to workers for collecting and burying 1,100 bodies that washed up on the banks of the Seine.

Reactions to the slaughter were mixed. Pope Gregory XIII ordered a celebration Mass to be sung and had frescos commissioned, one depicting the murder of de Coligny. King Phillip II of Spain, known for being perpetually dour and humorless, was said to have laughed upon hearing the news.

Average Catholics were shocked by the events. A backlash to extreme fundamentalist Catholicism grew. Membership increased in moderate Catholic organizations, and Protestantism experienced a wave of conversions. Monarchs in Protestant countries swiftly condemned the violence and threatened retaliation. Queen Elizabeth I of England, whose ambassador had barely escaped Paris with his life, was especially enraged.

Protestants had been leaving France for decades due to violence and persecution. Huguenots were subjected to forced conversions. They had their children taken from them and given to Catholic families. They were prohibited from practicing certain professions. Special taxes were levied on them. These and other indignities caused a steady exodus, mainly to Protestant countries like England, Switzerland, and the Netherlands. Prussia especially welcomed the refugees to rebuild a population and economy decimated by war.

Some Huguenots had already gone to the New World, one enclave eventually settling along the Saint John's river near present day Jacksonville, Florida in 1564. Later, in the seventeenth century, other Huguenot communities were founded in New York, Delaware, Pennsylvania, New Jersey, and Virginia. The British colonies welcomed these industrious and skilled refugees and even provided funds to help them relocate.

After the Saint Bartholomew's Day massacre, the steady stream became a flood. The effect on France's economy was notable.

Huguenots, largely members of a rising, prosperous, industrious, and creative middle class, took their skills and industry with them. By destroying the heart of French Huguenot society, France lost untold economic might.

To become king, Henri IV recanted his Protestantism and converted to Catholicism. He is rumored to have said, "Paris is well worth a Mass." Crowned in 1589, Henri IV became one of France's greatest monarchs, embarking on a great program of modernization, exploration, foreign alliances, and trade, significantly curtailing France's wars and their accompanying costs. Henri opened up New France in the Americas, sending explorers like Samuel de Champlain to claim land for France.

Henri also proclaimed the *Edict of Nantes*, declaring peace between Protestants and Catholics and granting Protestants rights as citizens of France. The document largely put an end to the Wars of Religion, although future monarchs would resume persecution of Protestants. After Louis XIV revoked the Edict of Nantes in 1685 by the Edict of Fontainebleau, even more Protestants fled France. All of this persecution over two centuries likely contributed to the decades of economic stagnation, poverty, and famine that led directly to the French Revolution of 1789.

### *Perfume*

> *"....the peasant stank as did the priest, the apprentice as did his master's wife, the whole of the aristocracy stank, even the king himself stank, stank like a rank lion, and the queen like an old goat, summer and winter."*
>
> — Patrick Süskind, *Perfume: The Story of a Murderer*

Catherine brought a large retinue of Italians with her: ladies-in-waiting, maids, pages, cooks, etc., and of course, Ruggiero, her astrologer. She also brought with her someone who would launch an entire industry for France: René Bianchi (René de Florentin), her personal perfumer. De Florentin became a favorite of the teenage Catherine by creating a scent he called *Acqua della Regina* (Water of the Queen).

Prior to Catherine's arrival, perfume was largely unknown in the French court, while Italian nobles had been using perfume for more than a century. The origins of perfumes lay in Egypt before coming to Europe in the 1300s from Arabia. Modern *par fume*, (literally "by smoke") was first fashioned in Hungary, and was known as "Hungary Water." Created by blending scented oils with alcohol, perfume became fashionable in Renaissance Italy among the wealthy. Italians refined the production of scents, which made their way to France with Catherine.

While de Florentin maintained a shop off the Pont Saint Michel, he also had a laboratory in the Louvre connected to the queen's apartments via a secret passage to protect the formulas for his rare and marvelous scents from being stolen. Catherine and de Florentin introduced to the French court the Italian fashion of perfumed gloves, known as "sweet gloves."

Leather gloves were then very popular, but adding perfume to the leather was difficult, largely because the tanning process of the day used animal urine, which gave the gloves a smooth texture and a foul smell. Perfumed gloves became all the rage in the French court, and the demand for signature scents kept de Florentin busy.

In fact, the demand became so great, an entire industry sprung up to supply the raw materials for the scents that went into making perfume.

Flowers like jasmine, lavender, and rose were used, along with scents like musk and bergamot, fruits, woods, and other substances. Although today the famous perfumeries—Chanel, Galimard, Dior, Fragonard, Houbigant, Caron, and others—are headquartered in Paris, the French perfume industry is actually centered in the small village of Grasse, northwest of Nice. High up in the hills off the Mediterranean coast, Grasse has the mild climate important for the natural aromas that are needed to produce fragrances.

Currently, the French perfume industry involves more than sixty different companies, employing some 3,500 people in Grasse alone. Grasse has kept up with current trends by manufacturing modern (and cheaper) synthetic scents, but its natural fragrances are still key to Grasse's fame.

Grasse is also home to the International Perfume Museum and the Fragonard Museum, which offer free guided tours. At perfume museums and ateliers in Grasse (or at the ones in Paris), for about €55 you can spend several hours learning about the art of perfumery, and try your hand at building a signature perfume of your own.

France's multi-billion-dollar perfume industry started with Catherine de Medici and her master perfumer. Today, the fragrance sector is second only to cosmetics in France's health and beauty industry. The global fragrance market is expected to grow to $70 billion by 2022, and France leads the world as the largest fragrance producer and exporter. *L'Oréal* alone had a total market share valued at 14 percent in 2013.

### *Ballet*

The first *ballet de cour* took place in 1573 when Catherine introduced this new, Italian form of entertainment to the French court. In those days, the dance was not performed by professional dancers but by her courtiers and ladies-in-waiting. It was not done on a stage, but in the great hall of the palace with the spectators standing alongside. The first performance so stunned the French that they swore the dancers looked as though they were flying, and the "Flying Squadron" was born.

The words *ballet* and *ball* come from the Italian *ballare* meaning "to dance." Dancers wore masks and costumes that were quite restrictive—beautiful to look at but difficult to move in. Dance steps were rudimentary: little hops and slides, elaborate curtsies, strolling promenades, and turns. Ballet shoes were unknown, so dancers wore formal dress shoes.

*Fig. 84 - King Louis IV as Apollo, the Sun King "Ballet de la Nuit," by Henry de Gissey (1653) (courtesy Wikimedia, public domain)*

During the reign of Louis XIV, the king himself performed in the dance with professional dancers taking over after the king and the courtiers finished. Louis was one of the great innovators of baroque ballet, which evolved to become classical ballet. In 1661, he established the *Académie Royale de Danse*. The Académie formed the standards for the various styles of dance, established the five classical ballet positions, and began to examine and certify dance teachers.

Over time, the court dances grew so large and elaborate that eventually performances were put up on a stage so larger audiences could watch the spectacles. Ballet spread to other countries, notably Russia. French and Russian styles began to emerge.

In 1909, Russian theatre producer Serge Diaghilev brought Russia's most talented dancers and choreographers to Paris. Together with composers like Igor Stravinsky, singers, and set designers like Pablo Picasso and Henri Matisse, he formed the Ballet Russes. Based in Paris at the Théâtre Champs-Elysées, the Ballet Russes featured the Polish dancer and choreographer Vaslav Nijinsky.

They toured America and Europe, once performing in the Hall of Mirrors at Versailles, taking ballet back to its earliest roots, while simultaneously launching ballet into the twentieth century. The Ballet Russes' premier of a new ballet, *The Rite of Spring* (*Le Sacre du Printemps*) in 1913, with choreography by Vaslav Nijinsky and music by Stravinsky, shocked audiences, causing a riot at its premiere. Ballet grew popular in America when, in the 1930s a few of Diaghilev's dancers settled in the US. George Balanchine, founder of the New York City Ballet was among the best known.

Catherine introduced other innovations to France, which then spread to the rest of the world. New fashions came to the French court, such as women wearing stylish high-heeled shoes. Other Italian innovations followed. Forks as an eating utensil were unknown prior to her arrival. Italian cuisine, with pastas and "exotic" vegetables like tomatoes and zucchini, also became more widely known.

Had Catherine not accomplished her forty-year-plus political balancing act, with the help of her astrologers, Nostradamus and Ruggiero, France and the world today would likely be very different. We can only guess at the full extent of Catherine de Medici's influence on us all.

Certainly the world would not have seen a mass exodus of Protestants from France, which in turn strengthened the economic growth of other countries and contributed to France's economic troubles in the centuries that followed. We would not have ballet as we now know it. Nostradamus would likely not be the household name he is today, but might have remained merely a provincial doctor with an eye on the future.

Queen Catherine Maria Romula di Lorenzo de' Medici was one of the most influential women in history. She deserves to be recognized more widely. Yet, other than the judgment of some historians who have treated her harshly, the most lasting memorial to her is the peculiar lone column at the edge of Les Halles in Paris, *en'cased in iron* and shrouded in mystery.

# Chapter 10
# The Phantom's Lake

*"There are 2,531 doors and 7,593 keys; 14 furnaces and grates heat the house; the gas-pipes if connected would form a pipe almost 16 miles long; 9 reservoirs, and two tanks hold 22,222 gallons of water.... 538 persons have places assigned wherein to change their attire. The musicians have a foyer with 100 closets for their instruments."*
— Excerpt from *Scribner's Magazine*, 1879

STEP INTO BOX 5, please. The orchestra has just started playing the swirling music of tonight's opera and the curtain is about to rise. Time to take your seats...but wait. What is this? Someone, a man, is in the box. He has not removed his top hat nor his cloak. He is sitting very still and intently watching the unmoving curtain, waiting for it to disappear up into the proscenium and for the stage to be flooded with light. You move to ask what he is doing in your box, but something stops you. Instead, you quietly back out and say to the usher, "Please find us another seat."

You are at the Paris Opéra House, known as the *Palais Garnier*. It is April 1910, and the man in the top hat is Gaston Leroux. He has just published his book, a tale which was serialized the year before in a popular magazine, *Le Gaulois*. The book is called, *Le Fantôme de l'Opera* (*The Phantom of the Opera*). He is here tonight, as he is every night when there is a performance, looking for the character he made famous: the Phantom of the Opera.

Gaston Leroux (1868-1927) was a French investigative journalist who would swear until his dying day that the story he unfolded was not fiction, but a true account of events that actually happened in the years after the Palais Garnier Opéra House first opened in January 1875. To emphasize this assertion, the book's prologue begins:

> IN WHICH THE AUTHOR OF THIS SINGULAR WORK INFORMS THE READER HOW HE ACQUIRED THE CERTAINTY THAT THE OPERA GHOST REALLY EXISTED
>
> The Opera ghost really existed. He was not, as was long believed, a creature of the imagination of the artists, the superstition of the managers, or a product of the absurd and impressionable brains of the young ladies of the ballet, their mothers, the box-keepers, the cloak-room attendants or the concierge. Yes, he existed in flesh and blood, although he assumed the complete appearance of a real phantom; that is to say, of a spectral shade.

Leroux goes on to write:

> The events do not date more than thirty years back; and it would not be difficult to find at the present day, in the foyer of the ballet, old men of the highest respectability, men upon whose word one could absolutely rely, who would remember as though they

> happened yesterday the mysterious and dramatic conditions that attended the kidnapping of Christine Daaé, the disappearance of the Vicomte de Chagny and the death of his elder brother, Count Philippe, whose body was found on the bank of the lake that exists in the lower cellars of the Opera on the rue Scribe side. But none of those witnesses had until that day thought that there was any reason for connecting the more or less legendary figure of the Opera ghost with that terrible story.

Leroux strongly emphasizes that his account is factual. He even asserts he has a "duty as a historian" to tell the tale. Was there really a Phantom of the Opera? Is the story true? Is there a lake? Did the chandelier fall? Did Christine Daaé and the Count, the "opera ghost" and the Persian (the Phantom's faithful servant) actually exist? To answer these questions, we need to leave M. Leroux in Box 5 and travel back a few decades, before the opening of the opera house, back to the winter of 1857-58....

Charles Louis Napoleon Bonaparte (Emperor Napoleon III) loved the opera, and on a cold January night he was just arriving via carriage at the *Salle Le Peletier*, located on the rue le Peletier, to attend the Opéra de Paris. The Opera had been housed there in "temporary" quarters since the last opera house burnt to the ground in 1821. Le Peletier was inadequate for most productions, but talk and plans for a new opera house had come and gone.

As fate would have it, as the emperor stepped from his carriage into the narrow street, a would-be assassin rushed toward him. The emperor's bodyguards whisked Napoleon III into the opera house, and his attacker was apprehended.

Emperor Napoleon III, along with his Prefect of the Seine, Baron Georges-Eugène Haussmann, had already started turning Paris into one big construction site, bulldozing entire neighborhoods and erecting new railway stations, hospitals, and aqueducts, designing parks and gardens, and creating the wide boulevards for which Paris would become famous. The assassination attempt was enough to compel Napoleon III to add one more building project to the list: a new opera house—one with a private entrance the emperor could use to safely enter and exit the building.

By imperial decree, a site was chosen in 1860 and a design competition was announced that December. Each entrant to the competition was to create a motto to summarize their vision. Young Charles Garnier entered his plans and designs under the Italian motto *Bramo assai, poco spero* (Hope for much, expect little). Garnier was a graduate of the prestigious *École Royale des Beaux-Arts de Paris*, studying extensively in Rome, Greece, and Turkey.

Chosen as one of the finalists out of some 170 entrants, Garnier had to contend with political, stylistic, and engineering challenges as well as personal attacks. The Empress Eugénie was annoyed that her preferred candidate—the great architect Viollet-le-Duc, then in the process of restoring Notre Dame to its Gothic glory—did not make the cut as a finalist. She confronted Garnier, a relative unknown.

"What is this?" she demanded after seeing his plans and sketches. "It is not a style; it is not Louis Quatorze, nor Louis Quinze, nor Louis Seize!"

"Why, ma'am," replied Garnier, "it is Napoleon Trois." (Napoleon the Third)

And so it was. The style that became known as *Napoleon III* or *Second Empire* was eclectic, taking freely from Gothic, Renaissance, and the Louis XV and Louis XVI styles. Émile Zola, no fan of either the emperor or the empire, called it, "The opulent bastard child of all styles."

Garnier and his contemporaries made innovative use of modern materials, such as iron frameworks and glass skylights, combining them with the architectural elements of the French Renaissance, Palladian, and French Baroque architecture, while giving it all a strikingly new coherence and harmony.

Garnier was also sometimes subjected to harsh public ridicule for his humble origins and his looks. His father, Jean, had been a blacksmith, wheelwright, and coachbuilder before moving to Paris and finding work renting out horse-drawn carriages.

A young but promising student of the École Royale des Beaux-Arts de Paris, Garnier won the Premier Grand Prix de Rome in 1848 when he was just twenty-three.

The era was a period of great upheaval, politically, socially, economically, and culturally. Lines were drawn between those who saw Garnier as an upstart, taking prizes and commissions that ought to go to his betters, and those who saw him as a shining example of a new egalitarianism being ushered in amid a wave of new wealth and the destruction of the old structures of class, nobility, and entitlement.

Construction on the opera house that would eventually bear Garnier's name began in 1862, in an area just off the Boulevard des Capucines. The project quickly ran into problems. The foundation had been dug deep to support the immense structure, especially in the rear where the stage would be located. It had to be high enough to allow scenery as tall as fifty feet to be raised and lowered. But while excavating the foundation, groundwater flooded the site.

*Fig. 85 - Portrait of Charles Garnier.*
*(anonymous circa 1880, courtesy Wikimedia, public domain)*

Nothing the builders tried worked, including running pumps twenty-four hours a day for eight months.

Finally, Garnier hit upon an ingenious solution: he would double the foundation. The inner foundation would safely hold the water, keeping it from undermining the building's structural foundation. Simultaneously, the water pressure in the reservoir would prevent more groundwater from flowing in. And as an added benefit, the ensuing lake could serve as a ready source of water should a fire break out, an all too common occurrence in theaters and opera houses.

So, one mystery is already put to rest: Yes, there is a lake under the Paris Opera House that still exists today. It is some sixty yards long and up to twelve feet deep in places. It is even home to a species of laré fish, ghostly white and blind, living in the perpetual darkness of the cellars and fed by opera house employees.

The cavernous cellars and the underground lake must certainly connect to the larger underground passages found around the opera and beyond to the subterranean labyrinth well known beneath Paris. It doesn't take much imagination to realize how easily the Phantom could enter and exit the opera house unseen, making a home down there on the banks of the lake, hidden away from the world.

The Palais Garnier encountered other obstacles before it was completed, including financial and political ones. And a war. Emperor Napoleon III unwisely engaged in a fight with Prussia, resulting in the Franco-Prussian war of 1870. All construction on the opera house was halted for more than a year.

The war went badly for the French. Its army was quickly defeated and the emperor captured on September 2nd at the Battle of Sedan. On September 19, 1870, the Prussian army encircled Paris. The city refused to surrender, and so began a terrible months-long siege.

Nothing came in or went out of Paris from September 19 to January 28, 1871.

The situation became dire as December temperatures dropped to -15°C (5°F). The Seine froze solid. The city suffered shortages of wood and coal. The City of Lights went dark. Communication with the outside world was almost entirely cut off. Balloons were tried, but were easily shot down, as were carrier pigeons. Letters stuffed into iron balls were floated down the Seine.

Soon food ran low, and medicines, yet the Parisians still refused to surrender. They began to forage for whatever they could find to eat, including cats, dogs, rats, pigeons, and eventually, the animals at the Paris Zoo in the Jardin des Plantes, including Castor and Pollux, the zoo's beloved elephants.

After several months with no sign of weakening Parisian resolve, the Prussian army bombarded Paris with its heavy guns. This assault caused the city finally to surrender and the Prussians entered Paris at the end of January 1871.

The defeat marked the end of the Second Empire. Sadly, Charles Louis Napoleon Bonaparte would never set foot in the Palais Garnier or see one of his beloved operas in the Paris Opera House. When the emperor was captured at the Battle of Sedan, the Empress Eugénie fled the city ahead of the Prussian advance. The emperor was deposed two days later. Released by the Prussians in 1871, he "retired" to England where he died and is buried in St. Michael's Abbey, Hampshire.

Into the power vacuum created by the fall of the Second Empire, Republican and other "radical" deputies in the National Assembly proclaimed the Third French Republic and swiftly formed a "Government of National Defence" to continue the war. As the

Prussian army descended on Paris, this new government packed up and fled to Tours. Surrounded and besieged, Parisians endured the harsh winter and famine while their new government abandoned Paris.

Within two months after the end of the war, in March of 1871, a revolutionary movement rose up against the new government, a movement known as the Paris Commune. The "Communards," as they were also called, were dedicated to principles of equality and fulfilling the ideals of the French Revolution and those espoused by the radical young thinker, Karl Marx. The Paris Commune marks the world's first attempt at governing under the principles of Communism.

The Paris Commune never had a chance, barely lasting two months. By mid-May, the Republicans and the French army moved into Paris in a bloody and brutal show of force, fighting street to street, neighborhood to neighborhood, to take back the city.

*The New York Times* reported on May 26, 1871:

> At 5 o'clock in the afternoon, the Versaillists [French government troops] carried the Opera-house. The people rush out clapping their hands, and give wine and money to the troops. Over Paris hang pillars of dense smoke so many that they cannot be counted. Now and then a sudden sharp crack, followed by a dull thud, is heard; a convolvulus-shaped volume of smoke rises, as from Vesuvius in eruption, and Paris rocks to its center.

The end of the Paris Commune marked the beginning of *La Belle Époque,* which lasted from 1871 until the start of the First World War in 1914.

*Fig. 86 - Barricades of the Paris Commune, April 1871. Corner of the Place de l'Hôtel-de-Ville and the Rue de Rivoli. (courtesy Wikimedia, public domain)*

During *La Belle Époque*, the Eiffel Tower, the Paris Métro, the Paris Opera, and the Basilica of Sacré-Cœur were all built. The Impressionists—Lautrec, Manet, Monet, and Renoir—were beginning their ascent. Debussy, Saint-Saëns, and Bizet were composing vibrant new works. Rimbaud, Zola, and Proust were rising literary stars. And Leroux was writing *The Phantom of the Opera*.

*Fig. 87 - Rue de Rivoli after the suppression of the Commune, May 1871. In the distance is the Hotel de Ville, which was set on fire. (courtesy Wikimedia, public domain)*

What does the Paris Commune have in common with the Phantom? The unfinished opera house, centrally located in the heart of Paris, was a focal point for Communist activity and saw some of the heaviest fighting that ensued as the French government took back the city. Some of the worst battles took place at the Place de l'Opèra and the nearby Place Vendôme, where the Communards tore down the column and statue that were erected to celebrate Napoleon's victory at Austerlitz.The Communards stored food and ammunition inside the opera house and held prisoners in its cavernous cellars. The Communards' use of the opera house and its underground labyrinth is vital evidence in Leroux's case to prove the Phantom really existed.

> Christine opened a box, took out an enormous key, and showed it to Raoul.
>
> "What's that?" he asked.
>
> "The key of the gate to the underground passage in the Rue Scribe."
>
> "I understand, Christine. It leads straight to the lake. Give it to me, Christine, will you?"
>
> "Never!" she said. "That would be treacherous!"

As Christine Daaé says to Raoul in Chapter Eleven, "Everything that is underground belongs to him!"

"Paris has another Paris under herself," Victor Hugo wrote in 1862, in *Les Misérables*. Indeed, countless books have been written about the mysteries of subterranean Paris. From the catacombs in the south to the maze of tunnels in Montmartre, underground Paris has fascinated people for centuries. The subterranean world in and around the opera is where the Phantom lives and rules unchallenged.

Christine and Raoul retrace the route of the Communards' secret way in and out of the opera house:

"We were to go by the Communists' road and through the trapdoor."

The Communists' road—the tunnel the Communards used to move troops, armaments, and prisoners—ties the historical events of the Paris Commune to the Phantom, the vital evidence being presented by Leroux, the investigative journalist.

With the war with Prussia over and the Paris Commune defeated, the opera house was finally completed in 1874. On January 5, 1875, it was officially named the *Académie Nationale de Musique—Théâtre de l'Opéra*, and the Palais Garnier was formally inaugurated with a lavish gala performance by the opera company, the orchestra, and the ballet company.

Leroux's tale chronicles the years soon after the opera house opens. He immediately answers the question on everyone's mind: Did the Phantom really live? Leroux answers with a resounding "Yes!" But can it be proven? Leroux certainly tries, using his evidence and pasting together the historical events. Whether the opera ghost really existed or was a figment of Gaston Leroux's imagination will probably never truly be known.

But we can at least put the question into perspective, using what survives today to help us understand the enthralling mystique and romance of the Phantom. Just like Christine Daaé, we have been held captive by the Phantom. So what evidence *does* Leroux give us that we can verify? Can we trace the outlines of reality in the mystery of the Phantom?

### *Peasant Girl Becomes an Opera Diva*

The character of Christine Daaé is a good place to start. She is beloved by the Viscount Raoul de Chagny, by the Phantom, and by the opera-going public. But who was she? Was she a character Leroux made up or a real person, with only "her name changed to protect the innocent"?

Many believe that character of Christine Daaé was modeled on the real-life opera star Christina (or Christine) Nilsson. Similarities between Nilsson and Daaé lead us to that conclusion: Christine Nilsson *was* Christine Daaé. Most obviously, both Nilsson and Daaé were blonde-haired, blue-eyed Swedish opera singers who trained in Paris.

Christine Nilsson was born in August 1843 in Sweden and died there in 1921, like Daaé. Nilsson's brother, Karl, was a violin player. In the novel, Daaé's father is a violin virtuoso. Both these budding singers came from poverty, being poor peasant girls who sang for their supper. Both were discovered singing in the marketplace. Both Daaé in the novel and Nilsson in reality were taken under the patronage of men who recognized their talent and gave them formal training.

*Fig. 88 - Christina Nilsson, the real Christine Daaé (courtesy Wikimedia, public domain)*

In Nilsson's case, she was discovered by the magistrate Fredrik Tornérhjelm while she was singing in a market in Ljungby. He was so taken by her raw talent that he took charge of her training. In the novel, Christine Daaé is discovered in a market in Ljimby:

> The nearer he drew to her, the more fondly he remembered the story of the little Swedish singer....
>
> There was once, in a little market-town not far from Upsala, a peasant who lived there with his family, digging the earth during the week and singing in the choir on Sundays. This peasant had a little daughter to whom he taught the musical alphabet before she knew how to read. Daaé's father was a great musician, perhaps without knowing it. Not a fiddler throughout the length and breadth of Scandinavia played as he did.... Then the father, who cared only for his daughter and his music, sold his patch of ground and went to Upsala in search of fame and fortune. He found nothing but poverty.
>
> He returned to the country, wandering from fair to fair, strumming his Scandinavian melodies, while his child, who never left his side, listened to him in ecstasy or sang to his playing. One day, at Ljimby Fair, Professor Valerius heard them and took them to Gothenburg.
>
> (Chapter Five: The Enchanted Violin)

Both sopranos ended up in Paris where they studied, Nilsson for four years before she first appeared at the Théâtre Lyrique in 1864, making her début as Violetta in Giuseppe Verdi's *La Traviata.* Her success was not immediate, however. In fact, one contemporary gave a very unenthusiastic review of her performance.

In *A Star of Song! The Life of Christina Nilsson* by Guy de Charnacé, published in France in 1868 as *L'Etoile du Chant*, the author recalls:

> Her Scandinavian accent, at this time very apparent, also offended the Parisians....
>
> ...although her debut had been much talked of, it did not produce the expected effect. In reference to the impression she then made on me, I find the following lines in my journal: A slender blonde...an actress intelligent but yet a novice, with an accent too northern for a Parisian boudoir.... An unequal singer, with very brilliant notes in the higher scale, dull and feeble in the intermediate, while the lower notes are veiled. Such, to me, appeared Mile. Nilsson in the role of Violetta....

However, four years later in March 1868, Nilsson appeared as Ophelia in Ambroise Thomas' *Hamlet* to thunderous applause and universal acclaim. After this triumph, she quickly rose to worldwide fame, performing throughout Europe and North America. Composer Peter Tchaikovsky heard her sing the role of Margarita in Gounod's opera *Faust* in Moscow in 1872, and praised her performance as one which epitomized the vision of *Faust's* author Goethe. Nilsson made such an impression she even appears as a brief mention in Leo Tolstoy's novel *Anna Karenina*.

There seems to be only one significant difference between Christine Nilsson and Christine Daaé. Nilsson never performed at the Palais Garnier Opera House. Her Ophelia was staged at the old *Salle Le Peletier* in the last years before it burned to the ground in 1873. There is some evidence that she was scheduled to make an appearance at the Palais Garnier, but she mysteriously cancelled.

Clearly, Christine Nilsson is the novel's Christine Daaé, the poor Swedish peasant girl with the raw singing talent, whom the Phantom transforms into the greatest soprano of the age. Her real-life career so closely mirrors that of the novel's heroine that we can conclude there was a real Christine who enthralled audiences in the great opera houses of Paris.

Gounod's *Faust* debuted in March 1859, at Théâtre Lyrique with Marie Miolan-Carvalho, the aging soprano who might have inspired Leroux's character Carlotta. Critics of her performance in the role of Margarita were cruel, describing her voice as thin and shrill.

Early in the novel, Daaé sings the role as Carlotta's understudy. Her performance is unexpectedly remarkable, with a passion so great she faints on stage after finishing the song. Later on, Raoul hears her talking to someone in her dressing room. She said, "I gave you my soul tonight." Christine has become suddenly famous and a rival to Carlotta.

The Phantom will have no other sing the role. He sends a note to the house managers insisting that Christine Daae sing the role of Margarita. He threatens:

> The part of Margarita shall be sung this evening by Christine Daaé. Never mind about Carlotta; she will be ill....
>
> If you refuse, you will give *Faust* to-night in a house with a curse upon it.
>
> Take my advice and be warned in time. O. G. [Opera Ghost]

Carlotta, a spoiled prima donna, has been the lead soprano of the Paris Opera for many years. At her home on the Faubourg St. Honoré she receives a similar note among her correspondence:

> If you appear to-night, you must be prepared for a great misfortune at the moment when you open your

> mouth to sing...a misfortune worse than death.
>
> The letter took away Carlotta's appetite for breakfast. She pushed back her chocolate, sat up in bed and thought hard.

Carlotta and the theater managers decide not to heed the Phantom's warnings, so she performs that night. In the midst of her performance, the Phantom puts a "frog" in her throat.

> At that moment, at that identical moment, the terrible thing happened... Carlotta croaked like a toad:
>
> "Co-ack!"
>
> Every one felt that the thing was not natural, that there was witchcraft behind it. That toad smelt of brimstone. Poor, wretched, despairing, crushed Carlotta!
>
> (Chapter Seven: *Faust* and What Followed)

***The Deadly Chandelier***

The opera house's great chandelier is more than twenty feet tall and made of bronze with golden crystals. Installed in 1874, it was gas-lit with some 340 gas nozzles. Electrification came in the 1880s with some 320 light bulbs.

The chandelier becomes a symbol for many (some would say evidence) that the rumors of an opera ghost were real. On May 20, 1896, during a performance of *Helle*, as the first act came to a close and the aria reached its crescendo, a counterweight from the great chandelier came crashing down into the audience, killing one person.

In the novel, the entire chandelier falls, the fulfillment of the Phantom's curse when the managers ignore his ultimatum to let Christine Daaé sing *Faust*. As the audience's tumultuous uproar grows, and Carlotta's mysterious and persistent "co-ack" prevents her from singing, the Phantom exclaims:

> SHE IS SINGING TO-NIGHT TO BRING THE CHANDELIER DOWN!
>
> With one accord, they raised their eyes to the ceiling and uttered a terrible cry. The chandelier, the immense mass of the chandelier was slipping down, coming toward them, at the call of that fiendish voice. Released from its hook, it plunged from the ceiling and came smashing into the middle of the stalls, amid a thousand shouts of terror. A wild rush for the doors followed.
>
> The papers of the day state that there were numbers wounded and one killed. The chandelier had crashed down upon the head of the wretched woman who had come to the Opera for the first time in her life....
>
> (Chapter Seven: *Faust* and What Followed)

In fact it was a counterweight that came down when a wire snapped after being weakened by a fire. The counterweight injured a number of people and killed one, the unlucky Madame Chomette, the concierge of a nearby boarding house, who was excited to see her first opera.

The falling chandelier is the dramatic climax to Act I in Andrew Lloyd Webber's production of *The Phantom of the Opera*. The spectacular stage effect brings to life Leroux's embellishment of an actual, historical event that caught the attention of the world. The Phantom rules the opera house, and he will not be disobeyed!

**TRAGEDY AT THE OPERA.**

**Details of an Accident at Paris That Almost Caused a Panic.**

Paris Dispatch to The London News

When the accident at the Opera occurred Mme. Rose Caron was singing at the close of the first act of "Hellé." It was noticed that the lights had been fluctuating in an extraordinary manner, causing much annoyance as well as apprehension on the part of the audience.

The enormous chandelier is balanced by eight counterweights, each hanging from

*Fig. 89* - New York Times *article, June 7, 1896 (courtesy* NY Times *Machine, public domain)*

***Skeletons and Phonograph Records***

The discovery of skeletons in the cellars of the opera house during Leroux's time makes the reality of the Phantom a historical "fact" we can believe in:

> And, now, what do they mean to do with that skeleton? Surely they will not bury it in the common grave!... I say that the place of the skeleton of the opera ghost is in the archives of the National Academy of Music. It is no ordinary skeleton.
>
> (Epilogue)

Leroux asserts at the start he can prove the discovered skeleton is not a victim of the Paris Commune. It is the remains of the opera ghost.

> It will be remembered that, later, when digging in the substructure of the Opera...the workmen laid bare a corpse. Well, I was at once able to prove that this corpse was that of the Opera ghost...it is now a matter of supreme indifference to me if the papers pretend that the body was that of a victim of the Commune.
>
> The wretches who were massacred, under the Commune, in the cellars of the Opera, were not buried on this side; I will tell where their skeletons can be found in a spot not very far from that immense crypt which was stocked during the siege with all sorts of provisions....
>
> (Prologue)

While there are no historic accounts of bodies being unearthed at the Paris Opera, in 1907, recordings were made and sealed away in the cellar to preserve the voices of famous singers of the day. Leroux weaves this historic fact into the story.

Indeed, Leroux refers to an actual event: twenty-four wax phonograph discs were hidden away in the deepest levels of the opera house, containing the voices of the opera singers of that day: Nellie Melba, Adelina Patti, Emma Calvé, and the great Enrico Caruso. On Christmas Eve 1907, Alfred Clark, president of the Gramophone Company, donated the recordings to be sealed away in a room in the opera's vast sub-cellars with strict instructions that they not be opened until the year 2007. This was a gift to the future as well as a clever marketing ploy. Clark's Gramophone company was promoting its new flat wax discs (records) as a superior medium to the round wax cylinders that Edison pioneered.

A few years later, more recordings were added, along with a gramophone, some foresighted person realizing that in the future technology would likely change. And in 2007, the recordings were unearthed. Someone had stolen the gramophone and a few of the recordings were damaged, but those voices from the past sang in the Phantom's mysterious lair one hundred years later.

This event is so important that the novel starts and ends in the chamber where the recordings were interred. In his novel, Leroux alleges workers came upon a body in 1907 while they were preparing one of the vaulted chambers to house the phonograph recordings.

The corpse, as Leroux asserts, was not one of the victims of the Paris Commune imprisoned in the cellars, but that of the real Phantom of the Opera. Erik, dejected, disfigured, and in despair from his unrequited love, went to his rooms in his underground lair and sealed himself up where he died of starvation and a broken heart.

*Fig. 90 - Paris Opera officials prepare to seal away wax discs, recordings of the era, to be reopened in 100 years (courtesy Opéra National de Paris, public domain)*

### *Gaston Leroux and Erik: The Reporter and the Living Corpse*

Leroux gives us a good deal of biographical information about Erik, the man he claims is the opera ghost. He tells Erik's story, a child disfigured and hidden away from the world who came to possess many talents.

> Erik was born in a small town not far from Rouen. He was the son of a master-mason. He ran away at an early age from his father's house, where his ugliness was a subject of horror and terror to his parents. For a time, he frequented the fairs, where a showman exhibited him as the "living corpse." He seems to have crossed the whole of Europe, from fair to fair, and to have completed his strange education as an artist and magician at the very fountain-head of art and magic, among the Gipsies.

Leroux, born in 1868, initially was going to be a lawyer, but instead became a reporter for *L'Echo de Paris*. In his newspaper career, he was a court reporter, a theater critic, and a field reporter who covered the 1905 Russian Revolution for *Le Matin*. He did in-depth reporting on the Paris Opera, and its role as a stronghold of the 1871 Paris Commune and the basement cells where their prisoners were held. Inspired by the stories of Edgar Allan Poe and the detective mysteries of Sir Arthur Conan Doyle, he began writing his own detective stories, the most famous of which was *The Mystery of the Yellow Room* (1907).

The character of Erik was inspired by a rumor heard around Paris: One of Garnier's architects, a man actually named Erik, had asked the designer for permission to live in the half-completed building after the foundation and main supporting structure of the Palais Garnier were completed. As the opera house began to rise from the rubble, Erik was granted permission to live on site in one of the vaulted cellar rooms. Supposedly, he lived there from then on.

After the opera house was completed, Erik was rarely seen and soon forgotten except for this vague rumor.

Like Christine Nilsson/Christine Daaé, Erik is based in a reality embedded in the novel. Erik, born in Normandy, had a birth defect that rendered his face horribly disfigured. His mother found him so difficult to look at that she made him wear a mask.

Eventually, Erik's parents abandoned (or perhaps sold) this young child to a traveling circus troupe for their freak show. When the show was in Persia, Erik, now a young man, escaped, living there for several years and working as an assistant to an architect where he excelled, made a good living, learned much, and built up some wealth.

He also acquired skills in some of the darker arts, which saved his life in the Middle East more than once. He finally returned to Paris and applied for work building Garnier's masterpiece. No longer the traumatized child, but a man who had seen much of the world, Erik carried himself with dignity. He still wore the mask made especially for him, and although he worked in a dusty and dirty construction site, he was always impeccably dressed in fashionable clothes. He gained some measure of respect for his work and his bearing, despite his deformity. He eventually moved into the chamber under the opera house.

> ....the viscount and I arrived without obstacle in the third cellar, between the set piece and the scene from the Roi de Lahore. I worked the stone, and we jumped into the house which Erik had built himself in the double case of the foundation-walls of the Opera. And this was the easiest thing in the world for him to do, because Erik was one of the chief contractors

> under Philippe Garnier, the architect of the Opera, and continued to work by himself when the works were officially suspended, during the war, the siege of Paris and the Commune.
>
> (*The Persian's Narrative in Chapter XXI, Interesting and Instructive Vicissitudes of a Persian in the Cellars of the Opera*)

The resemblance between the real-life Erik and Leroux's Phantom doesn't end there. Like the Phantom, Erik loved the Opera and was often in attendance in the years after it opened. Whether he still lived in the caverns deep underneath was a mystery. Many think he did. But he had a favorite box from which to watch the performances: Box 5.

He also fell in love with one of the opera singers and had his love rejected. Distraught, he was never seen at the opera house again...or at least not seen clearly. Many thought they saw him in a shadowy hallway or caught a glimpse of his cloak as they rounded a corner. Nobody knew for certain what became of Erik.

When you come to the Paris Opera House for an evening performance, the lights will be bright, and the gold will shine in the ceiling of the Grand Foyer. Everyone will be dressed in their finest, and all will be a swirl of elegant gowns, jewelry, tuxedos and evening wear, top hats and canes. The bell will ring, signaling the performance is about to begin, and the gay crowd will make their way up the *Grand Escalier* to their seats. Perhaps you will look at your ticket and realize your seat for tonight's performance is in Box 5. As you pass through the doorway, the shiny brass plaque on the door will catch your eye: Loge du Fantôme de l'Opera.

Your companion will not see it, but will feel a chill, give a shudder, and remark that this box is a bit too chilly for them. Could they find us another place to sit? You go ask the attendant if perhaps there is seating elsewhere? As you leave Box 5, you hear a muffled voice say: *Have a pleasant evening....*

## Travelers' Tips

 **Métro Station Pont Neuf, Line 7 (Quai du Louvre)**

### *Take an Opera House Tour*

Anyone interested in opera, history, *La Belle Époque*, architecture, or who enjoys grand opulence (or is fascinated by the story of *Le Fantôme de l'Opèra*) will want to take a Paris Opera House tour. The "Opera Garnier After Hours" is an amazing behind-the-scenes tour that takes place in the evening, after the building has closed to the public, on days when there is no performance scheduled. The tour affords a front row seat to the mysterious workings of the opera house, and allows you to visit places that are off limits to the public. Self-guided audio tours do not afford access to certain areas of the opera house, like the auditorium, where you will only be able to peer through a window and you won't get to see the famous Marc Chagall ceiling.

While access to the cellars and the Phantom's Lake is prohibited, one can sense the eerie, mysterious energy in the quiet corridors and in the auditorium that opera goers must have felt when the opera ghost haunted the place.

*Fig. 91-94 - Inside the Paris Opera House (photos by the author)*

*Fig. 92 - The View from Box Five*
*(photo by the author)*

***Read Leroux's Book***

Until one can travel to Paris, Leroux's book is a wonderful way to visit the Paris Opera House. Leroux makes the entire building a stage for his operatic tale, taking us from the lowest depths of the cavernous cellars to the heights of the roof, with Apollo and his steeds and the sweeping view of the Paris rooftops. Leroux's story provides numerous details about the opera house, the ghost, and the historical events surrounding them—details too involved to relate here, so I highly suggest reading the novel.

*Fig. 95 - Gaston Leroux*
*(courtesy National Library of France via Wikimedia, Public Domain)*

On top of being an engaging story, the novel will give you all the relevant information that "proves" the existence of the opera ghost. For almost a hundred years, tens of millions have enjoyed the movie adaptations of *The Phantom of the Opera*. Many millions are fans of Andrew Lloyd Webber's long-running 1986 musical. Yet few people have actually read the book. I confess I had not before I wrote this chapter. I found myself enthralled by Leroux's story and eager to know more.

In addition, several interesting places to visit are near the Garnier Opera House.

At 3 Boulevard des Capucines, you will find what is perhaps the most opulent Starbucks in the world, as befits its Paris locale. The building dates back to the seventeenth century and has been restored and refurbished with a glass and steel roof, restored eighteenth-century murals, brass trim, and parquet floors. Perhaps this was an annex for the opera house. Rumors say tunnels lead to the opera house for the dancers to make their way to the stage for performances.

At 5 Place de l'Opera is the Café de la Paix, a legendary place to dine along the Grands Boulevards. Boasting Napoleon III era decor, it first opened in 1862. Generations of artists, writers, musicians, composers, and of course, operagoers have spent hours there, deep in conversation and collaboration. The Empress Eugénie herself inaugurated the Grand Hôtel's opening. Here the café steps into history, mentioned in Ernest Hemingway's novel, *The Sun Also Rises*. It was frequented by ballet impresario, Serge Diaghilev, who often hosted lavish parties for his entourage and sometimes left without paying his bill. Oscar Wilde, Émile Zola, Victor Hugo, Sir Arthur Conan Doyle, and future king Edward, Prince of Wales all dined there.

A few steps in the other direction takes you to one of the Grands Boulevards, Boulevard Haussmann, which boasts two of the Grands Magasins (grand department stores) of Paris, Galeries Lafayette and Au Printemps.

## How Paris Shaped Our World

Leroux's book still reverberates today. Unsuccessful when it was first published, it soon went out of print. However, Hollywood was in its infancy, and the moguls who ran the studios were searching far and wide for good stories.

In 1922, Carl Laemmle, president of Universal Pictures, was on vacation in Paris. There he met Leroux, who gave him a copy. Laemmle read the book, instantly saw the possibilities, and bought the film rights. The subsequent silent film, released in 1925 featuring Lon Chaney as The Phantom and Mary Philbin as Christine Daaé, is today considered a classic. The scene when Erik plays the organ while Christine steals behind him and snatches off his mask is considered one of the most memorable moments in film history.

Especially shocking to audiences of the day was Lon Chaney's makeup. Chaney created his own looks and invented many makeup techniques. His Phantom was so disfigured and unsettling that sharp-eyed movie-goers will notice that the camera operator actually lost focus while filming the scene. Upon release, movie houses needed to have smelling salts on hand because some women fainted when Chaney's face was revealed.

Since that first production, the imaginations of millions of people have been stirred and delighted by this "Beauty and the Beast" love story that incorporates real people, real places, and actual events shrouded in mystery and high operatic drama. An underground world, a seductive yet horrible monster, a beauty both transfixed and repulsed—these themes go back to the Greek tragedy of Persephone held captive in Hades. *The Phantom of the Opera* plays upon it in ways that still hold us enthralled.

Perhaps, too, the genre of the grand opera has won some new adherents because of the novel, the films, and especially because of Andrew Lloyd Webber's musical, *Phantom. Phantom* opened at Her Majesty's Theatre in London's West End in 1986, and came to Broadway in 1988, winning the 1986 Olivier Award and the 1988 Tony Award for best musical. It currently holds the title of the longest running show in Broadway history, celebrating its ten-thousandth Broadway performance on February 11, 2012, the first production ever to reach this milestone. As of this writing, *The Phantom of the Opera* has been performed 13,605 times according to Internet Broadway Database. Three decades after *Phantom* first opened, the show has garnered more than seventy major awards and been seen by more than 140 million people in productions the world over.

Webber said of writing *Phantom*, "I was actually writing something else at the time, and I realized that the reason I was hung up was because I was trying to write a major romantic story, and I had been trying to do that ever since I started my career. Then with the *Phantom*, it was there!"

Leroux's novel is considered by many as the culmination of Gothic literature, a style which reigned from the late 1700s. Successfully straddling the line between Gothic horror and Gothic romance, *Le Fantôme de l'Opera* incorporates all the elements of both wrapped up in a classic, "Beauty and the Beast" story. Starting with Horace Walpole's novel *The Castle of Otranto, A Gothic Story* in 1764, the genre went on to include Edgar Allan Poe's short story "The Fall of the House of Usher" (1839), Emily Brontë's *Wuthering Heights* (1847), Robert Louis Stevenson's *Strange Case of Dr Jekyll and Mr Hyde* (1886), and Oscar Wilde's *The Picture of Dorian Gray* (1891).

And of course, France's own lion of literature, Victor Hugo, paid a huge homage to Gothic architecture in his novel *Notre-Dame de Paris* (1831), known to the English-speaking world as *The Hunchback of Notre Dame.* His title clearly indicates that the cathedral is the novel's central character, as Hugo cries out to save the decaying icon.

*Fig. 96 - Erik, The Phantom of the Opera (Lon Chaney) and Christine Daaé (Mary Philbin) in the 1925 film* The Phantom of the Opera *(courtesy Wikimedia, public domain)*

The edifice as a literary character is a part of many a Gothic tale, such as Charlotte Brontë's *Jane Eyre* (1847) and Bram Stoker's *Dracula* (1897). In many Gothic novels, the house or castle is full of human qualities, mysterious and eerie, full of malevolent secrets, with trapdoors, hidden passageways, and rooms that surprise and horrify the reader.

With gloom, fog, decay, death, and madness all central to the Gothic motif, Erik's home, the Palais Garnier, shares all these characteristics. Indeed, the opera house holds what is possibly the most haunting, mysterious and hidden place of all—Erik's secret lake.

The Phantom's Lake!

# Chapter 11
# The House of the Alchemist, Nicolas Flamel

(Fourteenth Century)

*"I knew it! I knew it!"*
*"Are we allowed to speak yet?" said Ron grumpily.*
*Hermione ignored him.*
*"Nicolas Flamel," she whispered dramatically, "is the only known maker of the Philosopher's Stone!"*
*This didn't have quite the effect she'd expected.*
*"The what?" said Harry and Ron.*
*"Oh, honestly, don't you two read? Look—read that, there."*
*— Harry Potter and the Philosopher's Stone,*
by J. K. Rowling

On a late summer evening in 1377, the small bell rang over the door of a shop that butted up against a medieval church in the heart of Paris. The sign over the door read *Écrivain, Libairie, Manuscrits Anciens*. No lamp burned within to signify that anyone was there at this late hour. The unlocked door opened easily. A woman cloaked in a robe and in darkness gave a furtive glance up and down the quiet street before she entered, closing it noiselessly behind her.

Under her cloak, the woman held a scroll covered in old leather, which she drew out as she called softly for her husband, the proprietor. Curtains in the back moved, and through them stepped Nicolas Flamel, scribe, bookseller, and purveyor of fine and ancient manuscripts. He went over to his wife, Perenelle, and gently took the ancient scroll from her hand. Perhaps this was it—finally—the last piece of the puzzle he needed, the one that would give him the answers he had long been seeking.

Going to the back of the shop, Flamel laid the bundle on the long, wooden worktable, gently undid the leather straps, and carefully unrolled the scroll. Using a glass tube filled with water, a surprisingly powerful magnifying lens that he had fashioned himself (an invention that would be attributed to René Descartes 250 years later), he focused his gaze on the ancient writings before him. As he did, these words came into clear relief: THE FIRST BOOK OF ABRAMELIN THE MAGE.

His heart leapt! Was this it? More testing and much reading needed to be done before he could authenticate the manuscript. If this indeed was the book of Abramelin the Mage, he would have, at long last, the answers he had been seeking, answers to questions thousands of years old, answers that he knew existed, but had not yet been able to prove.

He motioned to Perenelle to leave him and go home to rest. His lamps would burn all night and well into the next day....

Much is known of the life of Nicolas Flamel, but much is uncertain, and much is certainly the stuff of fiction. Who was he? How his life unfolded is a fascinating blend of truth, legend, myth, and imagination.

*Fig. 97 - Seventeenth-century engraving of Nicolas Flamel by Balthasar Moncornet (courtesy Wikimedia, public domain)*

Was Flamel really an alchemist who found the philosopher's stone? Did he possess the secret to immortality? Was he able to uncover the formula that turned cheap metals into valuable gold? Or was he just a wealthy and eccentric bookseller who lived an extraordinary life?

Some things are certain. Flamel was born in the year 1340 in Pontoise, just northwest of Paris, on the old Roman road between Paris and Rouen. Remnants of the city's medieval past can still be seen today.

Little is known about Flamel's early life. At some point, he came to Paris and became a scribe, someone who made copies of documents, an important and necessary function in those times.

In 1368, Flamel married Perenelle, a woman of some means, who was already twice a widow. This turn of fortune allowed Flamel to expand his business of buying and selling rare manuscripts and books by opening up a second shop.

As wealthy, prospering businesspeople and good Catholics, Nicolas and Perenelle were known for their generosity, giving to many charitable causes and to the church. In particular, they were significant contributors to building the medieval church of *Saint Jacques-de-la-Boucherie* (Saint James of the Butchers), built by the Butchers Guild and dedicated to Saint Jacques (St. James), brother of the Apostle John.

The Flamels lived and worked in the *quartier* (neighborhood) of the large and ornate church. This area had become—and would remain for centuries afterward—the site of the vast *Les Halles* marketplace. Here, butchers (*boucheries-charcuteries*), fishmongers (*poissonniers*), cheese mongers (*fromagers*), sellers of fruits and vegetables (*primeurs*), wine merchants (*marchand de vin*), and others came every day to sell the bounty of France that fed all of Paris. In the nineteenth century, Émile Zola immortalized this neighborhood and its people in his book *Le Ventre de Paris* (*The Belly of Paris*).

The Flamels gave so generously that their images were included in a stone tableau on the church façade. Mary depicted with the Christ Child has several people kneeling at their feet, two of whom are Nicolas and Perenelle Flamel. The church was expanded many times over the centuries. An immense tower, the *Tour Saint-Jacques*, which is more than 170 feet high (52 meters), was constructed between 1509 and 1523. When the church was destroyed during the French Revolution, only the tower remained, and stands today.

During this period of rising fortunes, Flamel recorded a dream he had. In it, an angel came to him holding a book. The angel said, "Look well at this book, Nicolas. At first, you will understand nothing in it neither you nor any other man. But one day you will see in it that which no other man will be able to see."

Sometime afterward, a book did come into Flamel's possession, an ancient manuscript written not on parchment or paper, but on thin but strong tree bark. He recognized it as the book from his dream. It contained text in Greek, Hebrew, and other languages he couldn't decipher, and symbols, drawings, and tables he could not understand. Not knowing exactly what he had, but knowing it to be more than an ordinary manuscript—he began working to translate the mysterious text.

*Alchemy Rediscovered and Restored* by Archibald Cockren claims to explain in Flamel's own words, the story of the manuscript:

> I, Nicolas Flamel, Scrivener, living in Paris in the year of our Lord 1399 in the Notary Street, near St.

> James of the Boucherie, though I learned not much Latin, because of the poverty of my parents who, notwithstanding, were even by those who envy me most, accounted honest and good people: yet by the blessing of God I have not wanted an understanding of the books of the philosophers, but learned them and attained to a certain kind of knowledge, even of their hidden secrets. For which cause's sake, there shall not any moment of my life pass wherein, remembering this so vast good, I will not render thanks to this my good and gracious God.
>
> After the death of my parents, I Nicolas Flamel, got my living by the art of writing, engrossing and the like, and in the course of time there fell into my hands a gilded book, very old and large, which cost me only two florins. It was not made of paper or parchment as other books are, but of admirable rinds, as it seemed to me, of young trees; the cover of it was brass, well bound, and graven all over with a strange sort of letters, which I took to be Greek characters, or some such like. This I know, that I could not read them; but as to the matter that was written within, it was engraven, as I suppose, with an iron pencil, or graven upon the said bark leaves; done admirably well, and in fair neat Latin letters, and curiously coloured.
>
> The book contained thrice seven leaves, so numbered at the top of each folio, every seventh leaf having painted images and figures instead of writing....

Flamel looked for someone to help him understand what he had. He guessed that this manuscript held secrets that could offer wealth and long life, perhaps even immortality. After all his attempts failed,

Flamel left Paris in 1378, traveling south along the Pilgrims' Road, known as *The Way of Saint James.* This medieval pilgrimage to the tomb of St. James in Spain began right outside of his door, at the Church of Saint Jacques-de-la-Boucherie.

Since medieval times, the church has been one of the main starting points of the pilgrimage known in French as the *Chemin de Santiago de Compostela*, or more famously in Spanish as the *Camino de Santiago*. Today, most pilgrims start their walk on the French side of the Pyrénées mountains. But historically, there were several routes, including the one commencing in Paris.

There are differing accounts of Flamel's journey to Compostela. Some say he searched twenty years before finding any answers. Most accounts, however, say that as he traveled from southern France into Spain he met a Jewish mystic, a *Jewish Converso* (one who was forced to convert to Catholicism). The man could read the scroll and told Flamel what was written on it. Flamel eventually made his way, by ship and caravan, back to France and home to Paris to begin his experiments, following the formulae written in the book.

Legends grew. Did Flamel actually become an alchemist and find the secrets of turning base metals into gold? While the truth may never be known, it is certain Nicolas and Perenelle, already well off, became even wealthier, wealthier than could be explained by her inheritance and the income one would expect from a bookseller.

However they acquired their riches, the Flamels lived a modest life. They did not squander their money on luxuries, something others might do with the ability to turn lead into gold. Instead, their lives were dedicated to charity. The Flamels, generous benefactors to the church of Saint Jacques-de-la-Boucherie, made significant donations to other churches for sculptures, chapels, and other gifts.

The Flamels were known to have endowed hospitals and to have given large sums to help the poor. They repaired old and neglected cemeteries and restored the front of Sainte-Geneviève-des-Ardents, a medieval church located where the *parvis* of Notre-Dame (the square in front of Notre Dame Cathedral) stands today. They gave large sums to endow the Hospice des Quinze-Vingts, and it is said that the patients of the Quinze-Vingts came regularly to the church of Saint Jacques-de-la-Boucherie to pray for Nicolas and Perenelle Flamel.

Perenelle died in 1397, leaving her estate to Nicolas. He continued on with his experiments and philanthropy until he died in March 1418. He was buried according to the carefully thought out wishes he expressed in his will in St. Jacques-de-la-Boucherie, the church he gave so generously to and under a tombstone he himself designed.

After the church was destroyed in the Revolution of 1789, the tombstone was lost for a time. It was found a few decades later. One story says it was discovered in a butcher shop, the butcher using the smooth back of the stone as a chopping block. The headstone now is housed in the Cluny Museum, where it can be seen today.

In the centuries after Flamel's death, a number of books purported either to be written by him or including his secrets surfaced. Early in the seventeenth century, *Le Livre des Figures Hiéroglyphiques* (*The Book of Hieroglyphic Figures*), appeared and was said to be the long-lost writings of Nicolas Flamel. Written under the pseudonym Eiranaeus Orandus, it was "rediscovered" by a publisher, P. Arnauld de la Chevalerie. However, many believe Chevalerie wrote the book himself and falsely claimed Flamel was the author.

Among other things, *Figures Hiéroglyphiques* shows the details of a tympanum Flamel designed and had made for the charniers of *Cimetière des Innocents*, according to fourteenth-century records.

*Fig. 98 - Tombstone of Nicolas Flamel, designed by himself. The tomb was in the church of Saint-Jacques-de-la-Boucherie and can now be seen at the Cluny Museum in Paris. (courtesy Wikimedia, public domain)*

The tympanum supposedly contained some of the secret signs and symbols of the ancient art of alchemy. Flamel paid for its construction in 1389. He also financed another in the charnier along the rue Saint-Denis in 1407; Perenelle's remains were laid to rest there, in a prime spot.

That infamous cemetery was not far from Flamel's shop. By the late eighteenth century, it had become such a foul, pestilent place, overflowing with the bodies interred over nine centuries, that the remains were removed to the Catacombs, along with those from Paris' other ancient cemeteries.

The book was quickly denounced as a hoax. One skeptic was Etienne Villain. In 1761, he claimed the book's real author was none other than the "discoverer" himself, de la Chevalerie.

However, to this day, many believe Nicolas Flamel was an accomplished alchemist. As word of Flamel's possible success in alchemy spread, a mystery was discovered. One night, grave robbers broke into St. Jacques-de-la-Boucherie and opened the Flamel's crypt to steal whatever riches they might find. According to legend, they found the tomb empty. This gave rise to the rumor that Nicolas and Perenelle are still alive.

## Travelers' Tips

Following the footsteps of Nicolas and Perenelle Flamel is surprisingly easy, despite more than 600 years separating us from the times in which they lived. Many of the sites they frequented or were associated with still exist in Paris. And although much of medieval Paris has disappeared, you can still get a sense of what their lives might have been like.

The Way of St. James (*Chemin de Santiago de Compostela*)

**Métro Station Hôtel de Ville, Line 1 — Tour Saint-Jacques, Rue Nicolas Flamel and rue Pernelle (4th arr.)**

Pilgrims leaving from Paris, northern France, and the Low Countries used this route. Not many modern pilgrims travel this way, today but some still do. This route, stretching some 1,500 kilometers (nearly 1,000 miles), is the one Nicolas Flamel would have taken, and you can still follow it. Starting at the Tour Saint Jacques, head south to the Petit Pont and across the Seine onto the rue Saint Jacques, which heads up the Mont Genevieve and out of Paris, southward.

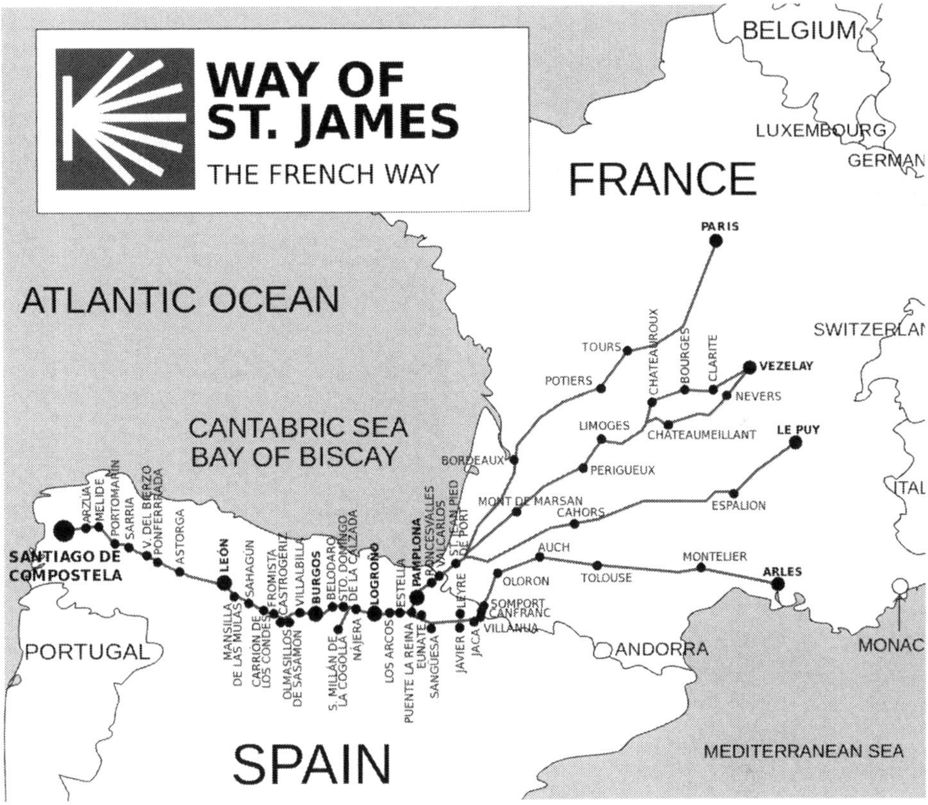

*Fig. 99 - The Medieval Routes in France of the Way of Saint James. One of the oldest and longest routes begins in Paris. (courtesy Wikimedia, public domain)*

### *Rue Saint-Jacques and Musée De Cluny*

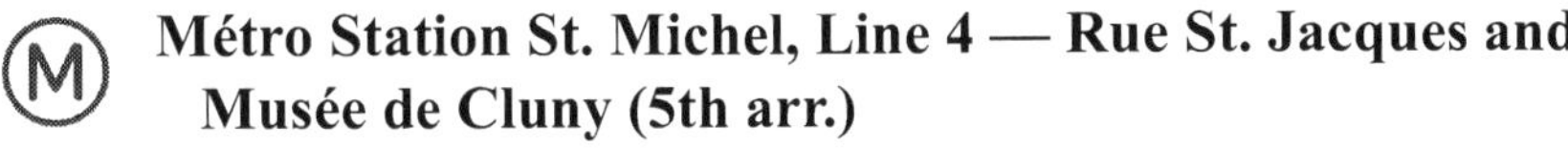

**Métro Station St. Michel, Line 4 — Rue St. Jacques and Musée de Cluny (5th arr.)**

Following the Pilgrims' Road along the rue Saint-Jacques, you can make a game of looking for scallop shells along the street. The scallop shells, the symbol of Saint James, mark the path, and trace the footsteps of Nicolas Flamel and thousands of others who have made this journey.

The rue Saint Jacques is the *cardo* (the principal north-south axis) of the Romans of 2,000 years ago, right under your feet! Along this road is the Sorbonne, the Lycée Louis-le-Grand, Saint-Séverin church, parts of which were built in the thirteenth century, and the church Saint Jacques du Haut Pas, a seventeenth-century building that is the burial place of the French astronomer Cassini.

*Fig. 100 - Dali Sundial—Surrealist artist, Salvatore Dali, himself installed this sundial along the rue Saint-Jacques in 1966 in a ceremony, hoisted up on a lift along with his pet ocelot, and accompanied by a brass band. Notice his signature in the bottom right corner. The face is in the shape of the scallop shell—symbol of the pilgrimage of St. Jacques de Compostella, adorned by Dalí's iconic flaring mustache. Sadly, the sundial does not work. (photo by the author)*

*Fig. 101 - Plaque on the façade of the church at 229 Rue Saint-Jacques in Paris' 5th arrondissement, stating that it is on the road to Saint Jacques de Compostela (photo by the author)*

On this street, the Dominican Order in Paris was started in 1218, in the Chapelle Saint-Jacques, which was located just near the Porte Saint-Jacques. Members of the Dominican order were known as *Jacobins* and later during the French Revolution, the Jacobins lent their name to the Jacobin Club, because that faction was based in another Jacobin monastery.

In 1470, the first printing press in France was set up on this street in a shop at the sign of the Soleil d'Or. Due to the proximity of the Sorbonne, eventually many printers, scribes, and booksellers followed.

*Fig. 102 - Rue Saint Jacques (photo by the author)*

***Musée Cluny—28 rue Du Sommerard***

The Cluny Museum, also known as *la Musée* national *du Moyen Âge—Thermes et hôtel de Cluny* (National Museum of the Middle Ages—Cluny thermal baths and mansion), envelops the visitor in medieval Paris and the life of Nicolas and Perenelle Flamel.

The museum building is a medieval Paris hôtel, many of which were being constructed at the time by the newly emerging wealthy class. Built for the abbots of the Cluny order in 1340, it was rebuilt in 1485. today's structure combines Gothic and Renaissance architecture. Mary Tudor, eighteen years old and youngest sister of England's Henry VIII, lived there in 1515, after her husband, King Louis XII, died three months after their marriage.

In addition to the site's extensive and well-preserved Roman ruins, the 11,500 square foot museum holds 23,000 European, Byzantine, and Islamic artifacts dating from the Gallo-Roman era, through the medieval period, and into the sixteenth century. Among the museum's collection is the tombstone of Nicolas Flamel, stolen from his resting place in the church of Saint James of the Butchers.

*Fig. 103 Musée de Cluny, Museum of the Middle Ages, and gardens (photo by the author)*

***The Oldest House in Paris***

 **Métro Station Rambuteau, Line 11 OR**

 **Métro Station Arts et Métiers, Lines 3 or 11, 51 rue de Montmorency (3rd arr.)**

Flamel built and owned several houses in Paris over his lifetime. The one at 51 rue de Montmorency, considered one of the oldest houses in Paris, was built after Perenelle's death in 1397. Flamel built the house not as a home for himself, but as a shelter to house the homeless. The house was completed in 1407.

Inscribed on a frieze below the ground floor cornice is an inscription in Middle French:

> *Nous homes et femes laboureurs demourans ou porche de ceste maison qui fut faite en l'an de grâce mil quatre cens et sept somes tenus chascun en droit soy dire tous les jours une paternostre et un ave maria en priant Dieu que sa grâce face pardon aus povres pescheurs trespasses Amen.*
>
> We, men and women, workers living in the porches of this house that was made in the year of grace one thousand four hundred and seven are, each of us, required by law to say every day one Our Father and one Hail Mary while praying to God that his grace brings forgiveness to the poor deceased sinners. Amen.

The house's facade became a historic monument in September 1911, and the house itself has generated much speculation about its design and the meaning of the images, text, symbols, and strange etchings on its façade. Today, the house is a restaurant, "Auberge Nicolas Flamel." It still attracts attention today beyond the visitors who come for the food. Some come to view one of the oldest houses in Paris, one around which mysterious and legendary stories have been woven for centuries. Others have broken into the house in search of the secrets they think may still be hidden within.

*Photos 104-106 - Images of the Nicolas Flamel house. The stone façade has reliefs of angels playing music (photos by the author)*

MAISON DE NICOLAS FLAMEL
ET DE PERNELLE SA FEMME
POUR CONSERVER LE SOUVENIR
DE LEUR FONDATION CHARITABLE
LA VILLE DE PARIS A RESTAURÉ EN 1900
L'INSCRIPTION PRIMITIVE
DATÉE DE 1407

***The Hospice of the Quinze-Vingts (Fifteen-Twenties)***

One of the many charities to which the Flamels donated generously was *l'Hospice des Quinze-Vingts*, a hospital for the blind founded in 1260 by King Louis IX (Saint Louis). Historians believe King Louis conceived of the idea of a hospital for the blind after encountering Crusaders who had gone blind in the hot deserts of the Holy Land.

The original hospital built by Philip II was just to the west of the Louvre fortress and outside the city's fortified wall. In 1356, when Charles V built a new wall, the hospital wound up in a new neighborhood on the rue Saint-Honoré at the corner of the rue Saint-Nicaise, a site roughly between the Palais-Royal and Place du Carrousel.

The name Quinze-Vingts means "fifteen-twenty," which in the bizarre French numerical system equals "three hundred (15 × 20 = 300). The name comes from the vigesimal (Base 20) numeral system used in medieval France and refers to the number of hospital beds for the poor blind residents of Paris.

In 1779, King Louis XVI and Cardinal de Rohan moved the Quinze-Vingts to its present location on the rue de Charenton. The hospital's new quarters are in the former barracks of the "Black Musketeers" (so named for the color of their horses), which had been disbanded in 1775.

## How Paris Shaped Our World

Some say there is nothing legendary about Nicolas Flamel and his amazing life. What we know—and we know quite a lot—is pretty mundane yet verifiable.

For example, we have evidence of his work as a scribe in the Bibliothèque Nationale in Paris, which contains a number of manuscripts copied in his own hand and some of his original works. Also, many official documents pertaining to his life are known and catalogued, including the marriage contract between Perenelle and Nicolas, proof of their many gifts and bequests, Pernelle's will, her sister's court action contesting it, and Nicolas Flamel's own will, written in 1418. While the story of Nicolas Flamel is based on solid fact and evidence—with perhaps a few embellishments and liberties taken—it is also true most myths and legends have their origins in substance and truth.

***Harry Potter***

One of Flamel's recognizable global legacies is perhaps the most modern one: his role in J. K. Rowling's Harry Potter series. Rowling's books have revived interest in the man and his life, and brought the name Flamel to millions upon millions of readers and moviegoers. Rowling recounts how she came upon Flamel's story in her early twenties. She then goes on to describe an almost mystical encounter that she had with Nicolas Flamel:

> I remember having a highly detailed and exceptionally vivid dream about Flamel, several months into the writing of *Philosopher's Stone*, which was like a Renaissance painting come to life. Flamel was leading me around his cluttered laboratory, which was bathed in golden light, and showing me exactly how to make the Stone. (I wish I could remember how to do it.)
> —"Nicolas Flamel" by J. K. Rowling, WizardingWorld.com

Indeed, of all the many wonderful characters that inhabit the world of Harry Potter, Nicolas Flamel is the only one drawn from real life.

Rowling included him in her very first book, *Harry Potter and the Philosopher's Stone*. Flamel appears again in the 2018 spinoff film, *Fantastic Beasts: The Crimes of Grindelwald*. Through her almost mystical dream visit with Nicolas Flamel, Rowling was inspired to use him in her work, and in doing so, she introduced him to millions of fans, reawakening interest in his life and legend.

***Flamel's (perhaps) Other Lives***

Besides the book *Le Livre des Figures Hiéroglyphiques*, other books have been attributed to Flamel, including:

- *Le Sommaire Philosophique* (*The Philosophical Summary*), first published in *De la Transformation Métallique*, Paris, Guillaume Guillard, 1561
- *Le Livre des Laveures* (*The Book of Washing*)
- *Le Bréviaire de Flamel (Flamel's Breviary)*

These may have been written by others using Flamel's name, but some people see them as evidence he was still active centuries after his reported death. Over the centuries, people have sworn they have seen Nicolas Flamel alive and well, including one incredible sighting at the Paris Opera in 1761.

One such personage rumored to *be* Nicolas Flamel was the Comte de Saint Germain who lived in the mid-1700s. Appearing in the French court sometime around 1748, Louis XV employed him for diplomatic missions. The Count also showed up in royal circles in England, Holland, and Germany where people who met him ascribed his origins variously to everything from Spanish or Portuguese to Romanian, Italian, or an Alsatian Jew.

The Count spoke fluent French, German, Dutch, Spanish, and Portuguese, with some facility in Russian and English. Others said he knew Mandarin, Latin, Arabic, Greek, and Sanskrit. He was also known as a prolific composer and musician, with many compositions credited to him. He was a writer, painter, and scientist. The Count seemed to be acquainted with everyone from Catherine the Great of Russia to Casanova. Voltaire himself described the Count as "The Wonderman, a man who does not die, and who knows everything."

*Fig. 107 - Left, An engraving of the Count of St. Germain by Nicolas Thomas (1783), in the Louvre, after a painting now lost. (courtesy Wikimedia, public domain)*

*Fig. 108 - Right, Was Richard Chanfray the Comte de Saint Germain? (courtesy Wikimedia, this file is licensed under the Creative Commons Attribution-Share Alike 4.0 International license)*

Myths and legends about the Comte de Saint-Germain were widespread throughout his lifetime and into the nineteenth and twentieth centuries. Many believed he was immortal, that he was Nicolas Flamel, or that he was the legendary "Wandering Jew." Naturally, speculation turned toward alchemy, and he was seen as someone who had discovered the secrets of immortality—the "Elixir of Life." Others pointed to him being a member of the mystical Rosicrucian sect.

Most recently, a man named Richard Chanfray claimed to be the still-living Comte de Saint-Germain. In 1972, he boldly appeared on French television claiming he was the legendary count. He sought to prove his claim by performing an alchemical experiment live on camera, supposedly turning lead into gold. In 1983, Chanfray left a suicide note in Saint Tropez. Mysteriously, his body was never found.

***Science, Alchemy, and The Arts***

Whatever the case and by whatever name, by the seventeenth century, Flamel had achieved legendary status within the circles of alchemy, science, mythology, occultism, and literature. Sir Isaac Newton referred to Flamel in his own alchemical experiments. One journal entry mentions, "the Caduceus, the Dragons of Flammel."

Newton's scientific experiments were often based on principles of alchemy. One fundamental theory of alchemy is that, in order to transmute lead into gold, one had to recognize that the basic building blocks of all matter were the same. Alchemists tried to break down substances into their simplest elements and then refashion them into other elements entirely.

In his explorations, Newton used these principles. In his "Opticks"—optical experiments, he succeeded in breaking down light into its component parts, discovering that white light is made up of the rainbow colors of the spectrum.

*Fig. 109 - Portrait of Isaac Newton by Godfrey Kneller (courtesy Wikimedia, public domain)*

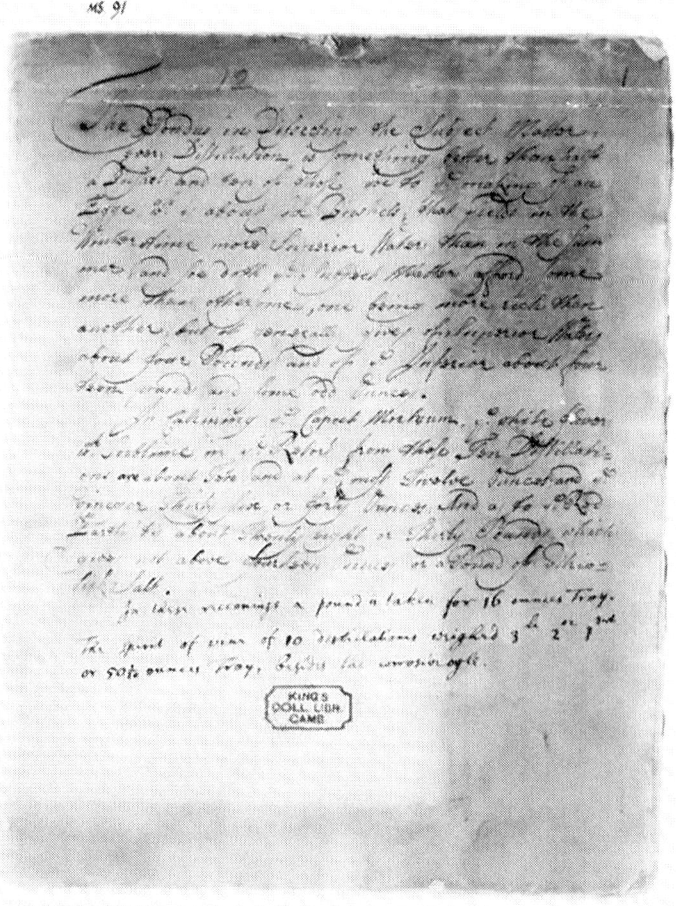

*Fig. 110 - Now take this secret that out of the Philosophers liquor are made two mercuries, a white & a red. And Flamel saith that the red ☿ must be kept to make the imbibitions to the red, & that he had erred in this point had it not been for Abraham the Jew. Others say that the white ☿ is the balm of the moon & the red of the sun: but how to get these Mercuries they tell not. If you have understood me I have given you light into this matter. (Keynes MS. 21, King's College Library, Cambridge University, courtesy* The Chymistry of Isaac Newton, *Indiana University at Bloomington, https://libraries.indiana.edu/databases/newton)*

Interest in Flamel continued into the nineteenth century. In Victor Hugo's 1831 novel *Notre-Dame de Paris* (*The Hunchback of Notre Dame*), the tragic character, Claude Frollo, is Archdeacon of Notre Dame, a respected scholar who speaks several languages and has studied law, medicine, science, and theology. In the novel, he becomes infatuated with alchemy, which leads to rumors he is a sorcerer. Frollo spends much of his time studying the carvings in Saint-Innocents cemetery trying to discover Flamel's secrets.

Hugo refers to Flamel again and again in recounting the history of the great cathedral and the imminent danger it faced of being lost to neglect, disinterest, and the ravages of time. At one point, Hugo writes:

> It is certain that the archdeacon often visited the cemetery of the Saints-Innocents, where, it is true, his father and mother had been buried, with other victims of the plague of 1466; but that he appeared far less devout before the cross of their grave than before the strange figures with which the tomb of Nicolas Flamel and Claude Pernelle, erected just beside it, was loaded.
>
> It is certain that he had frequently been seen to pass along the Rue des Lombards, and furtively enter a little house which formed the corner of the Rue des Ecrivans and the Rue Marivault. It was the house which Nicolas Flamel had built, where he had died about 1417, and which, constantly deserted since that time, had already begun to fall in ruins—so greatly had the hermetics and the alchemists of all countries wasted away the walls, merely by carving their names upon them. Some neighbors even affirm that they had once seen, through an air-hole, Archdeacon Claude

> excavating, turning over, digging up the earth in the two cellars, whose supports had been daubed with numberless couplets and hieroglyphics by Nicolas Flamel himself. It was supposed that Flamel had buried the philosopher's stone in the cellar....

Into the late nineteenth and twentieth centuries, Flamel continued to intrigue and inspire. Composer Erik Satie delved deeply into mystical and esoteric beliefs, which connected him to alchemy and to Flamel. This, in turn, greatly influenced his eerie and otherworldly musical compositions. Satie even founded his own religion based on the mysticism of the Rosicrucians.

Satie joined the Mystical Order of the Rose and Cross, a sect founded by a close friend of his. The connection of these occult, mystical societies with the European alchemists and with the Knights Templar was quite strong, stretching all the way back to the time of the Crusades. While Europe was in the Dark Ages, crusaders came into frequent contact with Arabian literature, mysticism, science, and culture, bringing much of their wisdom back to the West.

***The Way of St. James (Chemin De Santiago De Compostela)***

Flamel's search for someone who could read the inscrutable text that fell into his hands led him to take the mystical pilgrimage along the Way of St. James—just as millions have done over the centuries. The Way of St. James, along with other pilgrim routes to Jerusalem or Rome, was one of the most important Christian pilgrimages during the Middle Ages.

Legend holds that after St. James died, his remains made their way by boat to northern Spain, where he was buried in the city of

Santiago de Compostela. The origin of the pilgrimage is a story about a monk who followed a field of stars (probably the Milky Way) to a remote corner of Spain and discovered the long-lost tomb of St. James. In fact, in Spanish, the Milky Way is popularly referred to as *El Camino de Santiago*, and the name of the town, Compostela, means "field of stars."

The earliest records of the pilgrimage date to the ninth century. By the eleventh century, large numbers of pilgrims were coming from farther away. Pilgrims needed food, lodging, and often, medical care, so a number of "hospitals" were created along the way. Some say the very idea of a hospital originated here.

Nicolas Flamel started from the Tour Saint Jacques on a journey to find someone who could translate the manuscript of the Book of Abramelin the Mage, and thus began another journey into the secrets of the alchemists.

Whether Nicolas Flamel walks among us today or only in legend, one thing is certain: Nicolas and Perenelle Flamel were ordinary people who did some extraordinary things with their money. Their legend and the stories have filled our imaginations, the place where we can believe in the fantastic. Perhaps there is a philosopher's stone out there, if only in the idea that the ordinary can be transmuted into the extraordinary if we just open our eyes to the miracles right in front of us.

Even if you have never heard of Nicolas and Perenelle, they changed our world. Perhaps it is enough they gave us an example of how to live a long, healthy, and prosperous life—today and beyond our physical lifespan. In *On Becoming an Alchemist*, Catherine MacCoun writes:

> If you can uncover the hidden meaning of the various components; the beloved wife, the clueless scholars, the pilgrimage, the cemetery, the blood of the innocents, and so forth, you will be able to discern some sort of spiritual path leading to a result that is described metaphorically as "gold."

The journey in any myth, legend, or story is always an inner journey. The challenges we must overcome appear to come from without, but they are always inner challenges—to our beliefs, to our fears, to our stubbornness, pride, or ignorance. Perhaps the alchemist's quest to turn the base into the valuable is really *our* journey of enlightenment—our quest to turn our lesser instincts and gross animal nature into something divine, aka into "gold" that can then be used, *must* be used, to enrich and enlighten others.

Perhaps *this* is the immortality Nicolas Flamel sought.

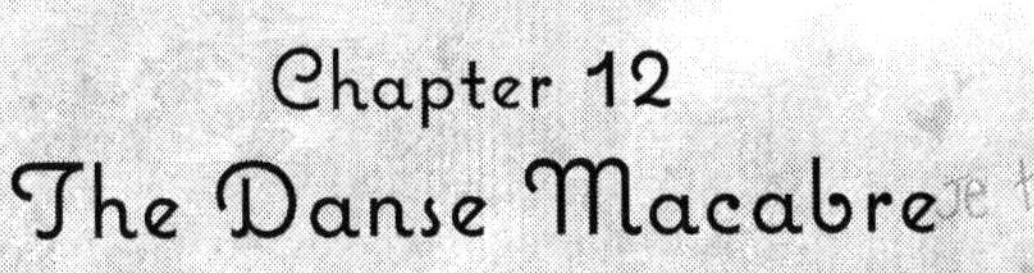

# Chapter 12
# The Danse Macabre

## (Fifteenth Century)

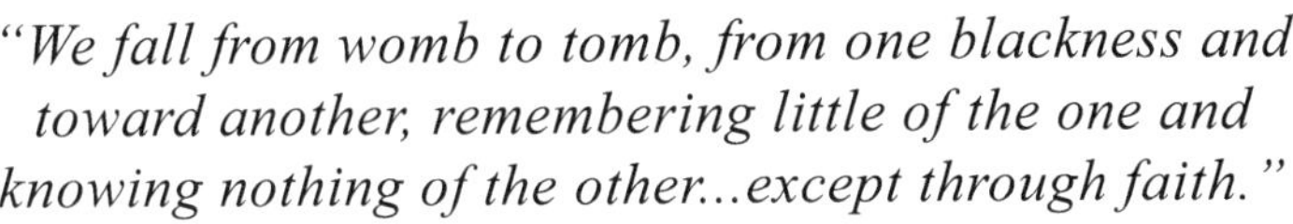

*"We fall from womb to tomb, from one blackness and toward another, remembering little of the one and knowing nothing of the other...except through faith."*
— Stephen King, *Danse Macabre*

YOU KNOW YOU shouldn't go, but you go anyway. There's bound to be some girls there, with wine and beer and who knows what else, so you slip out of the room without your parents hearing and you head through the pitch-black streets. You know the way by heart.

The blackness is thick and so is the stench, getting stronger as you approach. Almost there now, you spot some low light from the flickering fires and can hear the laughter and music from the other side of the stone wall. It sounds like there's a good number of people already inside, which makes your heart race and quickens your steps.

Soon you reach the makeshift stile which you climb easily and noiselessly. No alerting the watch, who will take you and beat you, and maybe arrest you on this side of the wall. But even the most stouthearted guard would never venture over to the other side…not at night.

You drop down and hear the crunch under your feet. Bones, large and small, shift as you straighten up and head toward the firelight and the revelers. Rats scurry. The noxious odor will disappear in a minute or two as you begin to sing and dance and laugh and fondle the women—it is fun with these people, some who are total strangers and others whom you've known your whole short life.

The women look pretty in the firelight, as long as they don't smile and show their teeth. They think the same thing about the boys. Later in the night, even that won't matter as the real fun, the real dance, begins….

*Fig. 111 - Charnier (bone storage) built into the walls at the St Innocents Cemetery in Paris; this fifteenth-century mural depicts the "Danse Macabre" decorating the walls behind the arched structures. (Wikimedia Commons)*

Paris' Holy Innocents' Cemetery was a graveyard for nine hundred years, but also much more. Besides being the largest of dozens of parish cemeteries where the people of Paris buried their dead, these medieval cemeteries were also lively social gathering places. Vendors would sell there because it was church property, and their wares could not be taxed. Important announcements were sometimes made to the people of the city. Prostitutes often plied their trade.

In, "Pictorial Representations of the Medieval Christian Cemetery," Danièle Alexandre-Bidon writes:

> All important events take place at the cemetery: declarations or elections municipal, justice, public sermons by the preaching brothers, theatrical games, but also walks and games for adults or children, wandering doctors who collect medicinal herbs, or prostitutes in search of a client, stray animals, or the many economic activities or crafts, butchers, potters, metal-workers, the presence of taverns, market stalls, etc. Almost nothing of this is represented in the images of the [holy] books of hours, as if a taboo was placed on any representation of secular activities in the most sacred space: this is indeed the case both in works of piety, intended for prayer, such as the books of hours, as in illustrations of secular books. And yet, everyday life in the cemetery does not seem to have shocked anyone...except the liturgists, who have long fulminated...against the impious flippancy of women who gossip while walking on the dead... or the bishops who reinforce, apparently ineffectively, the prohibitions against setting up markets, fairs, and shops of all kinds, in the Christian cemetery....

And at night, all manner of activities went on. In the early Middle Ages, when life expectancy was short, many people did *not* try to avoid death at all costs but were determined to make whatever short life that they had bearable—and by whatever means were available. Something dark and sinister and mysterious could be found by venturing into the cemeteries at night and engaging in wild behaviors, away from the watchful eyes of parents, friends, and neighbors, the constable, the priest, and perhaps even God.

Out of the medieval attitude about life and death—about life's brevity and death's inevitability—sprang the concept that became known as the *Danse Macabre*. The *Danse Macabre* became fixed in the medieval mind and spread throughout Europe, popularized by a mural painted along the wall of the charnel house (a place where bones are stored) of Paris' Saint Innocents cemetery. The mural, long since lost, portrayed this simple idea: that every person, no matter how high or low their rank, will eventually dance with Death.

A similar tradition of cemetery-festivities can be found today in the Mexican celebration known as *Día de los Muertos* or the Day of the Dead. Although much tamer than the *Danse Macabre*, this observance bears some resemblance. People go to cemeteries to be with the souls of the departed, building altars and bringing things to decorate them, bringing the favorite foods and beverages of their departed loved ones, photos, and other mementos.

The three-day *Dia del los Metros* is designed to entice the souls of loved ones to come and visit their family and friends. When the departed show up, they will hear the prayers, the conversations, and the funny and meaningful reminiscing that the living do over the dead.

The families clean the graves, placing orange marigolds, which are thought to attract the souls of the dead. Toys are brought and children are encouraged to make or bring things for the dead children, who are called *los angelitos* or "the little angels." Pillows and blankets are left at the cemetery so the deceased can rest after making the long journey back home from the netherworld. In many places, people will spend the night camped out among the graves of their family, singing, talking, and eating at the grave site.

In Madagascar, the Malagasy people celebrate a ritual known as *Famadihana* or "the turning of the bones." The bodies of the ancestors are removed from the family crypts, wrapped in fresh silk cloths with their names written on them, so they will be remembered. People dance while carrying the corpses, celebrating the dead person's life. The ritual of dancing with the dead is a way of including the spirits of ancestors in Malagasy culture, believing their ancestors will help protect and bless the family if they are properly cared for.

The family festivities of the *Día de los Muertos* and *Famadihana* are perhaps echoes of the happenings in the medieval cemeteries of Paris eight hundred years ago. In the Middle Ages, the average person was well acquainted with death, much more so than we are today. It was an age when life expectancy was a mere thirty-five years old, a time when about 12 percent of children died before the age of five, and when women frequently died in or soon after childbirth. Death was a constant presence, looming close for everyone.

Engaging in drinking, fornicating, fighting, dancing, and otherwise having raucous parties in medieval cemeteries where death and illness were ever-present made sense to the youthful, medieval mind which reasoned: *I am likely not going to live very long, so I may as well have as much fun as I can, while I can.* Of course, death was to be feared, but at the same time, a fatalistic attitude pervaded society because the specter of death was close at hand. "Eat, drink and be merry, for tomorrow we may die," was the watchword of the day for many.

The site of The Holy Innocents' Cemetery (*Cimetière des Saints-Innocents*) had been a place of burial since Roman times. The church and its cemetery were consecrated in the ninth century and named for the biblical event of the slaughter of the innocents by King Herod. Late in the twelfth century, King Philip II had a wall built around the cemetery to keep out grave robbers and dogs, who scrounged among the shallow graves. Saint-Innocents soon became one of the most sought-after cemeteries in Paris. It was believed that King Philip II brought back soil from the Holy Land to the cemetery when he returned from the Third Crusade.

Decades stretched into centuries and the number of dead rose, amplified by many epidemics, like the Black Plague from 1346 to 1353 and again in 1466, when some 40,000 died in Paris. To make room for the newly deceased, those long dead were exhumed and replaced with fresh corpses. The cemetery wall became a *charnier* or charnel house, with bones packed into the walls and roofs, often in patterns both artful and decorative, in a manner similar to the one seen today in the Paris Catacombs.

To get a good idea of a medieval cemetery, picture Act V, Scene I in Shakespeare's *Hamlet*. Hamlet, walking in a graveyard, picks up a skull to make a point about life and death: "Alas, poor Yorick. I knew him, Horatio…." he begins. Shakespeare is depicting the reality of a medieval cemetery—bones lying about, bodies lying not far below the surface, dug up by animals, by grave robbers or by gravediggers removing the older bodies so that fresher corpses could be put in the ground.

**Travelers' Tips**

**1 Avenue du Colonel Henri Rol-Tanguy, Line 6 or 4**

### *The Paris Catacombs*

Create your own "Day of the Dead" (*la jour de la Mort*) tour starting at the Catacombs. Then head to the site of the ancient cemetery, today marked by the Fountain of the Holy Innocents. After a stop for lunch in the Les Halles area, plan to spend a pastoral afternoon in Pére Lachaise cemetery.

Formerly called the *Place d'Enfer* (Place of Hell), the square Denfert-Rochereau was renamed to honor Colonel Pierre Denfert-Rochereau, commander of the forces of Belfort, France. The name was changed after the Franco-Prussian War of 1870, and helped lift the spirits of the Parisians demoralized after their defeat, *and* it had the added benefit of keeping the traditional name of the area.

Look for the majestic Lion de Belfort in the center of the Place. This statue is a smaller, bronze version of a monumental sandstone sculpture in Belfort, France, by Frédéric Auguste Bartholdi, the sculptor of the Statue of Liberty. In Belfort, the lion symbolizes the heroic defense of the city, which endured a 103-day siege by Prussian forces (December 1870 to February 1871). Forty thousand Prussian troops were held off by 17,000 French men and women, only 3,500 of them military. They were led in the defense by Colonel Denfert-Rochereau. It was a defining moment in French history. Originally designed so the lion would face east toward Prussia, the statue at Belfort looks west. The plans were changed after the German government lodged a protest.

*Fig. 112 The "Lion de Belfort," Place Denfert-Rochereau (photo by Jebulon, Courtesy Wikimedia, file licensed under Creative Commons Attribution-Share Alike 3.0 Unported)*

The *Place d'Enfer* was located inside the wall of the Farmers-General. Built between 1784 and 1791, the wall of the *Ferme générale* encircled Paris. Some fifteen miles (24 kilometers) long, the outline of the wall can be seen today by following the routes of Métro lines two and six. The wall was not built for city defense, but to keep untaxed goods from being smuggled into Paris. When you see the entrance to the Catacombs, alongside it is a stone building, one of two customs houses that flanked the *barrière* or tollgate of the wall.

Today, the Catacombs draw 700,000 tourists each year. Only 200 people are allowed in at one time. Head counts are strictly kept so no one is left behind, lost in the maze of tunnels. You have to buy timed tickets in advance and add an audio guide, or upgrade to a guided tour led by an experienced guide.

*Fig. 113 - Tollhouse at the Place d'Enfer and, to the right, the entrance to the Paris Catacombs (photo by the author)*

You must be prepared for three things before entering into this fascinating and mysterious underground ossuary:

**Stairs**—The tour starts and ends via a winding staircase with 243 steps. After walking down 130 steps, nearly twenty meters (over sixty-five feet), you reach the cool, damp underground "Empire of the Dead." Going down can be dizzying but not terrible. However, what goes down must come up. At the exit, you will have to climb some 113 steps. In between is a walk of a mile or more (one-and-a-half to two kilometers).

The Catacombs are not wheelchair accessible and require a considerable stair descent, a mile walk, and a strenuous stair climb.

**Environment**—Deep underground, the air stays a constant 57 degrees F (15 C). A jacket or sweater is a good idea, even on warm summer days.

*Fig. 114 - Staircase down to the Catacombs (photo by the author)*

Also, the underground passages are a bit damp, and the uneven footing can be slick. Good, comfortable footwear is highly recommended.

*Fig. 115 - Bones from the old cemetery of St. Jean (photo by the author)*

*Fig. 116 - Entering the Catacombs*
*"STOP This is the Empire of the Dead*
*(photo by the author)*

While the tunnels are fairly roomy, those with claustrophobia might want to think twice about going down. Once in, you are committed to walking all the way through to the exits.

This is just a friendly reminder that this tour is not for the faint of heart, because in addition to damp, cold tunnels and the stairs to climb, there are also....

**Dead People**—Did we mention this is the Empire of the Dead? The remains of some six million souls rest here. If that is not your cup of tea (or in France, your *tasse de café*), skip the Catacombs.

*As a strict reminder: Do not touch or try to remove the bones!*

If you choose to experience this sublime and macabre subterranean walk, know that you are immersing yourself in the very heart of Parisian history, mystery, and beauty.

The French, never content to be strictly utilitarian, brought beauty, philosophy, and their existential sensibilities to bear on the practical matter of transferring the bones of the Paris cemeteries—nearly six million people, and almost one thousand years of history—to this final resting place. There are many educational displays that tell the story of where and when the bodies were disinterred and moved. Stone plaques throughout the Catacombs indicate what year each tunnel was repaired and which street is above. Other stone tablets encourage visitors—in poetic, religious, and philosophical musings—to contemplate and meditate on the meanings of life and death.

These tunnels were once quarries and most of the stone for the buildings of Paris came from these tunnels that date back to Roman times. Ironically, the very ground that built Paris eventually became so honeycombed with tunnels that in the mid-eighteenth century, the streets around the *Place d'Enfer* began to cave in. People thought the mouth of hell was indeed opening up under their feet!

The fascinating story of the labyrinth of tunnels and the Paris Catacombs will be told in a future book, but suffice to say, a visit to this underground "Empire of the Dead" is an amazing way to spend a few hours in the company of the dead souls of Paris long past.

The Catacombs' exit is some distance away from the entrance, and it is a direct walk, ten- to fifteen-minute back to the Place Denfert Métro station.

***Cemetery of Saint Innocents***

**Métro Station Les Halles, Les Halles — Place Joachim-du-Bellay/Fountain of the Innocents (*Cimetière des Saints-Innocents*) Rues Berger, de la Ferronnerie, de la Lingerie and Rue Saint Denis (1st arr.)**

Châtelet-Les Halles is the largest métro station in all of Europe. To reach the Fountain of the Innocents, come up out of the métro station through either Exit 10, *Place Sainte-Opportune* or Exit 1, *Porte Marguerite de Navarre.*

With today's modern, sanitized experiences of death, it is hard to fathom the revolting horrors that unfolded here over many centuries. The imposing stony silence of the fountain stands as a silent witness to the bodies that piled up here for nearly 900 years. Despite complaints for a few hundred years, nothing was done until the putrefaction, the horrid smell, and the threat to health and safety became critical for the entire city, and especially intolerable in the area of the great Paris market, *les Halles.*

By the late sixteenth century, the cemetery was no longer burying bodies individually, but throwing them unceremoniously into pits and lightly covering them up. These rotting corpses poisoned the air with a stench that was more than an annoyance. It was downright pestilential. Houses, shops, and the markets at les Halles in proximity to the cemetery suffered terribly. People could not store food. Broth and milk went bad almost immediately; wine turned to sour vinegar. One risked illness and even death just breathing the fetid air or touching the cemetery's damp walls.

Louis-Sébastien Mercier (1740-1814), a prolific author and an early pioneer in the genre of science fiction wrote extensively about the conditions in Paris in his day. In *The Forbidden Best-Sellers of Pre-Revolutionary France*, Robert Darnton, says of Mercier,

"There is no better writer to consult if one wants to get some idea of how Paris looked, sounded, smelled, and felt on the eve of the Revolution." Mercier's most popular novel was, *L'An 2440, rêve s'il en fut jamais* (*The Year 2440: A Dream If Ever There Was One*). Published in 1771, it has been reprinted more than twenty-five times.

Mercier was a keen observer of the political, social, and economic life. In his epic twelve-volume work, *Le Tableau de Paris* (1781–1788) he chronicles Parisian life in the years before the French Revolution, and describes Paris cemeteries this way:

> The stench of cadavers could be smelt in almost all churches; the reek of putrefaction continued to poison the faithful. Rats live among the human bones, disturbing and lifting them, seeming to animate the dead as they indicate to the present generation among which they will soon stand....

*Fig. 117 - Portrait of Louis-Sébastien Mercier (1740-1814), French writer, by F. B. Lorieux (courtesy Wikimedia, public domain)*

*Fig. 118 - All that remains of the infamous cemetery is the Fountain of Saint Innocents in the center of the Place Joachim-du-Bellay. The square is named after du Bellay, a French poet and literary critic, who lived from 1522-1560. The cemetery of Saint-Innocents was adjacent to les Halles, the marketplace on this site, in an area bordered on the north by Saint-Eustache church. (photo by the author)*

Further insight into the unhealthy conditions in Paris at the time can be gleaned from Mercier's description of the unpleasant state of affairs at the hospital Hôtel-Dieu on nearby Île de la Cité:

> Hôtel-Dieu has all it takes to be pestilential (contagious), because of its damp and unventilated atmosphere; wounds turn gangrenous more easily, and both scurvy and scabies wreak havoc when patients sojourn there. What in theory are the most innocuous diseases rapidly acquire serious complications by way of the contaminated air; for that precise reason, simple head and leg wounds become lethal in that hospital. Nothing proves my point so well as the tally of patients who perish miserably each year in the Paris Hôtel-Dieu...a fifth of the patients succumb; a frightful tally treated only with the greatest indifference.

In 1780, after ignoring the problem for 200 years, an incident finally caused the local authorities to act. A restaurant owner on the rue de la Lingerie went down into his basement. To his horror, found his cellar overflowing with corpses in various stages of decay. Overnight, the wall had given way under the pressure of the expanding cemetery. This event caused the government to close the cemetery (over the protests of the church) and make plans to remove all the remains.

To make matters worse, the area around Saint-Innocents was *the* marketplace for all of Paris, Les Halles. It grew here as a result of the long-standing practice of people selling and buying in cemeteries. As far back as the eleventh century, this area, then called the Little Fields, or *Champeaux*, was a marketplace. The church controlled the market until 1137, when Louis VI stepped in to share in the revenues the marketplace produced. Philip II completely took over the market in 1183 and built two market halls, or *halles*. His wall encircling the city included the market, and it quickly went from being on the edge of Paris to becoming the city center.

What started out as a market for dry goods grew as farmers, fishmongers, wine merchants, cheese mongers, and others set up food stalls. By the fifteenth century, les Halles was the wholesale market for all of Paris—*The Belly of Paris (la Ventre de Paris)* as Émile Zola's novel title referred to it.

The area underwent a major renovation in 1851, as a part of then President Louis Napoleon's plan to modernize the city along with his Prefect of the Seine, Baron Haussmann. The entire marketplace at Les Halles was finally demolished in 1969, the grounds excavated and modernized. It is said that to rid the area of hundreds of years of animal fat and blood, rotting vegetables, fish, cheese, and other detritus from the markets, the excavation had to go down hundreds of feet.

Today, Les Halles is a large park and promenade with an immense underground shopping mall.

***Père Lachaise Cemetery***

**Métro Station Gambetta, Line 3**

At Place Gambetta, take the rue Père Lachaise to the north gate of the cemetery. I find that this is a better entrance to visit the cemetery. If you enter from the lower entrance, you have to walk uphill through the cemetery. Stop at one of the nearby flower shops to pick up a guide map that will lead you to the gravesites of famous people.

The history of this pastoral and verdant cemetery is fascinating. Once Holy Innocents and others were closed in 1780, and the bodies were moved to the Catacombs, there was a need for new resting places for the dead. In the early 1800s, attitudes about death were changing. Soon, several new, much larger cemeteries were built on the outskirts of Paris by order of Emperor Napoleon, including Montmartre, Père Lachaise, Montparnasse, and Passy.

Père Lachaise was the largest opening in 1804. The first burial on the grounds was of a five-year-old girl on May 21 of that year. At the time, people thought the cemetery was too far from Paris, so it attracted few people. Also, people wanted to be buried in a church graveyard. This new cemetery was secular and non-denominational. As a result, most Catholics would not inter their loved ones there because the ground had not been consecrated by the Catholic Church.

The administrators made a plan to improve the cemetery's standing in the eyes of Parisians. They had the remains of two lions of French literature moved to Père Lachaise: Jean de La Fontaine, author of many fables, including "The Crow and the Fox" (*Le Corbeau et le Renard*), and the playwright Molière, the "Shakespeare of France." The plan worked, and the number of burials began to increase.

In 1817, the remains of the famous lovers from medieval times, *Pierre Abélard and Héloïse d'Argenteuil*, were brought to the cemetery along with their monument—a canopy that had been made from the abbey of Nogent-sur-Seine. Tradition holds that lovers, or those looking for love, place their letters in the vault to honor these "star-crossed lovers" or to enlist their aid in finding true love.

Today, the grounds hold upwards of one million, with many more who have been cremated and placed in the columbarium. Many famous people rest here, including Gertrude Stein and Alice B.

Toklas, Oscar Wilde, Franz Lizst, Marcel Marceau, Isadora Duncan, American author Richard Wright, and singer-poet Jim Morrison of The Doors.

*Fig. 119 - Lithograph of the Les Halles area (Le quartier des Halles) by Theodor Josef Hubert Hoffbaueren (1849). The market stalls are scattered throughout this vast area; you can see some in the upper left. On the lower right is the Fontaine-des-Innocents. Saint Eustache church is centered at the top. (courtesy Wikimedia, public domain)*

Beyond the famous, the north end of the cemetery holds monuments to victims of various tragedies, including the Holocaust.

The Communards' Wall (*Mur des Fédérés*) is where 147 Communards, the last defenders of the Paris Commune, were massacred on May 28, 1871. That day concluded the "Bloody Week" (*Semaine Sanglante*) in which the Paris Commune was crushed. The wall today is a rallying point for the French political left. Ironically, Adolphe Thiers, the French president who was responsible for putting down the Commune and initiating the "Bloody Week," is buried nearby in the cemetery. His tomb is often vandalized since anger still exists over the events of 1871.

*Fig. 120 - The Wall of the Communards,*
*site of the last stand and massacre of the Communards*
*(photo by the author)*

An afternoon spent in Père Lachaise is a pleasant way to combine Paris' mystery and history, bringing together the pastoral beauty of a rural area once outside of Paris with the artists, politicians, musicians, and ordinary people who populate this necropolis.

The end of your "Day of the Dead" tour will leave you a bit tired and footsore, but also in a frame of mind to contemplate the beauty and brevity of life, and perhaps provide incentive to make the most of the time you have on Earth. As one of the signs in the Paris Catacombs reminds us:

*Quod fuimus, estis; quod sumus, vos eritis*
*What we were, you are; what we are, you will be.*

Contemporary images of the day give us a view of the charnel house at Saint Innocents, showing the skulls stacked in the upper tiers, while rotting corpses litter the burying grounds. The massive and mysterious mural known as *la Danse Macabre* can be seen at the back wall of the charnel house.

Commissioned and paid for by an unknown benefactor and painted by an unknown artist, the *Danse Macabre* was a series of murals and a poem extending along the rue de la Lingerie, ten or more alcoves of the *charnier*. The theme of the *Danse Macabre* was simple: No matter one's station in life, death takes everyone. Death is the great equalizer. Everyone will dance with death.

Meant to remind people of life's fragility, it also told people that, despite the riches and glories some might enjoy during their earthly lives, all eventually meet the same fate. Death comes to dance eventually with monarchs, beggars, popes, nuns, prostitutes, artisans, and peasants.

Since many people in those days could not read, the poem the image of Death, in the form of a skeleton or a hooded figure with a scythe or a sickle, was clear, sending a powerful message to those on the lower end of the scales. The bishops and nobility *seemed* secure and rich, happy, and powerful, yet Death was no respecter of either power, wealth, or station.

The mural itself is totally lost, but we know of the *Danse Macabre* through contemporary manuscripts that reproduce or otherwise refer to it. The author of the poem that accompanied the *Danse Macabre* mural has never been identified, but early accounts credit either Jean Gerson, chancellor of the Sorbonne at the time, or perhaps one of his students.

A diary, *Journal d'un bourgeois de Paris*, chronicles the years 1405–49. The anonymous author, an unknown priest says that the *Danse Macabre* mural was begun in August 1424, and completed during Lent in 1425, but never mentions the artist or the person who paid to have it painted.

From its origins in the cemetery Saint-Innocents, the fame of the Parisian *Danse Macabre* swept across Europe like the Black Plague, which some said it represented. The motif was popular, the images reproduced widely, and the poem translated into many languages. The sentiment of the *Danse Macabre* became a cultural icon in Western thought, taking hold in many countries and cultures.

A well-known versions of the poem was an English translation by the poet John Lydgate, written after he visited Paris sometime between 1426 and 1431, during the Hundred Years War. At the time, Paris and much of France was under English and Burgundian rule. Lydgate saw the murals of the *Danse Macabre* and wrote:

I toke on me

To translaten al

Owte of the frensshe

Macabrees daunce

(I took it on me
to translate all
out of the French
the Dance Macabre)

Returning to London, Lydgate's translation was incorporated into a Dance of Death mural commissioned by the London town clerk, John Carpenter, and painted along the wall in Pardon Churchyard at Old St Paul's.

In *A Survey of London*, written in 1603, John Stow gives a contemporary description of the London mural:

> There was also one great Cloyster on the north side of this church inuironing a plot of ground, of old time called Pardon church yard.... About this Cloyster, was artificially and richly painted the dance of Machabray, or dance of death, commonely called the dance of Pauls: the like whereof was painted about S. Innocents cloyster at Paris in France: the meters or poesie of this dance were translated out of French into English by Iohn Lidgate, Monke of Bury, the picture of death leading all estates, at the dispence of Ienken Carpenter, in the raigne of Henry the sixt.

The theme of the Danse Macabre took off across England, Scotland, Germany, Spain, and elsewhere.

Along with the mural in London, woodcuts and etchings similar to the *Danse Macabre* murals in Paris and London were created around the same time. Guyot (Guy) Marchant, a printer in Paris in the late fifteenth and early sixteenth centuries, put out five editions of the *Danse Macabre*.

In each image, Death leads one of the characters away and a conversation takes place, giving the reader/viewer a moralistic lesson on life and death. For example, in the image above, Death comes for a king. Death says:

Come, noble crowned king,
Renowned for might and prowess.
At one time you were surrounded
With great pomp and with nobility,

But now you leave behind
All heights. You are not alone.
You will have little of your riches:
The richest man has but a shroud.

The king replies:

I never learned to dance
Such savage steps and melodies.
Alas, one can look and think:
What good is pride, strength, bloodline?
Death destroys all—that's its purpose—
The noble along with the beggar.
He who thinks of himself the least is the most wise;
In the end one must become ash.

Nothing more remains of Saint Innocents Cemetery, except the fountain in the center of the Place Joachim-du-Bellay. The charnel houses were demolished in 1669 to widen the rue de la Ferronnerie. The cemetery was closed in the early 1780s, all of the remains moved to the Paris Catacombs.

Today you can trace where the wall of the arcade and charnel house stood on the south side of the cemetery, in a line roughly similar to today's rue Berger (formerly the rue au Fers), rue de la Lingerie, and the rue de la Ferronnerie. The fountain was in those days located at one corner of the cemetery, approximately where today's rue Berger and the rue Saint Denis intersect.

Fortunately, we can still see images of the mural published in 1485 by printer Guyot Marchant, showing each panel of the *Danse Macabre* and the accompanying verse. One original edition is housed today in the Library of Congress.

*Fig. 121 - Nineteenth century engraving of the Fontaine de Innocents, Bibliotheque des arts décoratifs, Paris (courtesy of Wikimedia, file is licensed under the Creative Commons Attribution-Share Alike 3.0 Unported license)*

Imagine Paris 600 or 700 years ago when it was not the City of Lights, but a dark city of noxious smells and overflowing cemeteries. Imagine this place in which you are standing as a playground for "dark deeds done in the dark." Then Paris was for the brave and the foolish, for the rats and the bones.

Hardly a Paris for tourists, but yet here you are. Are you ready to dance with Death? Maybe not today, but someday, hopefully not soon, the music will play, and Death will hold out a bony hand.

"Care to dance?"

*Fig. 122 - Pardon Church was demolished in 1549 along with its Dance of Death paintings. Saint-Innocents was completely destroyed in 1787. However, in Rosslyn Chapel, Scotland, a carving of the Danse Macabre can be found, likely modeled on the London mural, which came directly from the mural at Saint-Innocents. (Image from Heaths Picturesque Annual, 1835, by Roger Griffith, courtesy Wikimedia)*

*Fig. 123* The Dance of Death—*Michael Wolgemut, from the* Liber chronicarum *by Hartmann Schedel (1493)* *(courtesy Wikipedia, public domain)*

## How Paris Shaped Our World

### *Rural Cemetery Movement*

In the late eighteenth and early nineteenth centuries, the public health threat caused by Saint Innocents and other Parisian cemeteries was an urgent crisis. But emptying the cemeteries and moving the bodies to the Catacombs was only half the battle. New places also had to be found to bury the dead away from populated areas.

Meanwhile, across Europe and in America, the Romantic movement was taking hold in literature, poetry, music, and painting. By extension, it had a major influence on history, education, the social and the natural sciences, and other areas, such as politics. With

Romanticism influencing the arts and all aspects of life and culture—and with concerns for sanitation and public health—there arose a desire to create pastoral and more aesthetically beautiful cemeteries. Thus began the "Rural Cemetery Movement." The primary model for the movement was Père Lachaise Cemetery, which opened in 1804.

In the United States, Mount Auburn Cemetery in Cambridge, Massachusetts, was founded by the leaders of the Massachusetts Horticultural Society and opened in 1831. Described in contemporary accounts as a "pleasure garden instead of a place for graves," it evoked such beauty that it "almost excites a wish to die." Other notable rural cemeteries created around this time include Laurel Hill Cemetery in Philadelphia (1836), Green Mount in Baltimore (1838), Green-Wood Cemetery in Brooklyn (1839), Mount Hope Cemetery in Rochester, New York (1839), Bellefontaine Cemetery in St. Louis (1849), and the Albany Rural Cemetery in Albany, New York (1841).

Using British and French garden styles and landscaping features, Mount Auburn and other rural cemeteries embodied classic Romantic characteristics by using the elements of nature, woods, hills, plants, and natural paths, to create park-like romantic settings. Naturalism, a hallmark of Romanticism, was integral to the Rural Cemetery Movement.

Besides the desire to create pleasant, peaceful, and restful cemeteries for the dead, real public health concerns for the living propelled the rural cemetery movement. This concern was only made more urgent in the years during and after the American Civil War.

The rural cemetery movement took death out of the dark and grim churchyards of the Middle Ages and brought them into the Romantic age of beauty and peaceful repose. Moving away from mere boneyards, the shift in Paris from inner city cemeteries with the accompanying smell and unhealthful conditions, resulted in new, fresh, and airy places with trees and lawns, tranquility and beauty—places people actually wanted to visit to spend time in relaxation and contemplation. The rural cemetery movement allowed people to be in the presence of a restful death while enjoying life in peaceful, attractive surroundings. This was a far cry from places like Saint Innocents, where the presence of death was in the air and painted on the walls, ever reminding people of the horrible fate that awaited each and every one of them.

### *Inspiration in Art and Popular Culture*

The *Danse Macabre* continued to inspire people for centuries after it first appeared on the walls of the cemetery in Paris. Lydgate brought the poem and the mural to London, which sent the medieval idea of a "Dance with Death" across Europe at the dawning of the Renaissance and the Age of Enlightenment.

The *Danse Macabre* may well have been a factor in ushering in the Age of Enlightenment with its ideas of equality between the classes, with Death as the Great Leveler. As the image became well-known and widespread, it may have contributed to breaking down the inflexible, rigidly fixed class-based social structure. After all, the murals in Paris and London were highly visible pieces of art, not tucked away from the eyes of the common folk in a palace or a cloister, but publicly displayed in cemeteries visited by people from all stations. Subsequent books depicting the *Danse Macabre* were popular and disseminated widely.

As its fame spread in murals, carvings, and books, the theme's popular appeal took hold in the imaginations of millions. The rapid spread and popularity of the *Danse Macabre* motif throughout

Europe made it part of the zeitgeist of the late Middle Ages, into the early Renaissance, and beyond—as it still is today.

The idea of a *memento mori*, or a meditation on death, dying, decay, and mortality had existed in ancient Greece and Rome. Stoic Marcus Aurelius in his *Meditations* suggested people "consider how ephemeral and mean all mortal things are." Early Christian writings also contain instructions and lessons to the faithful about death and the fleeting nature of life.

We find meditations on life and death throughout various ages and in many societies. What makes the *Danse Macabre* stand out is its widespread appeal across cultures, perhaps because of its close association with the bubonic plague (Black Plague/Black Death), which also ripped through Europe, Asia, India, and North Africa, killing an estimated 75 to 200 million people. Images and ideas of death and dying changed significantly during this period. Trauma and suffering were rampant during the Plague, which radically shifted people's beliefs about everything from spiritual matters to matters of daily life, introducing new ways of artistic expression, especially a dark motif of painting known as "Death Art."

The theme of the *Danse Macabre* is echoed in sixteenth century art, such as *The Triumph of Death*, by Pieter Bruegel the Elder, which he painted around the year 1562. Death appears in the form of an army of skeletons who overrun all mundane human activities as the people in the painting flee or put up a futile resistance.

In Shakespeare's *Hamlet*, the scene in the graveyard is a meditation on death and the end to which we all eventually arrive. Hamlet starts his monologue:

Alas, poor Yorick! I knew him, Horatio:
a fellow of infinite jest, of most excellent fancy:

*Fig. 124* - Death Playing Chess *by Albertus Pictor. (c. 1480-1490, mural in Täby Church outside Stockholm, Sweden (courtesy Wikimedia, public domain)*

he hath borne me on his back a thousand times;
and now, how abhorred in my imagination it is!
my gorge rims at it. Here hung those lips that I
have kissed I know not how oft. Where be your gibes now?
Your gambols? your songs? your flashes of merriment,
that were wont to set the table on a roar? Not one
now, to mock your own grinning? quite chap-fallen?

This scene brings together Shakespeare's themes of corruption, death, and decay and echoes the *Danse Macabre*—life always ends like this. Indeed, even the greatest have been transformed into clay. Clay can be used to make a stopper for a beer barrel's bunghole. Hamlet concludes that this fate is a shabby end for titans like Caesar and Alexander the Great.

In the nineteenth century, French poet Charles Baudelaire, wrote his famous and notorious collection of poems, *The Flowers of Evil* (*Les Fleurs du mal*). The poems, written and rewritten over the years between 1840 and his death in 1867. He continuously wrote and revised *Les Fleurs du mal*, adding new poems and reinserting ones that were censored out of earlier editions.

Baudelaire deals with then taboo subjects: sexuality, sensuality, ideas of pleasure, suffering, mortality, and death. His book was swiftly condemned as offensive, a crime against public morality. Here we again find meditations on death as the great equalizer, something natural and normal, yet also something macabre that cannot be avoided. You cannot look, but you cannot look away.

A Carcass

My love, do you recall the object which we saw,
That fair, sweet, summer morn!
At a turn in the path a foul carcass

On a gravel strewn bed,
Its legs raised in the air, like a lustful woman,
Burning and dripping with poisons,
Displayed in a shameless, nonchalant way
Its belly, swollen with gases.
The sun shone down upon that putrescence,
As if to roast it to a turn,
And to give back a hundredfold to great Nature
The elements she had combined;
And the sky was watching that superb cadaver
Blossom like a flower.
So frightful was the stench that you believed
You'd faint away upon the grass.
The blow-flies were buzzing round that putrid belly,
From which came forth black battalions
Of maggots, which oozed out like a heavy liquid
All along those living tatters.
All this was descending and rising like a wave,
Or poured out with a crackling sound;
One would have said the body, swollen with a vague breath,
Lived by multiplication.
And this world gave forth singular music,
Like running water or the wind,
Or the grain that winnowers with a rhythmic motion
Shake in their winnowing baskets.
The forms disappeared and were no more than a dream,
A sketch that slowly falls
Upon the forgotten canvas, that the artist
Completes from memory alone.

Crouched behind the boulders, an anxious dog
Watched us with angry eye,
Waiting for the moment to take back from the carcass
The morsel he had left.
— And yet you will be like this corruption,
Like this horrible infection,
Star of my eyes, sunlight of my being,
You, my angel and my passion!
Yes! thus will you be, queen of the Graces,
After the last sacraments,
When you go beneath grass and luxuriant flowers,
To molder among the bones of the dead.
Then, O my beauty! say to the worms who will
Devour you with kisses,
That I have kept the form and the divine essence
Of my decomposed love!
— From *The Flowers of Evil* (William Aggeler Translation)

Classical pieces inspired by the mural are many. Frédéric Chopin's *Piano Sonata No. 2 in B-flat minor, Op. 35*, contains the world-famous *Marche funèbre*, or Funeral March. Published in 1840, it remains one of Chopin's most popular works. The first time it was performed by a full orchestra was on October 30, 1849, at Chopin's funeral beside his grave in Père Lachaise.

The French composer Camille Saint-Saëns wrote *Danse Macabre*, an orchestra piece, in 1874. Although panned by the critics at the time, it is today considered one of his greatest masterpieces. Saint-Saëns' *Danse Macabre, Op. 40*, takes its cue from the historical *Danse Macabre* and from an old French legend that Death comes on

Halloween night at midnight, playing a fiddle and calling all of the skeletons in the cemetery to arise and dance.

Moꝛs tua. moꝛs xp̄i. fraus mūdi. gloꝛia celi. Et doloꝛ īferni: ſint memoꝛanda tibi.

Credo q̄ redemptor meus viuit ꝛ in nouiſſimo die de terra ſurrecturus ſum et in carne mea videbo deum ſaluatorē meū

Vado moꝛi iudex: quia iam plures repꝛehendi Iudicium moꝛtis hoꝛreo. Vado moꝛi

Le moꝛt
Abbe: venez toſt: vous fuyez:
Nayez ia la chiere eſbaye.
Il conuient que la moꝛt ſuiuez:
Combien que moult lauez haye
Commandez a dieu labaye:
Que gros et gras vous a nourry.
Toſt pourrirez a peu de aye.
Le plus gras eſt pꝛemier pourry.

Labbe
De cecy neuſſe point enuie:
Mais il connient le pas paſſer.
Las: oꝛ nay ie pas en ma vie
Gardez mon oꝛdꝛe ſans caſſer.
Garde vous de trop embꝛaſſer
Vous qui viuez au demoꝛant:
Se vous voulez bien treſpaſſer.
On ſauiſe tard en mourant.

Le moꝛt
Bailly qui ſauez queſt iuſtice
Et hault et bas: en mainte guiſe:
Pour gouuerner toute police.
Venez tantoſt a ceſte aſſiſe.
Je vous adiourne de main miſe
Pour rendꝛe compte de vous fais
Au grant iuge: qui tout vng pꝛiſe.
Vn chaſcun porteras ſon fais.

Le bailly
Hee dieu: vecy dure iournee:
De ce cop pas ne me gardoye
Oꝛ eſt la chanſe bien tournee:
Entre iuge honneur auoye.
Et moꝛt fait raualer ma ioye:
Qui ma adiourne ſans rappel.
Je ny voy plus ne tour ne voye.
Contre la moꝛt na point dappel.

*Fig. 125* - Danse Macabre *painted under the mass graves of the Saints Innocents of Paris (1425) Reproduction of the original edition donated by Guyot Marchant, text and wood engravings (courtesy of Internet Archives, public domain Mark 1.0)*

One reason critics and the public greeted it so unkindly was the harshness of the music itself, which was jarring and unusual for the day. Because the solo violin is the devil playing, the violin's top string is purposefully tuned down a half a step, from E to E-flat. Known as a "tritone" or the "devil's interval," this discordant sound was strictly avoided in Western music. Saint-Saëns' deliberate use of the devil's interval was an affront to the day's musical standards. It has been used to great effect many times since. For example, Leonard Bernstein uses the same discordant two notes in the opening bars of "Maria" in *West Side Story*.

Saint-Saëns' *Danse Macabre* has been used in numerous productions, from the *Danse Macabre* ballet choreographed by Anna Pavlova to an episode of *Buffy the Vampire Slayer* where the piece plays an integral role in "Hush," (season four, episode 10, 1999). When Giles (Buffy's mentor) explains to Buffy and the gang how to kill the monsters (in pictures and pantomime, because the monsters have stolen their screams), he plays *la Danse Macabre* on a boombox.

Franz Liszt took Saint-Saëns' piece and transcribed it in a score for piano in 1876. Earlier, in 1849, he wrote "Totentanz" (*Danse Macabre* in German), a work for solo piano and orchestra. Liszt composed pieces such as "Totentanz" and "Funérailles" because he was fascinated with death, religion, heaven, and hell. Musicologist Alan Walker says in *Franz Liszt: The Virtuoso Years 1811–1847* that Liszt frequented "hospitals, gambling casinos, and asylums" in the Paris of his youth, sometimes venturing down into prison dungeons to see the condemned prisoners.

"La Danse Macabre" also makes up the final movement in Shostakovich's *Piano Trio in E minor, Opus 67*. Written in the Soviet

Union in 1944, during World War II, and played at Shostakovich's own funeral, it combines happy and sad elements, echoing musical themes found in Jewish and Russian folk melodies. This *Danse Macabre* was a reaction to the brutality the Russians endured at the hands of the Nazis and from stories that were just emerging of the horrors experienced by the Jews and others in the concentration camps, including stories that prisoners were made to dance next to their own graves before being executed by SS officers.

In 1929, *The Skeleton Dance* appeared in theaters, the very first of Walt Disney studio's successful "Silly Symphonies" series. In the short film, four human skeletons dance, playing music in a graveyard. With original music by Carl W. Stalling and excerpts from Edvard Grieg's "March of the Trolls" from *Lyric Suite*, *The Skeleton Dance* has since become an unofficial anthem for Halloween and owes a debt of gratitude to *la Danse Macabre* and composer Camille Saint-Saëns.

The mural *Death Playing Chess* by Albertus Pictor inspired Ingmar Bergman's film *The Seventh Seal*, released in 1957. Itself an example of "death art," the film takes place during the plague years. A knight (Max von Sydow) and his squire return home from the Crusades to find Sweden ravaged by the plague. At one point, they visit a church where an artist is at work, painting a mural of the *Danse Macabre* on the church wall.

In 1981, prolific writer of horror and Gothic fiction, Stephen King, wrote a book titled *Danse Macabre* examining horror fiction in movies, books, television, radio, and the comics. King examines the entire genre, focusing as much on what is bad about modern horror stories as he does on what is wonderful. In it, King writes:

> But on another, more potent level, the work of horror really is a dance—a moving, rhythmic search. And what it's looking for is the place where you, the viewer or the reader, live at your most primitive level. The work of horror is not interested in the civilized furniture of our lives. Such a work dances through these rooms which we have fitted out one piece at a time, each piece expressing—we hope!—our socially acceptable and pleasantly enlightened character. It is in search of another place, a room which may sometimes resemble the secret den of a Victorian gentleman, sometimes the torture chamber of the Spanish Inquisition...but perhaps most frequently and most successfully, the simple and brutally plain hole of a Stone Age cave-dweller. Is horror art? On this second level, the work of horror can be nothing else; it achieves the level of art simply because it is looking for something beyond art, something that predates art: it is looking for what I would call phobic pressure points. The good horror tale will dance its way to the center of your life and find the secret door to the room you believed no one but you knew of—as both Albert Camus and Billy Joel have pointed out. The Stranger makes us nervous...but we love to try on his face in secret.

### *Ideas and Images About Death*

The Paris mural and poem of the *Danse Macabre* have forever changed our perception of death and how artists depict the personification of Death. Before the fourteenth century, Death was depicted as an angel—the Angel of Death. After the Black Death swept across Europe, the motif of the *Danse Macabre* ushered in a whole new way of depicting Death.

The Plague killed millions of Europeans, some estimates run to more than 50 percent of the population in some places. Like the scene in *Monty Python and the Holy Grail,* carts piled high with bodies were regularly hauled through the streets on their way to be burned.

*Fig. 126* - The Triumph of Death *by Pieter Bruegel, the Elder, located in the Museo National del Prado, Madrid (courtesy of Wikimedia, public domain)*

As a result, people's view of Death began to change. Death was no longer an angel. Artists now began showing Death as a skeleton—grim and grinning, carrying a scythe or sickle. Death was now a quick and efficient harvester of souls. Death became "The Grim Reaper," although the term was not used until it first appeared in 1847 in Robert Menzies' book *The Circle of Human Life*:

All know full well that life cannot last above seventy, or at the most eighty years. If we reach that term without meeting the grim reaper with his scythe, there or there about, meet him we surely shall.

*Fig. 127 - Statue in the Cathedral of Trier, Germany (April 2006, image by Jbuzbee, courtesy Wikimedia, file licensed under the Creative Commons Attribution 3.0 Unported license.)*

The *Danse Macabre* mural brought us the image of The Grim Reaper, an image we still use today.

The *Danse Macabre*, first seen in Paris in an immense mural and accompanying poem painted on the wall of the charnel house of the Holy Innocents Cemetery, is an eye-opening window into the medieval mind and a concept that helped change people's thoughts about their place in the world. If Death took monarchs, popes, and peasants, maybe there was not much difference between me, a subsistence farmer, and you, the priest or the prince, the pope, or the monarch.

Because much medieval art has been lost, the influence of the *Danse Macabre* has likely been grossly underestimated. We can see its echoes in later writings, painting, music, and in popular culture, and these echoes are significant.

But all that happens centuries hence and is well beyond my understanding. Tonight is all that matters, for tonight there will be firelight and dancing and more in the Saint Innocents, and I don't want to be late, because, well...life is short.

**CHAPTER ONE**

Figure 1. Interior view of the morgue in 1855 (Paris). Brown University, public domain

Figure 2. Two men making a death mask — Wikimedia Commons, public domain.

Figure 3. L'Inconnue de la Seine, Death Mask, public domain

Figure 4-5. Memorial to the martyrs of the deportation (photo by the author)

Figure 6. Welcome to Paris Plages (by the author)

Figure 7. Resusci-Anne by Laerdal Medical — This image was originally posted to Flickr by ~aorta~ at https://flickr.com/photos/25068028@N00/3990641321 File licensed under the Creative Commons Attribution 2.0 Generic license

**CHAPTER TWO**

Figure 8. *The Center of Paris in 1550* by Olivier Truschet and Germain Hoyau (public domain)

Figure 9. *The Pont Neuf, the Samaritaine and the Pointe de la Cité*, Nicolas-Jean-Baptiste Raguenet (1715-1793); painting at the Carnavalet Museum, Paris (public domain)

**CHAPTER THREE**

**CHAPTER FOUR**



**CHAPTER FIVE**

**CHAPTER SIX**

## CHAPTER SEVEN



## CHAPTER EIGHT

**CHAPTER NINE**

**CHAPTER TEN**

**CHAPTER ELEVEN**

**CHAPTER TWELVE**

# Works Cited

**BOOKS AND ARTICLES**

Allingham, Margery Louise. *Mystery Mile*. 1930.

Anonymous. "A Description of the Paris Morgue. " *Harvard Crimson*. February 1885.

Anonymous. *Journal d'un bourgeois de Paris*.

Aurelius, Marcus. *Meditations.*

Balzac, Honoré de. *Catherine de' Medici*.

Barnes, David S. *The Great Stink of Paris and the Nineteenth-Century Struggle against Filth and Germs*.

Baudelaire, Charles. "The Painter of Modern Life." *Le Figaro*. 1863.

Baudelaire, Charles. *Les Fleurs du Mal*. (*The Flowers of Evil*.) Trans. William Aggeler.

Benjamin, Walter. *Das Passagen-Werk*. "The Arcades Project." Harvard Press, 1999.

Bernier, François. *Travels in the Mogul Empire*. 1670.

Blake, William Blake. *The Marriage of Heaven and Hell*. 1790.

Breslin, Jimmy. *How the Good Guys Finally Won: Notes from an Impeachment Summer*. 1975.

Charnacé, Guy de. *L'Etoile du Chant*. (*A Star of Song! The Life of Christina Nilsson*.) 1868.

Cockren, Archibald. *Alchemy Rediscovered and Restored.*

Cooper, Thomas. *Thesaurus Linguae Romanae & Britannicae (Thesaurus of the Roman Tongue and the British*. 1578.

*Danse Macabre.* Trans. John Lydgate.

Darnton, Robert. *The Forbidden Best-Sellers of Pre-Revolutionary France.*

Dickens, Charles. *The Uncommercial Traveler*. 1860.

*Dictionnaire des Rues de Paris*. 1874. 2nd ed.

Doyle, Arthur Conan. *A Study in Scarlet.*

Dumas, Alexandre. *Marguerite de Valois.*

Flamel, Nicolas. *Le Bréviaire de Flamel* (*Flamel's Breviary*.)

Flamel, Nicolas. *Le Livre des Laveures*. (*The Book of Washing*.)

Flamel, Nicolas. *Le Sommaire Philosophique*. (*The Philosophical Summary*.) In *De la Transformation Métallique*. Paris, France: Guillaume Guillard, 1561.

Gilbert, Martin. *The Holocaust: The Human Tragedy.*

Heilbron, J. L. "The Measure of Enlightenment." *The Quantifying Spirit in the 18th Century.*

Heine, Heinrich. *The Works of Heinrich Heine*. Trans. Charles Godfrey Leland. Vol 14.

Houdini, Harry. *The Unmasking of Robert-Houdin*. 1906.

Hugo, Victor. *Les Misérables*. 1862.

Hugo, Victor. *Notre-Dame de Paris.*

Huxley, Aldous. *The Doors of Perception.*

Jacobs, P. L. Jacobs. *Curiosités de l'Histoire du Vieux Paris*. 1858.

King, Stephen. *Danse Macabre.*

*le Guide Topographique of C. Chevalier, Chef des bureaux de l'Administration des Pompes Funèbres de Paris.* (*Administrative Bureau of Funeral Homes*.)

Leroux, Gaston. *Le Fantôme de l'Opera. (The Phantom of the Opera)*. 1910.

MacCoun, Catherine. *On Becoming an Alchemist.*

Marion, Fulgence. *Wonderful Balloon Ascents; or, The Conquest of the Skies*. 1870.

Marion, Fulgence. *Wonders of Optics*.

McCann, Lee. *Nostradamus: The Man Who Saw Through Time*.

Menzies, Robert. *The Circle of Human Life*. 1847.

Mercer, Jeremy. *Time Was Soft There: A Paris Sojourn at Shakespeare & Co.*

Mercier, Louis-Sébastien. *L'An 2440, rêve s'il en fut jamais*. (*The Year 2440: A Dream If Ever There Was One*.) 1771.

Mercier, Louis-Sébastien. *Le Tableau de Paris*. 1781–1788.

Morgan, Janet. *The Secrets of Rue St Roch: Intelligence Operations behind Enemy Lines in the First World War.*

Nabokov, Vladimir. "L'Inconnue de la Seine." 1934.

Nostradame, Michel de (Nostradamus). "Preface." *The Prophecies*.

Orandus, Eiranaeus. *le Livre des Figures Hiéroglyphiques*. (*The Book of Hieroglyphic Figures*.)

Poe, Edgar Allan. "The Mask of the Red Death." 1841. *The Works of Edgar Allan Poe, The Raven Edition*. P.F. Collier & Sons. 1903.

Poe, Edgar Allan. "The Murders in the Rue Morgue." *The Works of Edgar Allan Poe, The Raven Edition*. P.F. Collier & Sons. 1903.

Poe, Edgar Allan. "The Mystery of Marie Rogêt." *The Works of Edgar Allan Poe, The Raven Edition*. P.F. Collier & Sons. 1903.

Poe, Edgar Allan. "The Philosophy of Composition." *Graham's American Monthly Magazine of Literature and Art*. April, 1846.

Poe, Edgar Allan. "The Purloined Letter." *The Works of Edgar Allan Poe, The Raven Edition*. P.F. Collier & Sons. 1903.

Rilke, Rainer Maria. *The Notebooks of Malte Laurids Brigge*. 1910.

Roberts, Étienne-Gaspard (Robertson). *Mémoires, Recreatifs, Scientifiques et Anecdotiques*. 1831-1833. 2 vols.

Rousseau, Jean-Jacques. *Discourse on Inequality.*

Rowling, J. K. *Harry Potter and the Philosopher's Stone*.

Sciolino, Elaine. *The Only Street in Paris: Life on the Rue des Martyrs*.

Selznick, Brian. *The Invention of Hugo Cabret*. 2007.

Shakespeare, William. *Hamlet.*

Stow, John. *A Survey of London*. 1603.

Süskind, Patrick. *Perfume: The Story of a Murderer.*

Varennes, Claude de. *Dressé pour l'instruction & la commodité tant des François que des estrangers*. (*France, Prepared for the Instruction and Convenience of Both the French and Foreigners*.). 1639. Internet Archives.

Vidocq, Eugéne François. *Memoirs*. 1828.

Walker, Alan. *Franz Liszt: The Virtuoso Years 1811–1847.*

Willis, Nathaniel Parker. *Pencillings by the Way*. 1835.

Zola, Émile. *Le Ventre de Paris*. (*The Belly of Paris*.)

Zola, Émile. *Thérèse Raquin.*

## MUSIC

Chopin, Frédéric. Sonata No. 2 in B-flat minor, Op. 35. (includes Marche funèbre, or Funeral March).

Jackson, Michael. "Smooth Criminal." *Bad*. Epic Records, 1987.

Liszt, Franz. "Totentanz" (Danse Macabre in German). 1849.

Liszt, Franz. "Funérailles."

Saint-Saëns, Camille. *Danse Macabre, Op. 40*. 1874.

Shostakovich, Dmitri. *Piano Trio in E minor, Opus 67*. 1944.

Webber, Andrew Lloyd composer. *The Phantom of the Opera.* 1986. Librettist Tim Rice.

## MOVIES

*Fantastic Beasts: The Crimes of Grindelwald.* 2018. Dir. David Yates. Starring Eddie Redmayne.

*Hugo*. 2011. Dir. Martin Scorsese. Starring Ben Kingsley.

*The Phantom of the Opera*. Dir. Rupert Julian. Universal Pictures. 1925. Starring Lon Chaney and Mary Philbin.

"The Skeleton Dance." *Silly Symphonies*. Walt Disney Studios. 1929.

*The Seventh Seal*. Dir. Ingmar Bergman. AB Svensk Filmindustri. 1957. Starring Max von Sydow.

*Le Voyage dans la lune*. (*A Trip to the Moon*.) Dir. Georges Méliès. 1902.

**ART**

Bruegel, Pieter the Elder. *The Triumph of Death*. 1562. Museo del Prado. Madrid, Spain.

Goya, Francisco. *The Sleep of Reason Produces Monsters*. 1797-9. Nelson-Atkins Museum of Art. Kansas City, Missouri.

Goya, Francisco. *Witches' Flight*. 1798. Museo del Prado. Madrid, Spain.

Goya, Francisco. *Witches' Sabbath*. Circa 1821-3. Museo del Prado. Madrid, Spain.

Pictor, Albertus. *Death Playing Chess*. Mural. Circa 1480-90. Taby Church, Taby, Sweden.

**VIDEO GAMES**

Williams, Roberta. *Phantasmagoria*.

**WEBSITES**

FacingHistory.org

Rowling, J. K. "Nicolas Flamel." WizardingWorld.com.

The Internet Archives

Wikimedia.org

Wikipedia.org

# About the Author

John Frederick is (or has been) an author, poet, musician, photographer, ordained minister, travel guide, spiritual student, spiritual guide, husband, father, grandfather, politician, chef, legislator, pool player, teacher, and pronoic dreamer.

He is the author of *Paris Histories and Mysteries* and *Prosperity Now! A 12-Week Journey to the Life of Your Dreams*, and is currently living the life of his dreams in Paris, France, with Manny and Erica, his teacup Yorkies.

*John at the Galimard perfumery in Grasse, holding his signature scent, Serenely*

If you enjoyed *Paris Histories and Mysteries*,
you might also enjoy John Frederick's first book:

*Prosperity Now!*
*A 12-Week Journey to The Life of Your Dreams*

ARE YOU LIVING the life of your dreams?

If not, why not?

I can just hear your reasons: I've got a kid. I've got a mortgage. I've got parents. But someday I will….

Stop with the excuses. It's time to answer that question with a resounding "Yes!"

John Frederick has discovered a spiritual path to living the life you want, and in this new book based on his popular course, he will lead you to the life of your dreams.

Are you asking, "How?" As John reveals, you don't even need to ask how. The Universe will supply the "How." You are simply responsible for supplying the dream, believing in your dream, and making the decision to manifest it.

Using ancient and modern spiritual principles, *Prosperity Now!* will guide you through a twelve-week journey to the life of your dreams. You will learn how to discard old, false, and negative ideas in exchange for uplifting, positive, and powerfully practical ideas that work.

Using examples from his own life, John will gently guide you to wake up to this reality: You are worthy and deserving of a fabulous life of your choosing. You can "Begin it now." Change your mind and watch your world transform to meet the new you! It all begins with *Prosperity Now!*

Available at online booksellers or ask your local independent bookseller to order it.

# Book John to Speak at Your Next Event

JOHN FREDERICK HAS been visiting and been in love with Paris since 1975. He is available for lectures, individual and group tours, full-day or multi-day guided Paris experiences, group events and discussions, speaking engagements, seminars, book clubs, media interviews, and other events.

Drawing on his forty-five-year infatuation with Paris and extensive research for his book, he has uncovered many *Paris Histories and Mysteries*—stories worlds away from the tourist sites, crowded museums, noisy boulevards, and other standard Paris attractions. On the back streets and in the cafés, John will show you a Paris few ever see, revealing the reasons behind the allure, the mystery, and the hidden history that make Paris the City of Lights, City of Love.

Through his multimedia presentations, John can transport you back in time—to the Belle Époque, the French Revolution, dark Medieval Paris, or ancient Roman Lutetia. The stories he weaves are part history, part mystery, and always relevant to our lives today. Far from cookie-cutter tours or presentations, John will tailor the material to your interests. And he will show you much more—things beyond your expectations.

Everyone has been to Paris, even if they have not physically visited the city. How? Because Paris is so much a part of the world's history and has affected so much of what we know, believe, and take for granted today. In truth, we see, hear, and experience many things without ever realizing they began in Paris. John will show you how the histories and mysteries of Paris are infused in the very air we breathe!

To inquire about booking John today for tours, walks, talks, or book readings and lectures, contact him at:

Parishistorymystery@yahoo.com

*Bonne journée!*

Made in the USA
Middletown, DE
03 October 2023